HEAVEN HIGH, OCEAN DEEP

HEAVEN HIGH, OCEAN DEEP

Naval Fighter Wing at War

TIM HILLIER-GRAVES

CASEMATE

Oxford & Philadelphia

Published in the Great Britain and United States of America in 2019 by
CASEMATE PUBLISHERS
The Old Music Hall, 106–108 Cowley Road, Oxford OX4 1JE, UK
and
1950 Lawrence Road, Havertown, PA 19083, USA

Copyright © Tim Hillier-Graves, 2019

Hardback Edition: ISBN 978-1-61200-755-7
Digital Edition: ISBN 978-1-61200-756-4 (ePub)

A CIP record for this book is available from the British Library

Printed and bound in the United Kingdom by TJ International

Typeset in India by Versatile PreMedia Services. www.versatilepremedia.com

For a complete list of Casemate titles, please contact:

CASEMATE PUBLISHERS (UK)
Telephone (01865) 241249
Email: casemate-uk@casematepublishers.co.uk
www.casematepublishers.co.uk

CASEMATE PUBLISHERS (US)
Telephone (610) 853-9131
Fax (610) 853-9146
Email: casemate@casematepublishers.com
www.casematepublishers.com

Front cover: An Avenger on Indomitable being loaded with bombs with a 5th Fighter Wing Hellcat in the background. (DM)
Back cover: A mixture of Hellcats and Avengers set off on Combat Air Patrols (CAP) and anti-submarine duties as the ship transits to the strike area in January 1945. (DM)

Contents

Acknowledgements

The idea for this book had its origins in my childhood when I became aware that my father had served as a pilot with the Fleet Air Arm, during and after World War II. Most veterans, I'm sure, kept a box of souvenirs gathering dust in the bottom of a wardrobe or stored in an attic. I remember discovering his and being fascinated by the photographs and all the other items he had kept – naval buttons and cap, wings, rank badges, log book, pilot's notes, letters, a starched collar covered with signatures, small pieces of a Seafire, a letter opener made of wood from HMS *Iron Duke* and much more. Then later I was enthralled when listening to him and my godfather, John Hawkins, talk about the Fleet Air Arm. These snatched conversations caught my imagination.

But it was in 1979 when serving with the Royal Navy, and studying at the Royal Naval College, Greenwich, that I truly began to immerse myself in the FAA's history. As part of a staff course we had to produce a paper analysing some aspect of naval operations. HMS *Ark Royal*, with its Phantoms and Buccaneers, had just been withdrawn from service, and the keel of a new *Ark Royal* had just been laid. It seemed an appropriate moment to consider the role of maritime aviation – past, present and future. This led me to the college library where an archive of papers, written by other students going back to the 1920s, and an extensive collection of books, waited me. Many months of study and analysis followed and my fascination with the subject grew; although I can't say that the staff paper I produced was anything more than mediocre – I seem to remember advocating the return of big carriers with fixed-wing jets! But the seed was sown and a desire to write about my father and godfather's experiences soon followed.

In many ways calling myself the author is to claim too much. Editor might be more appropriate. In essence, the book condenses the memories of others, with me providing a broad view of events that puts their reminiscences in context. I only hope that I played my part as well as they played theirs. And there were many of them:

Hank Adlam, Gordon Aitken, Bill Atkinson, Joe Barber, Richard and Priscilla Bigg-Wither, Alan Booth, Ken Chapman, Brian Cork, Stan Farquhar, Bill Fenwick-Smith, Bill and Betty Foster, Richard Goadsby, Lionel Godfrey, Pat Godson, Bernard and Jean Graves, Norman and Kathleen Hanson, Rosemary Harrington, John and Peggy Hawkins, Ronnie Hay, Jim Little, Norman Luard, Dick Mackie, Alex Macrae, Cappy Masters, Noel Mitchell, Koa and Al Murdoch, Barry Nation, Richard Neal, John Northeast, Jack and Rae Ruffin, Les Rouse, Gerry Salmon, Fraser Shotton, Douglas Smith, Mike Tritton and John Winton.

In addition to their memories, these wonderful contributors added photographs, articles, copies of official documents and log books they'd retained, personal and squadron diaries and so on and gave me permission to copy and use the material they held as I saw fit (the source is denoted by their initials beside each item included or by direct reference to them in the text). In fact, Dick Mackie and John Northeast could probably have been called the 5th Fighter Wing's archivists, so extensive were their collections.

I would like to thank Kathleen Hanson, in particular, for permission to quote from her husband's book *Carrier Pilot* and John Winton for allowing me to quote from *The Forgotten Fleet*. John also, very generously, sent me copies of correspondence he had collected when researching his exceptional book and gave me permission to use it with due credit being given. This included material sent to him by Admiral of the Fleet Sir Philip Vian RN, particularly papers he collected and notes he made for his own book *Action This Day* (published by Frederick Muller in 1960 to whom I also thank for their permission to quote from the Admiral's book).

Although it is now more than 20 years since I consulted them I must thank the Naval Historical Branch of the MOD and the New Zealand Defence Force (HQ). In both cases they very patiently answered my questions, offered advice and sent me copies of many interesting papers.

Copyright is a complex issue and often difficult to establish, especially when a photo or item exists in a number of public and private collections, all of which could, in theory, claim ownership. Most material in this book was provided by the people listed and copyright has been assigned to them where appropriate. Rigorous checks have been made to ensure that each picture or item has been correctly attributed, but no process is flawless, particularly when these things are now more than 70 years old and the originators probably now long dead. If an error has been made it is unintentional. If a reader wishes to affirm copyright, please contact the publisher. I apologise in advance if a mistake has been made.

Introduction

It was the saddest of days. Two funerals in a few short weeks was too much to bear. But fate is rarely kind and now my father and aunt were being buried together; one in a coffin the other in an urn. Endings and beginnings are always entwined and today was no exception – tragedy and hope in a relentless cycle allowing little time to stop, remember and mourn.

Having stood and watched the grave being closed, I walked the short distance to where my car waited to drive the short distance to my mother's house to talk and reminisce about the dead. But as I did so my godfather, John Hawkins, emerged blinking into the sunlight from the church's lobby and we both turned to observe the gravedigger at his work. But John was a man of understanding and compassion and in the last few weeks of my father's life, when cancer had eaten into his body and soul, we had often spoken. At other times we'd simply sat with the dying man hoping to give him some comfort in the most terrible of circumstances. But my father's despair was only too apparent, and John and I could only exchange the occasional glance, impotent to relieve his suffering.

My father and godfather had both been Fleet Air Arm pilots, though rarely spoke of their experiences. Both, it seems, looked to the future and the possibilities it held. By nature, I look backwards, so didn't share this optimism. I like to think this is because I am the product of two generations whose lives were shaped by war and the social upheaval it created. To understand them I needed to see these events clearly and preserve what I could as a constant reminder of their suffering and their achievements. But it was much more than this. The past is often more real to me than the present or future. John being a perceptive man understood this and had remained at the church to offer me some solace by conjuring up a memory of the past to engage my curiosity and see possibilities in the future.

He had gathered together a number of aging magazines and slipped these into my hands with the words 'see if you recognise anyone in the pictures'. With so many other things occupying my mind we walked to our cars and

I placed his gift on the back seat and silently gritted my teeth for what lay ahead. As the days unwound, there was little time to grieve as a thousand other things filled my thoughts. But bad days pass or time simply deadens the impact of sorrow. Gradually you emerge into some sort of reality, to gather your thoughts and seek a new balance. It was just before Christmas, when the days drew in and winter truly approached, that the light John had struck in those dark July days began their illumination.

There were four magazines each with Royal Navy-themed pictures on their covers – all from the war years. Their subject was clear, pilots under training, then on operations in the Atlantic, Mediterranean and Pacific, with a photocopied page from an Australian magazine celebrating the Fleet's arrival in Sydney and containing interviews with some of the crew. Wartime propaganda of course, but they still captured the spirit of these young lives in all their shades none the less. I looked through them carefully and spotted John, encased in a mocked-up cockpit, being trained as a fighter pilot. But in each magazine there were a sea of other faces, all seemingly far too young to be in the middle of a war where death and disfigurement were constant companions. Old men and the mad make wars and the young and innocent are sacrificed to their vanity.

Once drawn in to this reflective pool I found it impossible to look away from the pictures and wondered about the lives caught in these momentary flashes of a camera's shutter. I also thought about the photographers seeking some anonymity behind their lenses – part of life before them, but coldly capturing images of those soon to die as though from another place, protected by the sense that they were only doing their jobs.

As I looked through these pictures a few words from John Keats' poem *Endymion* came to me:

> But such love is mine, that here I chase
> Eternally away from thee all bloom
> Of youth, and destine thee towards a tomb.
> Hence shalt thou quickly to the watery vast;
> And there, ere many days be overpast,
> Disabled age shall seize thee, and even then
> Thou shalt not go the way of aged men;
> But live and wither, cripple and still breathe
> Ten hundred years: which gone, I then bequeath
> Thy unknown bones to unknown burial.

And so just before Christmas 1993, my curiosity aroused, I spoke to my godfather and asked him about his days as a Fleet Air Arm pilot. Inevitably such questions as why, where and how came to mind and in his answers the story of the 5th Fighter Wing began to unfold before me. John was diffident in describing the role he'd played and deflected my interest in his service to broader issues once we had moved beyond the basic facts – trained as a fighter pilot and flew Hellcats from the deck of HMS *Indomitable* from March 1944 to May 1945. He hadn't kept in contact with his comrades in arms, attended reunions or appeared to have looked back in any comprehensive way since leaving the Navy. But as we spoke he did express interest in their respective fates. Did they all survive the war, how had their lives unfurled and more? In particular, he recalled his last Commanding Officer, 'Gammy' Godson, who had remained with the wing when many of his pilots returned to the UK, their tour of duty having ended. John gave no reasons for his interest in Godson, though I was left with the impression that they had been friends.

Some years earlier my father had given me a copy of John Winton's *The Forgotten Fleet*, which described the Royal Navy's campaigns in the Far East and Pacific in the last two years of the war. It was and remains the most important account of these complex and dangerous operations. Having talked to John I re-read this classic book and found a single reference to him and his CO:

> On the 16th April, *Indomitable* lost a Hellcat pilot, Langdon, who had been so successful four days earlier, was shot down over Ishigaki; and Lt S C Barnet, RNVR, and his crew whose Avenger was hit by a 20mm shell over Hegina. However, that afternoon Lt Cdr Godson and Sub Lt E J Hawkins, RNVR, both of 1844 Squadron, shot down a Myrt just as it was itself stalking and about to attack an American Privateer aircraft.

A small clue had emerged to explain John's continued interest in Godson – he had been his wingman, when together they had destroyed an enemy aircraft. It was a relationship forged in combat, when under great stress. Sadly, Winton's book recorded Godson's death on 12 May, when John was on HMS *Illustrious* heading for home. It wasn't until 1994 that he knew of his CO's fate. Such are the vagaries of life in wartime, when relationships can go through many evolutions in a very short time – literally ships that pass in the night.

From this small beginning I began to trace the lives of all the men who had fought with the wing. It was a search that led me, down many opaque paths, to a farm in Pembrokeshire, with lunch and conversation fuelled by a lot of wine, meeting and befriending someone who would influence me in the years ahead over creams teas in Cornwall. Then there would be lunches in Starcross, morning coffee in the Bear Hotel, Devizes, lunch beside the Avon in Bath, tea in the Ritz, then Dundee, Manchester, Largs and many more places in the six years that lay ahead. Each meeting gave me greater insights into lives spent on the edge of a visceral, but often exciting ordeal.

But there were other sources too. Quite early in the war British Forces had recruited soldiers, sailors and airmen from across the Empire to fight in mixed units, supplementing the large number who joined up and fought in regiments, ships or squadrons established under their own national flags. The 5th Fighter Wing was no exception and had Canadians and New Zealanders amongst their numbers, as did many other FAA squadrons. I was able to trace, correspond and occasionally meet many of these surviving veterans, and the families of those who were killed.

There were so many people who very generously gave their time, happy to recall past lives for the benefit of an interested stranger. From this friendships grew or were renewed, as old comrades made contact with each other, sometimes for the first time in half a century. I was lucky to be involved in this process, but as the years passed their number quickly diminished and by the late 1990s, when I planned to begin writing their story, very few were left and the youngest survivor was 75 years old. As so often happens the pressing needs of family and career conspired to thwart my best-laid plans. Seventeen years passed as though in a flash before semi-retirement allowed me time to look through all the 5th Wing material again, listen to many hours of taped conversations and re-read individual accounts. These echoes quickly re-engaged me and made it seem important to complete a mission now in its third decade of gestation. During this long wait all the surviving veterans who had befriended me had passed away, amongst them John Hawkins who died on 24 November 2001.

CHAPTER ONE

Learning to Fly, Learning to Fight, Learning to Die

When I came of age and volunteered to join the forces I remembered my father's experiences in the trenches – the mud, rats, squalor and horror – and decided to become aircrew instead. Death could be just as sudden and violent, but, at least, you had a clean bed at night, regular meals and 'home comforts' to make the whole thing tolerable. And after basic military training at HMS *St Vincent* we sailed for Canada and the States to learn to fly. For an 18-year-old with a sweet tooth this escape from rationing was akin to going to heaven. But we were soon disabused of any innocent fantasies we may have had about the future, seeing too many of our friends killed or injured whilst under training.

Instructors were never backwards in letting you view the results of students crashing because they'd failed to follow the advice they'd been given. There is nothing more sobering than seeing the remains of a cockpit and the offal that had once been a laughing happy go lucky young boy. (Bernard Graves, S/Lt (A) RNVR)

War demands sacrifice and soon strips those who fight of their youth and their innocence. There is nothing so demanding as armed combat and the bravest and the best will always answer a call to arms when their country is threatened. The Fleet Air Arm always seemed to attract a very high proportion of volunteers eager to do their duty, but many who came forward did not always understand where their honour and courage might lead them, with death often intervening in this path to self-realization. As an anonymous American officer recorded in a press article, having come across a Nazi death camp in the big push across Germany in 1945:

It was only then I truly understood why we had been fighting. Up to that point the enemy had seemed just like us, but in field-grey uniforms led by a madman with a Charlie Chaplin moustache. The realisation was sudden and brutal in the extreme. We had been fighting and dying in large numbers for 10 months by this stage and thought we had seen every horror man can perpetrate on man, but this gave us strength to carry on and seek a better world.

For the average recruit the process of enlistment began with a wish to do 'one's bit'. Many saw themselves in a particular service, but were disappointed to discover that war and bureaucracy soon dictated other destinies – to different services, even into industry. But some made it through, particularly those who volunteered to become aircrew where attrition rates and turnover were always very high. For this generation the wish to fly was strong. The 1920s and 1930s had been a time when aviation and the exploits of Great War fighter aces had fired many young imaginations. The press, finding a ready market for these stories, soon latched on to this growing interest in aviation and began reporting all aspects of its development. New technologies, the long-distance flights of Lindbergh, Amy Johnson and many others, air displays, particularly the Royal Air Force (RAF) pageants at Hendon, and air combat as portrayed in Hollywood movies all found a place in contemporary literature and culture. There was much to capture impressionable young minds eager for excitement. For most this interest simply resulted in scrapbooks full of press cuttings and photos, and so it might have remained but for the threat, then reality of war.

When speaking to those who survived, it was noticeable how many of their lives had followed this path, and also how many of them had been influenced by small travelling 'airshows', where a pilot in a single biplane could drop into a field nearby, perform a few 'stunts' then offer joyrides for a few shillings. Such close contact made thoughts of flying professionally seem more real. But they were also influenced by the highly publicised development of new monoplane fighters for the RAF which appeared in the last few years of the 1930s. The images of new Spitfires and Hurricanes were mesmerising and quickly engaged men eager to fly. The Royal Navy (RN) and its air arm also had glamour but lagged far behind in developing such advanced aircraft, relying on types more suited to the last war than the next. Many senior naval officers were still in thrall to battleships and failed to invest sufficiently in better aircraft, in so doing condemning many men to fly, fight and die in hopelessly outdated machines. In this they displayed a poor understanding of the changing face of war, unlike the American and Japanese navies, who pressed ahead with greater ambition and skill.

In the late 1930s the RN was still largely populated by men and women who had chosen to serve in the navy as a career. There were reservists, but insufficient to meet the rapidly increasing demands of an expanding fleet. With war seemingly unavoidable, despite Chamberlain's hollow prediction of 'peace in our time', the Admiralty began to recruit more officers on short service commissions for all its branches, with many destined for the Fleet Air Arm. The response was enormous and vacancies were soon filled by men, mostly in their early twenties.

Academic qualifications didn't seem to be of paramount importance, though school matriculation or attendance at a public school did help, as did some professional training. Being presentable, well-spoken and having a sporting background also gave applicants a head start. Nowadays, with better diet and health, the services have a much wider pool from which to draw their recruits, but by 1938 a legacy of poverty, poor diet and austerity had taken its toll. So large were the problems that many applicants failed on health grounds alone, resulting in worried recruiters highlighting the shortage of fit men to fill the many vacancies. With war soon to be a reality this didn't bode well for the mass 'call up' that would surely follow and could continue to undermine Britain's ability to fight effectively.

With this is in mind it wasn't surprising that those selected in 1938 came from the middle or upper middle classes. There was also the issue of snobbery to consider. In peacetime the officer class held themselves to be a cut above the rest and demanded certain standards of behaviour, even the way you spoke, by its members. Candidates from public schools naturally fitted into this narrow, restricted view of the world. But others had to acquire these new 'skills' if they were to be accepted. Many veterans I interviewed commented on this aspect of their new lives. They'd felt it necessary to enhance their family and school backgrounds, speak in clipped accents and generally behave as though from the 'top drawer'. For many it was a front they felt necessary to adopt for the rest of their lives as though it was a badge of acceptability. War diluted these attitudes to a certain extent, but social mobility was then a little understood concept and social barriers were still a long way from being demolished in such a class-ridden society.

For those lucky enough to pass through the selection process, and be granted commissions, basic naval training followed, with midshipman or sub lieutenant insignia adorning their uniforms. Learning to march, salute and behave as officers were key to this process, and became known as the 'knives and forks' course, with the Royal Naval College at Greenwich chosen as the venue, rather than the more traditional, well-established route through Dartmouth. Once completed these newly minted recruits were transferred to RAF training establishments where they began the more difficult process of becoming pilots. Many would fail, some becoming observers or transferring to the general list for service afloat. Less than a third would go on to gain their wings.

By the time these early recruits had become pilots Britain's defeat and invasion had become real possibilities. With the RAF desperate for aircrew to make good losses over France and Belgium, many naval aviators were seconded to Fighter or Bomber Command in June 1940, leaving the FAA squadrons seriously depleted of new pilots for a time.

Three young men who would play leading roles in the story of the 5th Fighter Wing were swept up in this rush to arms. Tommy Harrington, Dennis Jeram and Mike Godson all found the thought of flying with the Navy almost impossible to ignore, especially when faced with many monotonous or dreary peacetime alternatives. They were typical of the sort of men the Fleet Air Arm hoped to attract – fit, active, sporting, intelligent, brave, but most of all hard fighting by nature. Or as Dickie Cork, a high scoring aval ace and one of their contemporaries, succinctly put it in a letter written in 1943 when he himself was training men as fighter pilots: 'They have to be ruthless and capable of killing in combat without regret or too much soul searching.' And he was right. War demands men like this if it is to be fought successfully, especially when faced with German and Japanese fanatics or equally hardened men.

Born in June 1915, Tommy Harrington was the oldest of the three. He transferred to the navy in 1938, as part of the Fleet Air Arm's expansion plans, having completed pilot training as a member of the Royal Air Force Voluntary Reserve. Alan Marsh, a fellow student, later recalled the impact he made:

> We were co-pilots and it soon became obvious to me that he was quite exceptional and was a master of his craft. His expertise had the effect of making one try harder and he undoubtedly inspired everyone who served with, or under him, to give of their best.

In the early months of the war Harrington served with 758 and then 774 Squadrons training air gunners at Aldergrove, north-west of Belfast. Finding this work less than inspiring he re-mustered as a fighter pilot with 801 Squadron, flying dual role two-seater Blackburn Skuas from Detling. These heavy and underpowered aircraft had some success as interceptors when attacking German bombers, but were found to be no match for German fighters. As casualties quickly mounted, including eight out of 15 on one operation alone, they were relegated to second-line duties. But before then Harrington helped cover the evacuation from Dunkirk and then flew from Hatston, in the Orkneys, and HMS *Furious*, on operations against the Germans over Norway. These encounters proved quite sobering experiences especially when faced by the enemy's more modern single-seater fighters, as Marsh again recorded:

> His skill as a fighter pilot undoubtedly saved him on two occasions when he was attacked by ME 109s and he flew back to Hatston riddled with bullet holes. On the second occasion a bullet had passed through his cockpit canopy, missing his head by inches.

With the Fleet Air Arm rapidly expanding to fight on many different fronts, Harrington was promoted to lieutenant and appointed to 800 Squadron flying Fairey Fulmars from HMS *Victorious*. She was the third of a new class of fleet carrier and within days of commissioning, in May 1941, was assigned to track and attack the German battleship *Bismarck* on its foray into the Atlantic. With only nine Swordfish and six Fulmars available the carrier could only be of marginal use, but they were desperate times. Four aircraft were lost in the appalling conditions whilst searching for the enemy. Two men were later rescued by SS *Ravenshill*, a passing merchant ship. But Harrington, with his observer Sb Lt Staveley, did manage to find *Bismarck* shortly after the Swordfish had attacked leaving the German battleship trailing oil. He shadowed it briefly, but with his fuel running low returned to *Victorious*. *Bismarck* continued on and attempted to reach Brest, but was sunk on the 27th by gunfire, having been disabled by aircraft from *Victorious* and *Ark Royal*.

Harrington remained with 800 Squadron until 1942 and was then posted to RNAS Yeovilton as an air gunnery instructor, where he remained until early 1944. Here he gained experience of many new types of aircraft entering service, including the Grumman Hellcat, an aircraft he would soon be flying on operations.

One of those he commanded later recalled Harrington and the effect his leadership had upon them:

> He was a typical product of the pre-war Royal Navy – disciplined, organised and unflinching. He led by example, but was seen by many as being too hard-nosed at times, and rarely allowed us to glimpse any other side of his personality. But he knew what he was doing and instilled these qualities in all of us from the first. In the months ahead his professionalism and training allowed us to flourish as fighter pilots and saved many lives that a more gung-ho attitude might have forfeited. (John Hawkins, S/Lt (A) RNVR)

Dennis Mayvore Jeram was born in Buckinghamshire during November 1917 and joined the navy on a short service commission in late 1938. After basic training at Greenwich he and 38 other recruits began their pilot's course, with the RAF at Gravesend, gradually progressing from Tiger Moths to more advanced aircraft. Winter and the crush of new pilots under training restricted their flying time, but in March he was awarded his Pilot's Badge and returned to the Navy for assignment. But with invasion a strong possibility and after sustaining heavy losses in the retreat to Dunkirk, the RAF needed as many pilots as it could get so in June he and 57 other naval aviators returned to the RAF.

They were posted to the operational training unit at Harwarden, near Chester, and began a short, sharp course in learning to fly and fight in Spitfires. He was then posted to 213 Squadron which operated Hurricanes from Exeter. Undaunted by this challenge, he discovered himself to be an accomplished fighter pilot, shooting down four enemy aircraft by September. With the threat of invasion lessening, and bombing raids moving from day to night, Jeram returned to the navy and was eventually posted to 888 Squadron which would operate from HMS *Formidable* until 1943. Promoted to lieutenant in early 1942, he saw service in the Mediterranean and destroyed two more enemy aircraft in the process before becoming an instructor. As the Fleet Air Arm began to re-equip with more advanced aircraft Jeram was posted to the United States in late 1943 where he visited both Grumman and Chance Vought to see and test their newest products – the Hellcat and Corsair. Being a pilot of note he would soon be accompanying these new fighters back across the Atlantic for use in front-line service.

Michael Stapylton Godson was born in Epsom Hospital, Surrey, on 24 August 1916, the second son of Edgar and Grace Godson, who lived in Godalming. After attending Charterhouse, and finding the thought of life working in the City too limiting, he joined the Royal Navy in early 1939. After Greenwich he followed the now well-established path to Gravesend and Netheravon for pilot training. Like many of his comrades he was seconded to the RAF following qualification as a pilot and was posted to RAF Newton Down, near Porthcawl in Wales. But after sustaining a serious leg injury he was transferred to RNAS Eastleigh for a period of recuperation. With the usual light-hearted attitude to disablement common in the services he acquired the nickname 'Gammy', which remained with him until the end of his life.

Recovery took some time, left him with a limp and kept him away from front-line service at sea or on land for a considerable time. Promoted lieutenant in September 1941 he was appointed to 792 Squadron, a fleet requirement, target towing unit based at St Merryn in Cornwall. After this he saw service in Dekheila before transferring to 809 Squadron, which was involved in the North African landings flying from HMS *Victorious*, before returning to the UK where the unit was re-equipped with Seafire Mk IIs.

By this time the RN was in the midst of its massive expansion programme and had many new squadrons working up in the United States, to be equipped with locally produced Hellcats, Corsairs and TBR Avengers. Most young men due to populate these new units were undergoing training in North America, but needed experienced officers to lead them.

Although his operational service had been limited by injury, 'Gammy' Godson was promoted to acting lieutenant commander and crossed to the States in July 1943 to take command of 1835 Squadron, which was due to be equipped with Mark 1 Corsairs. This posting lasted only three months before he was re-assigned to 732 Squadron then 1838 Squadron in June 1944, which was soon to embark, with its Corsair Mk 2s, to the UK then the Far East. In July the squadron was temporarily assigned to *Victorious* for an attack on Sabang, but was disbanded two months later to boost numbers in 1830 and 1833 Squadrons on *Illustrious*. Although losing his command he was quickly re-assigned to 1844 Squadron with its Hellcats on HMS *Indomitable*.

Everyone who knew Godson seemed to remember him with great affection and respect:

> No one could resist the infectious gaiety that made him the most charming of companions and the most popular of officers. He had the 'common touch', and young and old, high and low were fascinated by his perfect manners and perfect poise that made him the life and soul of every gathering. With a keen sense of the ridiculous he had a tender regard for the feelings of others, and his mirth was free from any suspicion of malice. It was a wonderful solvent of threatening discord or depression, and all but the most inveterate forms of pretentiousness and humbug melted before it. (Norman Luard, Commander (A))
>
> He led by example and pressed on no matter how difficult the circumstances. But at times he could seem reckless in his eagerness to get at the enemy and seemed to be blind to the risks, which, as his occasional wing man, I tried to discourage. (Bill Foster)

And so this early intake of pilots gradually gained experience and became leaders in a Fleet Air Arm almost unrecognisable from its the slightly gentrified pre-war self. But with war demanding ever increasing numbers of men, the Navy had to broaden its recruitment and selection process if it were to meet so many pressing needs on so many fronts. The Royal Naval Reserve had been created in the mid-19th century to provide a trained reserve of part-time sailors to be activated in the event of war. But this scheme didn't foresee the coming of world wars where millions of servicemen and -women would be needed. The Voluntary Reserve forces were formed in 1903, following the Boer War, to be activated when the nature of a war had been assessed and targets set for mobilisation. The scheme had proved itself in the Great War and in 1939 was resurrected and a new programme created to attract suitable recruits.

The Royal Naval Volunteer Reserve (RNVR) were quickly into their stride. Within weeks, posters could be seen at main line stations and on hoardings in city centres. One, in particular – placed above the main concourse at Waterloo in London and almost impossible to ignore – was remembered by many men who then went on to serve in the Fleet Air Arm. It was a recruitment campaign that stretched to New Zealand, Canada, Australia, South Africa and Rhodesia, through their own national VR schemes. The RAF tended to snap up most applicants in the latter three. But the navy proved more successful in the other two and guaranteed that a large number of men from these countries served in the Fleet Air Arm throughout the war.

Although conscription was given legal status by the 1939 National Services (Armed Forces) Act for men between the ages of 18 and 41, most applicants for aircrew training with the Fleet Air Arm were volunteers for the duration of the war. No 'press gangs' were required and the quality of men who came forward without any sort of persuasion was always high as a result. But before reaching flight training school many hurdles had to be negotiated and the process of sifting began with an application form, a medical, some tests and, finally, a formal interview with senior naval officers:

> After waiting many weeks I received a letter from the Admiralty inviting me to HMS *St Vincent* to be considered for the Fleet Air Arm. There the medics set about checking my blood pressure, hearing, lungs, heart, stature, posture and eyesight. But the tests also covered such things as depth perception and general health, some of which was rather embarrassing for an 18-year-old straight from home. It took about two hours and I was rated A1B, which meant that I was fully fit and qualified physically for flying training.
>
> After a hurried lunch in the mess I was called in front of a panel of three, chaired by a rear-admiral, in a rather imposing oak panelled room. I'd heard some apocryphal stories about these interviews and wondered how true they may have been. The one that had made me laugh most was the candidate entering the room, tripping over the carpet, then slowly rising from under a rather grand table to peak over the edge at his inquisitors. As he did so the admiral asked if he might prefer to join the submarine service instead!
>
> But in my case there were no funny incidents just a short greeting followed by a mathematics test, which as a trainee mechanical engineer I passed easily. There followed a few questions about aircraft, in which I was asked to identify a number of models, then I drew and described the main features of an aircraft carrier and the way they operated. All child's play for someone growing up in the 1930s with the Meccano Magazine as their bible. Finally, the Rear-Admiral asked me why I wanted to fly, did I want to be a pilot or observer and then few questions about naval history. My nervous and slightly naïve answers were greeted with a gentle smile, before I was dismissed and asked to wait outside. I sat in an anteroom and kicked myself, mentally, for 10 minutes reliving each moment of the interview and thinking 'did I really say that and Oh God! what about my London accent' and wishing I could start again. So when I was recalled back into their presence I was expecting the worst. But to my great relief was told that I was in and given a pep talk by the kindly Admiral eager to put me at my ease and encourage me to do my best! On the way home from Portsmouth Harbour Station to Waterloo I hung upside down from the luggage racks and did other silly things in sheer exuberance at my good fortune.
>
> I expected it to be a while before my call up papers arrived, but only waited three weeks, a pilot's course having a vacancy which I was asked to fill if available. And back to Gosport and HMS *St Vincent* I went in my best and only suit of clothes. I joined the pilo'ts course, Rodney Division in August and immediately fell under the spell of CPO Willmot, a Great

War veteran, and his deputy, PO Oliver. Two of the old school whose job it was to turn us into sailors, though not aviators. When there is a gathering of VR Fleet Air Arm veteran these two men always feature large in the reminiscences such was their impact.

Willmot's presence was very apparent to us from the start and each new entry was noisily instructed, often from the opposite side of the very large parade ground, to get doubling – a privilege only enjoyed by the current new entry division, who were easily recognised by their gaiters, belts and lanyards, from dawn to dusk. He was small in stature and not particularly neat in appearance. He had a round face and rosy complexion adorned with circular glasses, which he only took off for photographs, revealing a small trace of vanity in the process. We were told that during 1940 he had shot down a Luftwaffe bomber with a machine gun and this only added to his authority and mystique. I always remember him with a tolerant but long-suffering smile on his face, as though thinking, 'Oh God! Not again. What am I doing here with this lot'? But he did turn hundreds, if not thousands of raw recruits into something recognisable as sailors in a very short time and prepared us for what lay ahead. (Bernard Graves)

Very early in the war, when the RNVR was setting up training courses to absorb huge numbers of young men as aircrew, it was decided that recruits would be enrolled as able seaman. Only later when receiving their pilot's badges were they promoted to become officers. In pre-war days it had been very different with officer status being conferred from the first, whether an individual qualified as a pilot or not. But now, with so many being engaged in these schemes, the Admiralty didn't want to be swamped with too many RNVR officers, especially when such a high proportion of men on each pilot's course failed to make the grade. It was better, easier and cheaper to re-assign them without rank.

By 1940, with air space above Britain ever more crowded and dangerous, flight training was becoming increasingly difficult. There were very few places left where fledgling aircrew could learn their trade without interference from the Luftwaffe or getting in the way of their own operational squadrons or being shot at by trigger-happy gunners protecting cities and factories. For a while basic training carried on in the UK, so that the wheat could be separated from the chaff as soon as possible. But with facilities in Canada available, and the USA reaching its Lend-Lease agreement with the Churchill government, all this changed. With unlimited resources and facilities, the USA and Canada were far better places to train aircrew for the RN and RAF than the crowded skies of home. So from 1941 the bulk of new recruits began making the long, dangerous voyage across the Atlantic in convoys, after basic training at *St Vincent*:

The whole voyage couldn't be described as a pleasant experience. Apart from the normal hazards associated with war, the vessel was over-crowded, cold and uncomfortable. We finally arrived in Halifax on the bleak cost of Novia Scotia after 19 days at sea, various alarms having caused the ship to zig-zag its way across the Atlantic. Being limited to one meal a day, plus a pint of water did not contribute to our morale or well-being. We waited on the dockside in very chill air for quite a while until an RAF officer took charge and marched us to the main railway station where we boarded a huge steam train bound for Kingston, Ontario. The journey took 30 hours and we enjoyed the comfort of the carriages and their pull-down beds. To young men long used to rationing the meals were excellent and plentiful, with fresh fruit and candy bars thrown in.

We arrived in the early evening darkness and were taken by Royal Canadian Air Force trucks to the airfield beyond Kingston and home of No. 31 Service Flying School, which was one of a number of establishments that operated under the 'Empire Air Training Scheme'. (Lionel Godfrey, S/Lt (A) later Lt RNVR)

At a time when travel for most was limited to day trips to the coast, being decanted to foreign, though English-speaking lands opened many minds to a new way of life and new possibilities. It wasn't simply a case of leaving rationing, bombing and blackouts behind, though this was a great relief. Suddenly the world they had glimpsed at the cinema became a reality. The glamour and sexiness of Hollywood enhanced by the new world these young men now entered, away from family ties and the social restrictions on life in Britain. There were few who didn't take advantage of all that was on offer and grew up very quickly in the process.

But first the serious business of aircrew training had to be dealt with and the regime they found was organised, disciplined and ruthless in eliminating those who couldn't make the grade. But not all of these trainees remained in Canada. With the United States entering the war, after the Japanese assault on Pearl Harbor, their navy agreed to accept 30 RN cadets per month for training at Saufley Field, Pensacola, in Florida. There was little difference between the two schemes, but those trained in the States greatly benefitted from a warmer climate and didn't face the disruption of Canada's harsh and prolonged winters.

For the first six weeks the cadets attended ground school, learning about navigation, meteorology, the theory of flight, the mechanics of aircraft and more. At the end of each week there were written tests to ensure these 'school subjects' were being absorbed. But few, if any, were 'washed out' if they failed and were given more time and extra coaching to help them pass. When flight training began the thinning-out process would start in earnest and was pitiless, as much to preserve the lives of the students as the need to train effective pilots.

Surprisingly when flight training started it was often a student's first time in the air, such was the fledgling state of aviation in the 1930s and 1940s. But letting young men get so far into their pilot's course without establishing their fitness to fly, except by medical test, seems rather short sighted now:

It seemed that each week 1 or 2 men were scrubbed from the course, some because they couldn't overcome air sickness. Others simply couldn't judge heights properly when flying low, because their depth perception was poor. You could always spot them because they kept trying to land twenty feet or more above the ground, crunching the undercarriage each time or worse. Even those who got over these sort of difficulties struggled and were given time to improve, with more dual instruction, before being called to the flight commander's office to be 'chopped'. And so it went on until our numbers had reduced significantly.

Because we flew with instructors at this stage serious accidents were few and far between, but as we began to go solo casualties became more common, depleting our number still further. (John Hawkins)

For much of the war Tiger Moth biplanes were used to give cadets their first experience of flying. But as methods were refined they were replaced by the more advanced Fairchild PT-19 Cornell, a two-seater monoplane, which first appeared in 1939 and remained in service for ten years. No matter which aircraft was used though, time in Link flight simulators, where cadets learnt instrument flying in a safe environment, proved an essential addition to the training scheme. But it was in a Tiger Moth or Cornell that many cadets faced two memorable events – their first flight and their first solo – before moving on to more advanced types. Yet it was going solo that tried the student and instructor most and usually occurred after 15 or so hours of dual control:

It was a strange feeling to be alone in the cockpit without the reassuring presence of the instructor. There were certainly a few moments of panic when he'd hopped out, tapped me on the head and shouted 'one circuit then land'. But we had just completed an hour's flying in which I'd landed and taken off several times and he'd warned me that I'd go solo if everything went well.

I sat there for a few minutes gathering my thoughts and running through the cockpit drill. Then I ran the engine up, keeping a careful watch for other aircraft and any signal from flying control, and took off into a very slight wind. I swept around the airfield in a very broad turn at about 1500 feet enjoying the feeling of freedom, joined the circuit and landed with a couple of heavy bounces, then taxied over to where my instructor stood, his thumb up in the air. Later I tried to imagine his feelings at seeing another cadet land safely and decided that I wouldn't like to be in his position. There were a number of crashes – some fatal – and you could see how badly this affected the instructors. Self-examination and recriminations would have been unavoidable on these occasions. (Bill Foster, S/Lt (A) RNVR)

Once this milestone was passed the pace of training quickened, each element of flying being rehearsed and practiced until they gradually became instinctive. But with each step forward so the failure rate increased and struggling cadets continued to trudge, periodically, to the CO's office to hear their fate. Some transferred to observer courses or the RN's general list and others to the RAF, re-mustering as navigators, bomb aimers or air gunners. Some even relocated to the Marines or army, being eager to fight in any way possible before hostilities ended. But the sobering fact remained that only about a third of those who had assembled at *St Vincent* a few months earlier remained on the pilot's course and the attrition rate continued during more advanced training. Though now, with so much solo time included in the programme, accidents became more commonplace.

This training was pressured and unremitting, so leave, when it came, was enjoyed to the full and here these healthy young men, free of domestic ties, began to enjoy the fruits of Canada and the States. Many took to smoking and drinking with much enthusiasm, but tried to keep other youthful urges in check:

> Cigarettes and alcohol were cheap and plentiful and local people were invariably hospitable, so our time off duty was spent in bars being offered free drinks if we were in uniform. But in many ways we were naive and inexperienced and the Navy tried to make us behave as much for our own safety as the good of the service. We were lectured on the 'evils of drink' but also sexually transmitted diseases. I can still remember a wizened old Petty Officer's lecture with a most gruesome set of slides highlighting the perils of illicit sex. I don't think he believed it would do any good, so laced his talk with some basic advice – if you can't resist temptation use condoms and avoid prostitutes!
>
> Periodically the Navy would repeat these messages, colouring their advice with the added threat of court martial if we contracted an STD. They would also resort to telling us that there were untreatable forms of these diseases locally. I don't think we ever believed it and those who couldn't wait still dived in during their booze-filled leave.
>
> Flying and drinking don't go well together and our instructors were always on the lookout for those with hangovers. Once was forgiven, though we would be ticked off sharply and threatened with the chop. But repeat performances were treated more severely, so we learnt to behave sensibly up to a point. Flying was all that mattered to me and the thought that I might be grounded permanently and sent home was too much to bear. (Bernard Graves)
>
> When we were at Pensacola many local women would sidle up to us in bars for company. One in particular, who was a long way past her prime, seemed very keen and gradually progressed through our group of ten, displaying a less than innocent approach to sex. Finally she latched on to ......, who in his naivety fell for her. He was a romantic and thought he could save her, whatever that meant. We tried long and hard to dissuade him but to no avail and three weeks later they married in a local registry office.
>
> When training was over he was posted to one of the new Corsair Squadrons and was killed in combat during January 1945. His wife, who continued in her own very distinctive and well-supported way with the courses that followed, so we heard, became a widow and received a pension for life. I hope she gave him a few moments of happiness along the way, poor sod. (Gerry Salmon, S/Lt (A) RNVR)

The world is puzzling and exciting when still a teenager and the war added a thrilling but terrifying dimension that was almost impossible to resist. Despite the many pitfalls most grew up quickly and each stage of their training helped enhance their stature and maturity still further. As they progressed to the more advanced North American T-6 Texan, known to RN and RAF recruits as the Harvard, the surviving students moved one giant step closer towards the award of their 'wings'.

The Harvard was regarded by many as the ideal training aircraft. This single-engined, two-seater aeroplane had retractable undercarriage, was capable of 200 mph, could reach 24,000 feet and had more advanced systems to test the novice. But it was considered safe and predictable, continuing in service until the 1990s, with three remaining on the strength of the Empire Test Pilots School at Boscombe Down, such was their versatility.

As they reached this crucial stage in their training it became quite common for a pilot of note to visit the school to meet and chat to the students. Here many met two men who had featured large in their childhoods – Charles Lindbergh and Billy Bishop, the Great War ace. Both impressed with their easy style and their interest in young men so far from home. It helped in many ways that Lindbergh, although a civilian consultant to Chance Vought, had flown that company's Corsairs on a number of combat missions in the Pacific. Young men soon to face this ordeal could appreciate the words of someone with this first-hand experience.

Over the following weeks their hours on the Harvard quickly grew and the exercises became more testing. They included long-distance, cross-country navigation flights, night and instrument flying, aerobatics and formation flying. Time was spent learning and practising basic combat techniques, with students attempting to jump comrades or instructors in true fighter pilot style. It couldn't hope to reproduce the gut-wrenching sensation of true 'dog fighting', but it did open their eyes a little to what lay ahead.

And so the day arrived when each recruit faced their final checks, graduated and were awarded their pilot's badge. An important occasion carefully recorded in log books and marked with photographs and a 'fly past'. It also meant the end of their days as sailors and promotion to midshipman and then sub lieutenant in very short order. It was an occasion to be savoured and many took the opportunity for leave wearing their new uniforms:

> Some took the train to New York, but two of us managed to grab a lift in a C-47 which was heading south, the pilot circling Manhattan for our benefit before landing at La Guardia Field. It was our first time in the city, but we'd devoured so many films at the Odeon cinema in Worcester Park before and during the war that it all seemed very familiar.
>
> We were conscious of our new uniforms and officer status and made full use of this gaining access to Billy Rose's Diamond Horseshoe Club and the Copacabana. But we were shown the door from others when we started messing around when the band was playing. But 19-year-olds were going to have fun and we sure did.
>
> At this stage of the war it was common for Hollywood stars to visit some of the clubs in New York, where young servicemen gathered, as a morale booster. I met and chatted with

Rita Hayworth who was even more gorgeous and charming than on the silver screen. She was certainly worth fighting for. (Bernard Graves)

Flying training continued after leave but now these new officers began to move on to operational aircraft and awaited posting to new units. During training each student had been regularly assessed, with any particular skills noted by the instructors. During the Great War it had become clear that some pilots were better suited to specific types of aircraft and roles. They were equally skilled but flying fighters or bombers seemed to demand different abilities as well as personalities, so selection techniques were refined to take account of these variations. Today we would call this personality and skills profiling, but then these techniques were in their infancy and took a less measured approach. Yet by the time these new RNVR pilots began rolling off the production line their suitability for different roles had been established.

But how do you assess whether a pilot has the qualities required to be a fighter or bomber pilot, when air fighting was still in its infancy? The World War I aces, such as Manfred von Richthofen, left some clues – fly high where you could see the enemy clearly, use this height to swoop down like a bird of prey and get in close before shooting. In essence you needed good eyesight and reactions, a dominating position from which to attack, speed, good marksmanship and superior numbers, if possible. When World War II came fighters could fly much faster and climb much higher, but the same rules still seemed to apply.

A mystique seemed to surround the fighter pilot and Adolph Galland, the Luftwaffe ace, gave voice to this belief when he wrote: 'Only the spirit of attack, born in a brave heart, will bring success to any fighter aircraft, no matter how highly developed it may be.'

A fighting spirit and courage were essential of course, but there was much more required in an individual's make up. Dickie Cork saw the need for a killer instinct, whilst von Richthofen believed that aerobatic flying skills were of little value, regarding his aircraft as simply a means of manoeuvring his guns onto an enemy. Others thought that exceptional spatial and situational awareness were essential, coupled with an ability to think and stay calm when under stress, and so the list grows. Bill Foster, who flew and fought with the 5th Fighter Wing, probably best summed up the needs and stresses of being a fighter pilot in 1945, on carriers, when he wrote:

Experience, good eyesight and quick reactions mattered a great deal. The novice saw little in the air and took time to see what was happening around them. When new to air fighting everything just seemed to happen too quickly. Some never really acquired these skills no matter how hard they tried and were picked off before they knew what was happening. To others it came naturally and they prospered.

Tommy Harrington, who was a very experienced fighter pilot by the time I arrived, constantly reminded us of the basic principles of air combat – engage from above, fast and hard, get in close, shoot accurately, aim for the pilot, and climb away quickly. Don't follow the enemy down if you've damaged him to confirm a victory, weave, always look behind you, don't fly straight and level in the combat zone for more than a few seconds and always fly with a wingman.

But in addition to this, you needed to know the capabilities of your aircraft and how far you could push it. Knowing the strengths and weaknesses of the enemy was also important, though less so in the Pacific in 1945. By then Japanese casualties were high, their replacements of poorer quality and they focussed their limited resources too much on kamikaze tactics.

Flying fighters took a heavy toll on your body and there were no pressure suits then to protect you in high G turns. So being fit, avoiding late nights and alcohol were essential. For some this was a problem, especially in the cramped, noisy quarters on a carrier, where drink was readily available.

You had to be naturally calm at times of extreme stress. Overstretched nerves usually led to unnecessary risk taking. But as your hours flying in combat added up so the risk of battle fatigue increased and, inevitably, you had to be taken off operations for your own good. Some managed to disguise the effects of creeping exhaustion and carry on flying when it had become unsafe to do so. They were brave and didn't want to let anyone down, but it was still foolhardy to let them continue. I'm sure some were lost because of this.

The saying 'the quick and the dead', though clichéd, held many grains of truth.

It was the instructors' task to try and gauge whether a barely trained pilot was best suited to fighters or bombers, and often it was no more than instinct that guided them. Undoubtedly quotas were also applied at times, as was personal choice. So it was that each man found himself, by whatever means, moving on to the next stage of their lives in the Fleet Air Arm.

By 1944 the nature of carrier warfare and the aircraft available had changed enormously. No longer were aircrew going to war in aircraft whose performance lagged behind the enemy they faced. By degrees, other fighter options were tried. Some of the RAF's battle-hardened, but aging Hurricanes, went to sea and proved themselves in combat, particularly in the Mediterranean during 1942. The RN purchased a number of Grumman Wildcat fighters, under Lend-Lease, as another stop gap measure and these too proved successful for a time. But Britain, although beginning to invest in purpose built seaborne aircraft, struggled to produce machines as advanced and tough as those being developed in the United States.

To help fill the gap RAF Spitfire Mk Vs, then being superseded by the more advanced Mk IXs, were developed for service as Seafire Mk I, II and IIIs during 1942 and 1943. Designed to fly from grass fields and with relatively short endurance, the rigours of life at sea soon exposed their weaknesses, but, at that stage, it was the only British-built fighter available. Make do and mend seemed to be the order of the day and would have remained so but for the America aero industry and the greater ambition of the United States Navy (USN). With war in the Pacific being dominated by carriers and the Japanese being able to field many fine aircraft the USN had to compete. They made a massive leap forward with the Grumman F6F Hellcat and Chance Vought F4U Corsair during 1943.

These two fighters dominated carrier operations until the end of the war and became more than simply fighters in the process. They were also ideally suited to ground attack and bombing roles, both of increasing importance in an island-hopping war involving amphibious landings and ground support to troops.

Of the two the Hellcat was initially more successful. The Corsair proved difficult to land on carriers and so was assigned to land-based Marine units who operated it successfully. But these squadrons could only absorb a small part of the number being produced, leaving many newly built aircraft in store seeking customers. Senior RN representatives, in the States, soon became aware of this and sought agreement to acquire Corsairs, under Lend-Lease, for use by the Fleet Air Arm, even though their design seemed seriously flawed. At the same time, they also took steps to procure Hellcats and Avengers, such was the need for aircraft.

By this stage of the war the British carrier force was growing rapidly. In 1943 there were four modern fleet carriers available, with two more soon to be operational and another two with keels laid, due to enter service in 1946. In addition, 16 new light fleet carriers were under construction or planned, and there were more than 30 escort carriers in varying states of readiness all needing aircraft. At this time, the war seemed likely to stretch into 1946 or 1947, even 1948, such was the ferocity with which the Germans and Japanese fought. Faced with these huge demands, and a British aviation industry limited in its ability to produce aircraft of equal merit in sufficient numbers, the supply of American-built carrier aircraft to the Fleet Air Arm was essential if all the squadrons already in existence or planned were to be equipped effectively.

For the remainder of the war the navy's fighter needs were met by a mixture of Seafires, Corsairs and Hellcats. At the same time the Fairey Barracuda and Grumman Avenger would fulfil the TBR role, with Fairey Fireflys providing general support as strike and reconnaissance aircraft. It was a mixed bag and, to some, a poor solution, but the Admiralty accepted this plan as a fait accompli in the face of so many pressing demands and throughout 1943 and 1944 the programme gradually came together.

This was the situation faced by those selected to be fighter pilots when graduating from training schools in North America in the last two years of the war. Many returned to the UK to complete flight deck training and a fighter air combat course, but others undertook these final stages of their education in Florida, with the United States Navy. But the development programme was a dynamic one and occasionally often muddled by the sheer scale of the Fleet Air Arm's expansion. New, front-line Corsair squadrons were formed in the States, whilst Hellcat and Seafire units came together in Britain, with pilots often switching from one to another as needs ebbed and flowed. But, first, it was essential that the new fighter pilots complete all their training before being posted to a squadron

> Many of us waited around, taking leave or acting as general 'dogsbodies' at air stations, waiting posting. By this stage Fighter Pilot Training Schools had been set up and here you flew operational types in simulated combat conditions, under the direction of experts in the field. I was posted to Henstridge, near Wincanton in Somerset, which was equipped with Seafires and so fully expected to fly them from a carrier, in due course. Hellcats tended to be based at Yeovilton, with Corsairs in the States. But having spent a month learning all about Seafires I was then posted to a Hellcat Squadron. (John Hawkins)
>
> I was destined to fly Corsairs and completed my training on them at Quonset Point only to find myself posted to a Hellcat Squadron when reaching the Far East, which, with hindsight, was to my benefit. (Bill Foster)
>
> As always the Navy f...... up many postings. In my lighter moments I often wondered whether some poor souls ever arrived and spent the war travelling between ships or air stations being turned away each time and re-directed elsewhere! At different times I was heading for a Seafire Squadron then Hellcats and Corsairs in quick succession. Luckily 1838 Squadron took pity on me and allowed me to stay! (Gerry Salmon)

Whether by design or chance, pilots eventually completed their training and were posted to operational squadrons, with those destined to fly Hellcats seeming to be the most content. Through service in the Pacific, where they had won a deserved reputation as rugged, powerful fighters, word of their success quickly spread. When FAA pilots had an opportunity to fly them they quickly found these stories to be true; easy to control and formidable in combat. In time the Corsair would be equally admired, but early in their career the soubriquet 'bent-winged bastard from Connecticut', that many Americans attached to the type when first in service, created some prejudice. But with a few modifications and in the hands of the Fleet Air Arm's highly trained pilots, they soon proved themselves to be equally impressive flying from carriers. It was an example of perseverance and skill that American Navy pilots soon followed, revelling in the Corsair's other nickname 'whistling death', such was its impact.

And so the new pilots came to the end of their prolonged and often traumatic training. It was a path that had taken them from their homes in many different corners of the world to HMS *St Vincent* and through the hands of CPO Willmot, then Gravesend, Netheravon, Canada, the States and many other places. They now faced the reality of life on the front line and the cold reception of the oceans and a bitter, vicious enemy. Along the way they had seen many friends disappear, some because they lacked the necessary skills to become pilots, others to cemeteries in Britain or foreign lands. There had been many light and sexy moments to balance these horrors, but for men who'd barely started shaving let alone begun life it was still a great deal to ask and the future would demand even more. But young people then were more robust and absorbed much more because of it and selection had chosen some of the best of this generation to be fighter pilots.

With the benefit of hindsight many veterans played down the impact of these early months as though it lasted only a few days and involved very little effort. They tended to remember it in the same way young men do their years at university; a right of passage to adulthood, fuelled by testosterone and stimulants. Each passing month saw them change perceptibly, as their experience broadened and a sense of responsibility grew. They would stay young men, but an understanding born of danger, sacrifice and loss began to penetrate their being, making many wise beyond their years. The months of combat that lay ahead would test this mercilessly. But first they had to reach a squadron on active service and learn to become a small but necessary cog in the life of that unit.

5th Fighter Wing (1943–45)

Photographs of many of the pilots who served with the wing no longer exist or cannot be traced. Others are of such poor quality that their inclusion would serve little purpose. More may come to light in time, but the pictures presented here are the best that can be managed at the moment. (All photos in this group, DM/JN)

Dennis Jeram

Mike 'Gammy' Godson

Tommy Harrington

Barry Nation

Fraser Shotton

Noel Mitchell

Lionel Godfrey

Peter Fell   Richard Neal   R. J. Corkhill   John Habberfield

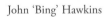

John 'Bing' Hawkins   Jack Ruffin   Edward 'Tug' Wilson

Harry Taylor   Bill Atkinson   Dick Mackie   Bill Foster

Brian Hicks   J. K. Thomson   Tim Schwenk

1839 Squadron in early 1945. (DM)

1844 Squadron, summer 1944. (JN)

Training

A sight familiar to prospective Fleet Air Arm naval airmen during the war, St Vincent. (BG)

During each course students would gather together for a group photo with instructors. Three future members of the 5th Wing are present here plus the Canadian Robert Gray who would be awarded the Victoria Cross for gallantry when flying Corsairs from HMS *Formidable* in August 1945. (THG)

CPO Willmot, minus his familiar round spectacles. To all the young naval airmen passing through his hands he became a legend to be recalled with great affection years later. (THG)

Gammy Godson's first solo flight in a Tiger Moth, based at the training airfield at Gravesend. (PG)

From callow youth to manhood in six months – you needed to grow up quickly if you were to survive. (BG)

Night-time exercises – an essential part of a of pilot's training programme. (DM)

Worth fighting for – my father's treasured snapshot of Rita Hayworth. (BG)

CHAPTER TWO

And so to War

During 1943 the Fleet Air Arm began to expand at an ever-quickening pace. With six large carriers and a plethora of other ships to serve any other of course of action would have been impossible to contemplate. But with so many different types of aircraft becoming available, or already in service, the programme was a complex one to administer. In each case the pressure to produce sufficient fighters and bombers had to compete with many other pressing demands placed on manufacturers in Britain and the States. The bombing war over Germany, the Mediterranean campaign and battles in many parts of the Far East and Pacific were absorbing vast numbers of men and ever diminishing resources. As Gordon Aitken, a fighter pilot serving with 1833 Squadron put it, 'the Fleet Air Arm had to suck on the hind tit to get even a fraction of what it needed.'

Each carrier received an eclectic mix of the best aircraft available, but it was a programme with huge uncertainties as the war fluctuated both one way then the other, causing leaders to switch their precious resources to defend or attack wherever an advantage could be exploited or disaster averted. Dominating everything were plans for the 'second front' in France, soon to become a reality. With so much activity and so many pressing demands the Navy slowly built up its forces, from different sources, and awaited assignments, which would inevitably be in the Indian Ocean and then the Pacific, as the Atlantic war began to die down.

For most these questions of high policy and logistics were shrouded in mystery and secrecy, so played little part in their day-to-day lives until active service beckoned. They saw the end result of these machinations with new Seafire, Corsair, Hellcat, Avenger, Barracuda and Firefly squadrons being formed, to sit beside or replace existing units that made do with aircraft many thought 'past it'. But these new squadrons had to find bases where they could form up and exercise. In the States, with so many establishments available there were few problems. The same couldn't be said of Britain where there were huge pressures on facilities, especially with so much activity in the crowded skies over the south and along the eastern side of the country.

For this reason, Corsair and Avenger squadrons tended to form and work up in the USA, near Chance Vought and Grumman factories, with the same thing happening in Britain with Supermarine and Faireys. Only the new Hellcat squadrons broke this mould, presumably because they were tried and tested and available in greater numbers for shipment overseas during 1943. In some ways they were regarded as a stopgap measure only. Corsairs and new marks of Seafire were seen to be the latest and most effective weapons becoming available, so would form the core of this new force. Therefore only one or two Hellcat wings were planned, though squadrons for operational service on escort carriers or for training purposes would also be formed. The 5th Fighter Wing came into existence in late 1943, for service on HMS *Indomitable*, a fleet carrier then undergoing refit in America. Initially it was planned that three new squadrons would make up this wing, but this was reduced to two, 1839 and 1844, when space considerations and a shortage of pilots were taken into account.

And so the posting system slowly came to life, drawing recruits from other squadrons, training establishments, home service or leave to man the new wing. For most it would be their first operational assignment, whilst many of the 'old hands' lacked combat experience. But there was a small hard core of very experienced men, led by Tommy Harrington and Dennis Jeram, the two new squadron commanders, to impart the important lessons they'd learnt in battle and try to get their pilots ready for action.

During the course of the war Northern Ireland had been home to many new squadrons. Here they were able to gain experience in a relatively peaceful setting and, at the same time, help protect shipping entering the Northern Approaches. Convoy and anti-submarine patrols could be tedious, but they were essential in protecting vulnerable freighters plying their essential trade to and from Britain's western ports. Many airfields had sprung up to support these operations and one at Eglinton, near Londonderry, became home for the two new Hellcat squadrons in November 1943. Although built for the RAF it was used by both services until May 1944 when the FAA became virtually its sole user, commissioning the establishment as HMS *Gannet*.

Noel Mitchell, who was posted as a lieutenant to 1839 Squadron, captured the spirit of these early months in Northern Ireland:

Some of us arrived at Eglinton on 15th November 1943. It was to our pleasurable surprise that we found Lt Cdr Jeram as our Commanding Officer – he was an excellent type.

We found a situation that had arisen many times before, in as much as we had no aeroplanes to fly. So for a week we sat on our backsides waiting for someone to 'extract their fingers'. Eventually, after several visits from the gentlemen of Flag Officer Carrier Training's staff to see how we were progressing we were supplied with ten new Hellcat MK1s.

After a week's flying, just getting our hands in, we got down to some serious training. Jerry, our CO, became somewhat bad tempered as the days passed because, now that the powers that be had given us aircraft, they had not thought about supplying us with spare parts and replacements. There was also the problem of getting 'hands' to do the work. I, as the Squadron's Stores Officer bore the brunt of his grievances. This in turn I put on the stores basher who immediately blamed the Station Main Stores, who in turn blamed the Admiralty, the latter blaming the Americans....

After much gnashing of teeth, we started our training, which consisted of formation and low-level flying and so on. Most of us had completed deck landing training, but needed to sharpen up our techniques according to the CO who wasn't too impressed, so we practised Aerodrome Dummy Deck Landings (ADDLs) with Jerry batting us down, swearing vociferously when we didn't reach his high standard. Tommy Harrington did the same for the 1844 boys when they arrived.

Both were very scornful of mistakes, but one incident with 'Habers' [Jack Haberfield] springs to mind that rendered them both speechless for a time. One day, with snow on the ground and a very cold wind coming off Lough Foyle, Jack came floating down after a short flight with his wheels up. It wasn't uncommon for new pilots to do this, but he was a very old hand and should have known better. We fired red signals, waved and cursed but still he came down, waving at us, some later said 'happily as though he didn't have a care in the world'. In his mind I'm sure the CO was already preparing court martial papers, but shelved these thoughts temporarily when the Hellcat did a belly landing and rushed over in a jeep to extract the 'happy' pilot. In fact, his undercarriage had failed and his landing was a text book one. Greatly relieved we adjourned to the Wardroom for a few drinks, whilst Habers went to see the MO for a check-up.

Air firing at a 15ft sleeve towed by a specially adapted plane or into ground targets occupied a great deal of time and caused a great deal of rivalry. Some virtually went within a few feet of the towed target in their eagerness to score as many hits as possible. All targets were assessed by Wrens, but particularly those for air firing which were recorded by cameras in the firing mechanism. There was much ribbing when these were played back to us, followed by instructions, sometimes polite, on how we might improve.

After a couple of months of this we not only learnt how to do things as a team as opposed to a group of individuals, but we became much better acquainted with each other. And each lunchtime and in the evenings we would meet in the wardroom and over a glass or two would discuss the day's flying and generally talk shop. It has always been said in the Navy that most business was done over a glass of gin, which probably accounts for it being so cheap!

Over Christmas 'Jimmy the One', Lt Commander Simon, 1st Lieutenant of the station, who was a great fellow organised a pretty hectic round of parties, which everyone was determined to enjoy to the full, it being the last chance we might have to do so.

With Christmas behind us we got down to more training, sometimes doing big escort exercises with 1844 Squadron, which meant instead of the usual 12 aircraft there were 24. As might be expected these exercises sometimes ended in complete chaos with aircraft flying in all directions, usually due to too many pilots giving orders and unnecessary nattering over the R/T. In fact, it is better to have no R/T than all the screaming and shouting that can go on with it.

Each Saturday afternoon we used to put on civvies and go over the border into Eire where the chief attraction was ham and eggs repeated as many times as we were able to eat. Customs were very strict on the return trip and used to stop the train every 20 minutes to make an extensive search. On one occasion Jerry, Dick Mackie, Habers, myself and some others were testing out these customs officials prior to smuggling some silk stockings, when I happened to say I had a pair. It looked as though things might get out of hand, so I tried to make clear that I'd been joking. They didn't believe me, took me out of the carriage to the station master's office where they stripped me naked and conducted a close search. It was a long time before we tried our hands at smuggling again.

It was on 31st January that we suffered our first casualty. Sub Lt Corkhill was killed instantly when his engine caught fire flying at low level near Ballymena and he hit a hill covered in cloud. This was indeed a tragedy which might easily have happened to any one of us.

Corkhill had been a keen duck shooter and this became a popular past time amongst the rest of us. All we had to do was wait over on the far side of the airfield just before dark and shoot them as they flew low over Lough Foyle. On one occasion when light was fast disappearing we heard a 'swish swish' of wings and opened up with our shot guns. Our target forced landed 30 yards away and was found to be a swan. However, nothing lost we hung it up and two weeks later it produced a fine dinner for 10 of us.

Early in 1944 we were told that our ship would be HMS *Indomitable*, for which everyone was thankful because she was a large carrier. This produced two trains of thought. One that going to a large fleet carrier meant we were due to go east. The other being that it didn't matter where we went as long as we had the biggest carrier to land on. There were many varied reasons for people wanting to go east – some to fight the Japs, others to travel, some to see their girlfriends and last, but not least, our New Zealand squadron members who would be one step nearer home. Some of them had been away for two years or more.

All this led to more parties and a little less flying as we seemed to be well in advance of our programme, or so it seemed until staff people kept popping in and asking why this or that hadn't been done.

In mid-February along came the Captain and Commander (Flying) from *Indomitable*. They put us in great spirits by telling us that we were well ahead of the ship and that, in all probability, we would get three weeks leave before joining her towards the end of April. All this made life extremely pleasant, but not for long. Four days later along came an Admiralty pink signal, one of those of which no one seems to know the origin, instructing us to proceed overseas.

John Hawkins, who by this time had taken up his secondary duties as 'Records and Link Officer' for 1844 Squadron and become its unofficial diarist, takes up the story:

Never has such a transformation been seen before. We started working like mad to get the aircraft serviceable. Stores were packed with the greatest speed and by 2 o'clock on the 25th the squadron was ready to move. Before lunch orders were given to fly all the aircraft to Belfast for embarkation on HMS *Begum*, Tommy Harrington added that we weren't to do a beat up of Eglinton or the city on the way. At 16.30 the whole Wing took off and was last seen heading towards Belfast in thick cloud. Claude (Westfield) and Jacky (Ruffin) were left behind to look after the troops and stores that would travel to Belfast by train the next day. That evening the boys proceeded to get as drunk as usual., but there was no hurry to sober up the morning after because *Begum* couldn't get alongside the loading jetty because of rough weather. So we stayed in Belfast at the Officers Club and had another party, which none of us will forget.

Finally, on the 27th *Begum* managed to get alongside and once the stores had been dealt with the loading of aircraft began. A very high wind was blowing the whole time and until the crews got used to it manoeuvring the aircraft proved difficult. However, 24 Hellcats were put down below in the hangar and then everyone started on 24 Barracudas belonging to 815 and 817 Squadrons, with five more being added later, plus four Wildcats. All of them were put in position, some with wings spread and others folded, on the flight deck.

Work went on throughout the night to get the ship ready, which allowed some of us time to get ashore for one last fling. But it would take until 2nd March for all the work to be complete and enable the ship to move outside the harbour where we dropped anchor to top up with fuel. At 5 am the next morning we set sail, with the Captain announcing over the tannoy that our destination would be Gibraltar, but gave us no further news.

A little later we rendezvoused with the rest of our convoy of ten frigates, one cruiser, HMS *Nigeria*, and HMS *Atheling* another carrier crammed full of Corsairs and more Barracudas – 'Fred's trick aircraft' again. Coming up the rear were a liner of the Empress type and two 'Kaiser's floating coffins' (USN escort carriers of poor repute).

As we headed south and out into the Atlantic, Beaufighters of Coastal Command provided cover throughout the day. A large swell built up which caused the ship to slow its pace, but a heavy sea mist fell which hid the convoy from prying eyes and U-boat attack, especially in the Bay of Biscay. Our passage to Gib was fairly uneventful, except for one suspected U-boat sighting which resulted in four depth charges being dropped without result. At 0130 on the 10th the Rock was spotted and into the Mediterranean we went.

And so the convoy made its way through the now calmer waters of this once very dangerous sea. With the war in North Africa over and Italy suing for peace in September 1943, there were few bases left from which the Germans could operate aircraft capable of striking well-protected shipping. There was still a chance of U-boat attack, but even that risk had diminished greatly in this confined sea, their navy seemingly focussing its boats in the Atlantic. There were alarms and counter-measures – depth charges and violent manoeuvring – yet no enemy attacked and no ships were lost

With little to do, time passed slowly under cloudless blue skies, so pilots wrote journals, played cards, caught up with paperwork or simply stood watch. Some wrote poetry, much of it bawdy but occasionally it tried to give voice to the lives they now lived and the nature of their war. Many years later John Northeast, sitting in the lounge of his farmhouse, recalled with sadness one entitled 'The Fighter Pilot', its author now long forgotten:

Not his, the realm of mud and mire,
Of pouring, drenching rain,

Or desert like a furnace fire
Of never ending pain.
Where men like overburdened mules
With hate-laden minds, intent
On blasting other stupid fools
On same intention bent.
Not his the sly, inconstant sea
That rages, then is still,
Where life meets death in secrecy
Beneath its iron will.
Where steely walls of floating death
Move pond'rously in war,
And, teeming with life-giving breath,
Are suddenly no more.
But these realms of heavenly vales exist
On golden, fleecy clouds,
Of ghostly, silvery vapour trails
Above earth's blood-lusting crowds.
Here riding in his sun drenched throne,
The world that's his, and his alone,
Here, high up in the roofless skies
The fighter pilot lives and dies.

John believed that many of his fellow pilots shied away from expressing themselves in this way, preferring to keep any piercing insights to themselves. Some saw this even before engaging the enemy, but most fell victim in time, influenced by the violence of combat and the loss of friends. Kill or be killed was their vow, but also their curse, though at this stage few realised what this meant.

Bill Foster, who joined 1844 Squadron later in the war as a sub lieutenant, remembered only too well the feeling of apprehension and uncertainty he felt as the day of his first mission gradually came closer:

All the training we undertook tried to prepare us for that day, but dress rehearsals were no substitute for the real thing. I wondered how I would feel or react. Would I be a liability to the others and let them down? Would I be shot down by flak or another fighter hidden from view? Worst of all would I be shot down in flames. One of our RAF instructors had suffered this fate in 1940 though he survived the searing flames that all but destroyed his hands and face. Although McIndoe and his team had worked wonders with plastic surgery, his scars were still appalling and a constant reminder of what we might face if our luck ran out. Some thought it better to be killed outright.

I also thought about killing the enemy and when the moment came whether I could 'pull the trigger', so to speak. Air to air combat was one thing, because we had the illusion of shooting at an aircraft, its pilot hidden from view, but ground strafing would be a much more personal affair and difficult for that reason. But when the moment came there was little time to reflect and I was thankful for that. Later I did think about the men I may have killed and wondered what sort of people they had been and the families they left behind. A feeling of guilt was unavoidable, but we had to do our duty and tomorrow it might have been my turn to die. I can't remember ever hating the enemy, even when word of Allied aircrew being executed came through. But some did and seemed to relish sending the enemy down in flame or, I'm told, shooting at those who had taken to their parachutes. Not that they often bailed out, preferring to crash into our ships instead if given a chance. Did I think them inhuman or alien? I didn't. I'd taken the opportunity to read about Japan just after Pearl Harbor and the fall of Singapore, so felt I understood a little of their culture and ways of life. These were different to our own, but contained strong elements of humanity, order and loyalty that we held dear in Britain. I'd also read of the barbarity they'd shown to people in the countries they had invaded and prisoners of war. The two images sat badly together, but didn't lead me to believe they were monsters, though the thought of being captured by them was troubling.

The convoy slowly crept towards Egypt with a brief stop for fuel at Port Said on the way, with each young man in the wing preparing himself, in these few weeks of relative calm, for what lay ahead. The *Begum* entered the Suez Canal during the night of 17 March and then docked in Port Suez (Tewfik) where leave was granted, allowing some to take the train to Cairo. A few days later their voyage continued down through the Red Sea into the Indian Ocean and Ceylon, for another short stay, before sailing for Madras, in southern India, where:

The aircraft were unloaded and towed down to a small landing strip on the beach to be made ready for flying. We'd now been told why we were there. The Imphal crisis in Burma led many to believe that India would soon be invaded, so we were sent out as part of the defence.

When the aircraft were ready we set off on a 35-minute flight to Ulundurpet, 90 miles away to the south of Madras. The countryside was flat, bare and parched as far as the eye could see, with hardly a tree in sight. Our living quarters were kadgire huts of the native type. Once more training started all over again. But during these exercises we lost S/Lt Starkey who was killed in a most unfortunate accident due to lack of oxygen at a great height. It was hard to believe that half an hour before he was with us and then suddenly gone forever. No one spoke about it but the same thought was in everyone's mind.

For eight weeks we struggled aimlessly on until, with no spares left and none to come, all our aircraft were grounded. The sick bay was full to capacity, mostly with cases of dysentery, and the food was atrocious. Our only amusement in this no man's land was a weekly visit to Pondicherry some 50 miles away, where we enjoyed a swim, good food and a bath. After travelling back on the hot dirty roads in the back of a truck we were dirtier than when we started out, but that didn't deter us at all.

After a while someone remembered us and we were moved to the air station at China Bay in Ceylon, where we spent two days doing ADDLs prior to deck-landing training on HMS *Unicorn*. The results of this probably show the state of mind we were in and the level of sickness that prevailed. Each pilot had to do three deck landings each and there were nine prangs or one crash for every 6½ landings. At that rate the wing wouldn't have had any aircraft left after two days and would have ceased to exist. Something had to be done.

With the aircraft left we flew to the Racecourse Aerodrome near Colombo to regroup. New aircraft arrived and others were repaired. And with this flying continued daily and we gradually recovered our health. (Noel Mitchell)

Lionel Godfrey remembered his time at Colombo very fondly, particularly the opportunities he had to practise dogfighting with RAF fighters:

We practised formation attacks on a Dakota, which pretended to be an enemy bomber, and we enjoyed pitting our Hellcats against the wiles of some Spitfires based south of Colombo. They were faster than our Hellcats, but not so manoeuvrable. We derived some satisfaction from allowing a Spit to get outside true firing distance on the tail of our fighters and then take violent evasive action as they lined up their camera gun to register a hit. By suddenly throttling back and reducing speed, as the same time as going into screaming tight turn to port or starboard, it was possible to get a Spitfire to overshoot its target and go whistling by at high speed in the wrong direction. It was not too difficult to keep these beautiful and speedy aircraft at bay.

And in the relative 'paradise' of Colombo, after Ulunderpurt that is, the pilots could recover their health and enjoy the night life whilst training hard during the days. Noel Mitchell continues:

Each evening we spent at the Galle Face Hotel or the Silver Fox Night Club, fully enjoying what was on offer.

Shortly afterwards Pete Fell, our Senior Pilot, left and I took his place. Fraser Shotton, my oppo in 1844 Squadron, and I with our flights took an RAF Photo Reconnaissance Course and learnt to take a series of pictures vertically from 20,000 feet or above. Eight of our Hellcats were specially equipped for the job, with two cameras in the belly of each aircraft and the controls in the cockpit. When operations began we spent a considerable amount of time flying over targets gathering information, with other Hellcats guarding our tails.

While we learnt the tricks of this trade the rest of the Wing continued practising deck landings and escorting Barracudas on dummy missions. During one of these, 1839 had its third casualty when S/Lt Blackie was killed.

John Hawkins who was flying on this exercise recalled the circumstances of this loss:

July 7th

The morning of the 'big job' and everyone was up with the lark. Our rendezvous time was delayed two or three times but at 0850 hrs six aircraft from 1839 and four from ours, flown by the CO, Colonel (Westfield), Tug (Wilson) and I took off and rendezvoused with the bombers. Colonel returned almost immediately with R/T and generator trouble. The target was a small force, five escorts and two fleet carriers, *Indomitable* and *Victorious* (just arriving in Ceylon after a long voyage from the UK).

It was much nearer than expected, but having found it everyone made their attack and started off from the rendezvous point. Then Blackie, a recently arrived New Zealander with 1839, called up and said he had engine trouble and was about to ditch. Valentine, another newcomer, watched him go down and said on his return that the landing seemed perfectly normal. Unfortunately, he failed to get out and nothing was seen of him again.

With these exercises coming to a crescendo, and *Indomitable* arriving in Ceylon, the day was fast approaching when the wing would be embarked on her to begin operations. For most it had been two years or more since they walked through the gates of HMS *St Vincent*. Along the way two thirds of these recruits had been 'washed out' before basic training had finished and loss of friends had become a regular, but still bitter, pill to swallow. In the last few days in Ceylon these young men busied themselves in readiness for the big event, sliding off in the evening to local bars and clubs to enjoy their pleasures. No one could know who might return or when, but the young can feel invincible and any doubts they may have had were swept away in a show of youthful resilience and exuberance.

On the 24th, *Indomitable* slipped anchor at Tricomalee and headed out to sea to rendezvous with the first of its Hellcats at 1630 hrs. But all didn't go well, as Noel Mitchell recalled:

> At 1615 hrs a great gaggle of aircraft under Lt Cdr Jeram (Tommy Harrington being grounded with a severe ear infection) set off bound for their new home. Visibility was poor and the ship couldn't be found and so the formation was sent to Katukuranda to start again. Mac and Frankie, Yellow 1 and 2, were by then short of fuel and returned shortly followed by 3 and 4. A new vector was given to the remaining aircraft and the ship was located. Jeram was the first to approach but on landing his hook pulled out and he promptly went through both barriers and just trickled over the bows. He was eventually picked up by one of the escorts and after some delay the remaining six landed on successfully.
>
> Dick Mackie and Bryan Hicks of 1839 took off at 0830 the next morning from the carrier to do a radar exercise and Bryan had the misfortune to prang the barrier on his return. At 1250 hrs five more Hellcats arrived from Colombo and all landed OK.

Gradually over the next few days the rest of the pilots joined the ship with no major incidents recorded and the wing began the process of familiarising themselves with life on the carrier. It was a process fraught with many difficulties, not least between aircrew and ship's crew, where friction became a regular part of day-to-day existence.

The Wing Forms (1943)

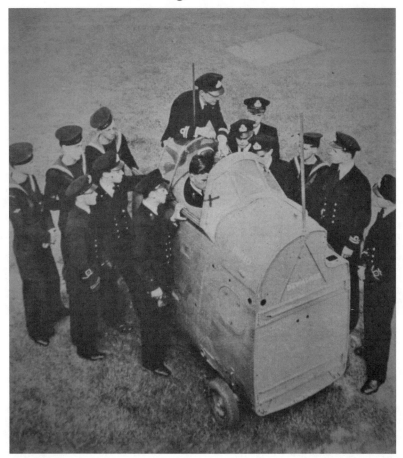

Heath Robinson personified – John Hawkins settles in to a mocked-up and pushable fighter cockpit as a young midshipman at RNAS Yeovilton. (JH)

John 'Jack' Haberfield buzzes the airfield at Eglinton in Northern Ireland in late 1943. In time this would become a familiar sight on many Japanese airfields as Hellcats thundered in at very low level to attack. (DM)

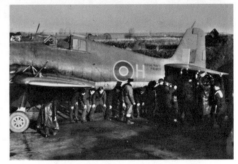

1839 Squadron's pilots get to grips with their aircraft in late 1943. (DM)

It was a hard life for aircraft maintainers whether on land or sea, the appalling weather at Eglinton was particularly memorable with its open-ended silo-type hangers. (DM)

By the time the 1839/1844 left Northern Ireland, the pilots were well acquainted with the Hellcat and each other. (THG)

HMS *Indomitable* leaves dock in the States before transiting to the Indian Ocean. (DM)

CHAPTER THREE

HMS *Indomitable*

When joining a large warship for the first time you are aware of a confusing mass of narrow, endless gangways, compartments, bulkheads, deckheads, ladders and water tight doors. There is an alien mixture of smells made up of oils and fuel, food cooking in the galleys, paint and sweat. Always in the background is a general clamour of noise caused by men rushing and bustling, indecipherable pipes broadcast throughout the ship, as though the speaker is holding his nose or covering his face with a cloth to obscure the words, and the whirling, throbbing sounds of machinery. The thought that comes to the novice's mind is clear, 'will I ever get used to this bloody awful place, let alone learn how to fight the enemy when the time comes?'

Of course, there is some order to it and by slow degrees you acclimatise and learn the language. But in those first few days your ship mates can seem as hostile as the ship itself, all seemingly smug in their knowledge and experience. But if you look closer you'll find that most members of the crew only really know their own departments, messes and 'action stations'. Beyond that they tend to have the same degree of ignorance as yourself.

A smaller ship can be bad enough but a fleet carrier or battleship is much worse, with many members of the crew living a troglodyte existence below decks when the ship is in an operational area. In these circumstances only a few would see daylight regularly and they tended to be on the bridge or in special deck parties – gunners and the like – or those concerned with flying. British warships, which should have been designed for service in the tropics, protecting sea routes around the old empire, rarely, if ever, made allowance for this in their design:

> In hot weather they became sweatboxes, where everything became damp and even the furniture seemed to ooze liquid. It was impossible to get cool and many slept on the flight deck at night if there was no flying. Due to a general shortage of fresh water showers only came on

at certain times and then only for brief periods. But even after standing under a cooling stream for a few seconds you began sweating again as soon as you'd towelled yourself dry.

Privacy was hard to come by as well and after flying in combat it was essential to find a peaceful corner where you could collect your thoughts. But you were always surrounded by other people and the sounds of the ship. At times it became unbearable. (Stan Farquhar, S/Lt (A) RNVR)

Cabin quarters – we had four bunks in each cabin and bed bugs lived permanently in each one. Ours were positioned under the flight deck and so there was plenty of noise as each aircraft landed on. Most of us picked up a dose of crabs all because of a lack of fumigation. Because of the intense heat water was in short supply for long periods and many pilots were quickly drained of stamina. They didn't look good either. The equivalent of bucket of water per person each day for all your needs – plus the occasional shower – was all we were allowed and did little to relieve the problems. But the wardroom and mess on *Indomitable* couldn't be faulted – nor the grog or the food. (Dick Mackie, S/Lt (A) later Lt RNZNVR)

A fighting ship wasn't a place for the faint hearted, the needy or those who suffered from claustrophobia.

By the time 5th Wing aircraft landed on its deck *Indomitable* had seen a great deal of action since its commissioning in October 1941. Built by Vickers-Armstrong, at their Barrow-on-Furness Yard, it was one of the four *Illustrious*-class carriers, but had undergone some redesign work to enable it to carry a greater number of aircraft. This meant that more hangar space was required, in this case in a double-decker formation, which raised the flight deck by 14 feet, giving *Indomitable* a slightly different appearance to the other ships in the class. At nearly 30,000 tons fully loaded, it could reach a top speed of 30.5 knots and cruise for up to 11,000 nautical miles between replenishments.

By comparison, American *Essex*-class fleet carriers were bigger – by 3,000–4,000 tons – and carried a considerably bigger complement of aircraft, often by a factor of times two or more. But it came at a cost. British carriers were built with more armour, particularly on their flight decks; USN ships didn't have the same degree of protection. This made ships like *Indomitable* far harder to sink or damage, though performance and hitting power suffered. In hot weather the heavy armour increased the oven effect inside, making the ships even more uncomfortable to live in. Yet, in time, when kamikaze attacks wreaked havoc on American carriers, *Indomitable* and the other *Illustrious*-class carriers survived similar onslaughts and could be repaired in the front line, without recourse to the support of distant shipyards.

Early in the war the Fleet Air Arm had suffered because the aircraft available for its squadrons were out of date or 'last year's RAF models'. Forced into seeking a fighter capable of defending themselves and the ships against enemy attack, aging Hurricanes were converted for shipborne life. These, in the experienced hands of pilots such as the Battle of Britain ace Dickie Cork, gave a good account of themselves when flying from *Indomitable*, but were at the end of their operational lives as front-line fighters. To supplement these fine, but dated aircraft the Navy had acquired a number of Grumman Wildcat fighters from the States.

After much sparring in the Indian Ocean, with the Japanese fleet, and in the Mediterranean, with the Germans and Italians, *Indomitable* finally engaged the enemy in serious combat. This came during August 1942 when, as part of Operation *Pedestal*, it, with two other carriers, two battleships, cruisers and other escorts guarding 14 merchant ships, attempted to force passage through the Mediterranean to help break the enemy's stranglehold on Malta. Many ships, including a carrier, were lost, but, before being bombed and severely damaged on the 12th, *Indomitable*'s aircraft helped give the enemy a bloody nose. Cork led the way with six 'victories'.

With British shipyards at full stretch *Indomitable* was redirected to the States for repair, after being patched up in Gibraltar, returning early in 1943 to see service in the Mediterranean again. But these were still dangerous waters and the enemy could still mount attacks with their well-established and equipped fighter and bomber squadrons. By this stage the Sea Hurricane had been superseded in naval service by Seafires. They were far less rugged than the Hurricanes and their undercarriage was a particular weak spot, but once safely in the air they could hold their own against all but the latest marks of German fighters. But even with this more potent weapon available the enemy got through. When supporting the landings on Sicily in July 1943 *Indomitable* was torpedoed by an enemy aircraft and crippled. It again made the trip to the USA for refit, once temporary repairs had been effected to make it seaworthy for the voyage across the Atlantic. It was whilst in America that Captain John Arthur Symons Eccles was appointed to command *Indomitable* and remain with the ship until December 1945.

Eccles joined the Navy in September 1916, when aged 18, as a cadet, just missing the battle of Jutland. He achieved rapid promotion in the inter-war years and was a captain, serving on HMS *Ark Royal* as executive officer, when war was declared in 1939. During 1940 and 1941 he commanded the aging light cruiser HMS *Durban*, as part of the Eastern Fleet operating in the Indian Ocean. Then in December 1941 he was appointed to be Director of Operations Division (Home) and it was from here that he joined *Indomitable*.

All those who met him were impressed by his strength, intelligence, compassion and humour. Although not an aviator himself, like all senior RN officers at the time, he fully appreciated their world and the stresses and strains they were under, so commanded them with patience, tact and understanding, often turning a blind eye to their youthful excesses and high spirits.

With repair work and modifications, including work to update its radar, taking seven months to complete, it wasn't until April 1944 that sea trials began. Once completed *Indomitable* was ready to return to the UK and take passage for Ceylon where four squadrons of Hellcats and Barracudas (815 and 817) awaited its arrival. In dribs and drabs the aircraft came on board and began the serious business of flying from a carrier. For most of the pilots this would be their first time, but for one of the experienced hands it proved to be his last in wartime service.

For some inexplicable reason Dennis Jeram landed badly, crashed through the barriers then went over *Indomitable*'s bows into the sea. He was quickly picked up unhurt but badly shaken. By July 1944 he had been flying operationally on and off for four years and seen a lot of killing and dying along the way. The law of diminishing returns applied to combat flying just as much as it did to troops fighting on the ground. Fighter pilots may have returned to clean beds and good meals at night, but flying in action with a sudden violent death only a breath away was a draining business. Senior officers and medics on board had learnt to look for signs of stress and changed behaviour, and often they had to look no further than mess bills and the level of drinking they exposed – a sure sign that an individual was trying to muffle the effects of anxiety. But there were many other indicators to measure the depth of exhaustion, even despair. Sleep became difficult if not impossible without sedatives. Eating properly fell by the wayside, with alcohol filling the gap. Popping Benzedrine tablets, an amphetamine, to boost alertness and performance, became a habit for some, but came with side effects not fully understood at the time. Often an individual displayed an over confidence – likened to a bulb burning brighter just before it dies. In this situation they often took unnecessary risks or ignored the advice of wiser minds with dire consequences, as John Hawkins recalled:

> We all knew the story of Anthony 'Judy' Garland, a very experienced fighter pilot, who came out to the Pacific in command of 1842 Squadron (Corsairs) on HMS *Formidable*. His state of mind seems to have been confused, to say the least. He swaggered about in a gung ho manner, ignoring the advice of friends and colleagues who understood the tactics of fighting in the Pacific and was killed by flak on his first operation; a ground strafing attack on Ishigaki. Afterwards it was said that he had all the obvious signs of battle fatigue and should have been taken off operations. Too late. In a better ordered world, his tiredness would have been identified and this experienced man been given the rest he deserved, but probably didn't seek. Being regular Navy probably didn't help. They had their career after

the war to think of and couldn't afford a blemish on their record or a suspicion that they didn't possess the right stuff, as the Americans called it.

Whilst there was compassion for those who had grown tired, fellow pilots, as young men often do, broke things down to a simple, even crude level, referring to those reaching the end of their tether as having the 'shakes' or the 'twitch'. It was their own language as were the time-honoured phrases 'going into the drink', 'bad prangs', 'gone west' for death in combat, 'sky pilots' for chaplains and much, much more. There was little time for sympathy and the betrayal of emotions, which some were concerned might become infectious.

Whether Jeram had fallen victim to this weariness is unclear, though his pilots suspected it to be true, but after this bad crash he was taken off flying duties, possibly at his own request, and left the ship on 10 August, his war over. He was sadly missed, though a shore posting probably saved this gallant man's life.

In the short term Noel Mitchell took command of 1839 but in August Fraser Shotton, senior pilot with 1844, was promoted to fill the vacancy permanently. But change was a constant feature of life in any squadron; crashes stripping their ranks with a terrible regularity. New people were always turning up to fill the gaps, with novices forced, by necessity, to become veterans very quickly.

When reaching Ceylon *Indomitable* joined the Eastern Fleet, which had been in existence for many years, with its carrier force under the command of Rear-Admiral Clement Moody, a veteran of nearly 40 years of service. A gunnery specialist by trade, he had taken command of HMS *Eagle* in 1937 and had been closely connected with the Fleet Air Arm ever since. During 1941 he was promoted to rear admiral and appointed second in command of Naval Air Stations, followed two years by a posting as second in command of Aircraft Carriers Home Waters. Though not an aviator himself he had developed a firm grasp of tactics and the different nature and needs of aircrew. Like John Eccles, he was a strong, capable and understanding leader who had the needs of his men at heart.

The wing's first few weeks on *Indomitable* passed quickly, with everyone working hard to get ready for their first operation. Noel Mitchell recalled how the days were spent and the new routines they learnt:

> The one thing we thought had finished started all over again – practice!
>
> When would it end? Eventually we all began to realise that in this game of chance we had little or no prospect of ever becoming perfect. In fact, there is so much that can go wrong to even the finest pilots that literally there is no such word. So we went plodding on doing dummy attacks on shore-based aerodromes in Ceylon with RAF fighters providing the opposition. These were awful bloody nightmares of total confusion.

And by slow degrees the novices began to understand the workings of the carrier. Early in the piece I gave lectures to all and sundry describing how the flight deck worked, and reminded them of the landing and take-off procedures. It went something like this:

The crash barriers are controlled by a Petty Officer who shoulders quite a responsibility. He can operate No 1 barrier independently, but 2 and 3 operate together. If, for instance, an aircraft lands well down the deck, the hook catching No 6 or 7 arrestor wire, the speed of the aircraft is such that it will pull the hydraulically controlled wire up the deck until the aircraft is brought to a standstill. If the barrier is left up the aircraft would crash into it, although engaged by an arrester wire. So it can be realised that the PO in charge has quick thinking to do. He watches the aircraft hook engage the wire and then lowers his barrier down so that the aircraft can run over the top without crashing into it.

This is what happens when an aircraft wants to land on.

The Captain turns the ship dead into wind so as to produce the right amount of wind down the deck. If there is a 17-knot wind and the ship is steaming at 24 knots the total wind speed is 42 knots (or 50 mph). The aircraft approaching to land will fly just above stalling speed (for the Hellcat about 65 knots) so actually touches down at a relative speed of 23 knots.

With the ship turned into wind the pilot is then instructed to land either by signals displayed on the port side or over the R/T. As he approaches the batsman guides him in and onto the deck. As the aircraft comes to a standstill two or more deck handling ratings run out and release the hook from the wire. Meanwhile during these split seconds, the pilot is busy putting his landing flaps up, selecting the hook switch and, if quick enough, unlocking his wings prior to them being folded as he taxies up the deck.

When the hook is clear of the wires the pilot is signalled to taxi forward, whereupon he opens up his throttle wide enough to overcome the 50-mph wind coming towards him. Once over the barriers they can be raised again to protect him from the next aircraft if it misses all the wires. More ratings rush out and push the wings into the locked position, as the aircraft is guided onto the lift and taken below or parked forward and made ready for another flight.

A fully worked up squadron should be able to land all 12 aircraft in about 1½ minutes. Or one every 8 seconds. But in reality, and in difficult conditions, the normal rate was 2½ to 3 minutes or about 14 seconds each. To achieve this the first aircraft should be just taxiing over the crash barriers as the second is touching down and taking a wire with its hook. As can be imagined this requires a great deal of practice and team work, because one small slip might mean instant death for anyone.

To some pilots taking off is the most difficult part, especially those with short legs who find it difficult to control the rudders and brakes. There is no doubt one can make a terrible hash of a landing and get away without even bursting a tyre, but in taking off the margin of error is greatly reduced. Two of the most hazardous points were undoubtedly a wet and greasy deck and the view prior to the tail of the aircraft coming up. On a wet deck an aircraft is often seen to go down the full length of the deck with one wheel fully locked by brakes to counter the swing caused by the throttle being opened too quickly.

To get the best view for take-off the pilot usually runs his engine up with brakes fully on until he feels the tail starting to lift. At that precise moment he jams the throttle fully open and lets go the brakes, by doing this he gets a clear view forward of the deck before actually moving. Modern fighters, but particularly Seafires and Corsairs, have long noses that obscure the view ahead and this has to be overcome by such means.

The maximum number of aircraft that can be ranged on deck and flown off at speed is about 30, of which 20 are ranged with their wings still in the folded position. In this mass take-off position, with the ship being turned into wind, Commander (Flying) waves a green flag from the island, whereupon the range controller, usually the batsman, waves for the deck party to take chocks away from the wheels of the aircraft first in line. At the same moment the pilot opens up the throttles with brakes on. Then the range controller waves him into position for take-off and, when happy that the carrier's bow hasn't dipped too deeply into a swell, signals him to go.

When the aircrew and deck-handling parties are trained to a high degree of efficiency and teamwork this whole process can see an aircraft off the deck every 6 seconds. But the deck party can ill afford to be slack with a 50-mph wind roaring over the deck and 30 aero engines making it impossible to stand up. So most work is done on all fours.

During August, ship exercises moved away from the coast of Ceylon across the Indian Ocean towards Sumatra. Before major operations began *Indomitable*'s two specially adapted PRU Hellcats were kept busy doing high-level passes over enemy territory to gather information, as Lionel Godfrey later recounted:

On the 15th August I took off on the first of my photographic reconnaissance missions at 25,000 feet. But at just above 5,000 feet, as I was making a slow, steady climb, the airscrew of my Hellcat stopped turning accompanied by a loud clunk. I checked the fuel supply which was being drawn at the time from my torpedo-shaped drop tank, but nothing appeared to be amiss.

Making a quick decision that some structural failure had occurred in the engine I jettisoned the extra fuel tank and then broke radio silence and broadcast 'Mayday! Mayday! Mayday! Am ditching aircraft in sea. Height now 3,000 feet and decreasing.' A brief acknowledgement of my distress call and a good luck message gave me the encouragement I needed to stay with my aeroplane rather than attempting to bail out. Speedily removing my flying helmet and unplugging its attachments to avoid entanglement, I jettisoned the cockpit hood and prepared to land in the ocean. Although I stalled tail down into the sea at a mere 65 knots it was like hitting a brick wall.

My straps and shoulder harness held me firmly in place as the aircraft's nose dipped sharply below the surface of the ocean and water poured into the cockpit. Just as I was about to release the holding pin of my harness the nose of the 'plane bobbed up out of the water and the whole aircraft settled on a fairly even keel. I leapt from the cockpit and stood on the starboard wing as I released and inflated the dinghy. By this time the Hellcat was beginning to sink and I quickly scrambled into the dinghy and began paddling frantically with my hands. I looked back and watched the tail rise into the air then the whole aircraft disappeared from sight beneath the waves. In all it had taken about 1½ minutes.

The contents of the dinghy were hardly inspiring. On the advice of a more experienced flier I always carried an extra pint can of water in my pack, and I thanked my lucky stars for taking this precaution. There was some chocolate and a bright red triangular flag attached to a telescopic pole, to signal one's position to rescuers. The waves were far larger and deeper in the troughs than they'd seemed from the air, and it was only when the dinghy lifted high on their crests that I could see the horizon over a tumbling blue-grey ocean.

The next 1-½ hours or so were the longest I'd ever experienced. I tried to stay calm in the confident expectation of rescue, but thoughts of sharks crept into my mind. Finally, to my inexpressible relief, I caught sight of something grey far away in the distance and hurriedly extended the pole, with the red flag on the top. Within seconds the dinghy flipped over and deposited me into the sea. I hadn't realised just how fiercely the wind was blowing, and it had taken just one gust to hit the flag and pole and cause the dinghy to over-balance. Soaking wet, I scrambled back into the dinghy and caught sight of a rescue vessel, its bow wave making it visible. Within minutes an Air Sea Rescue launch came alongside and I was lifted up to be dried out, warmed and cared for by its crew. Minus my watch, which had suffered irreparable damage from being immersed in the ocean, I was returned to *Indomitable* that evening, none the worse for my experience.

To this day I carry the cloth badge denoting membership of the Goldfish Club, awarded to aircrew who survived ditching in the sea.

Even before the enemy had been engaged, accidents such as this continued to take their toll of men and machines. But, as in Lionel Godfrey's case, most pilots managed to walk or swim away without serious injury and a short period of rest was all they needed to restore them to health. Undoubtedly these incidents, coupled to the rigours of flying in combat, had a cumulative effect, but for fit young men recovery was generally quick and they gained in experience along the way. But, as one pilot recalled, it was a 'game of blood' that would eventually have only one winner if a limit on operational flying wasn't set.

With regular reconnaissance flights over enemy-held territory becoming more frequent the level of intelligence being sought could only mean that *Indomitable*'s aircraft would soon be flying their first operational mission, codenamed *Banquet*. With this knowledge the air group practised and rehearsed their roles with added vigour, to such an extent that many aircraft had developed faults, as John Hawkins recorded:

The 16th was a busy day and the flight deck was littered with Hellcats all with different ailments. It took all day and well after dark for all the work to be completed and the aircraft struck down into the hangars. The same thing happened the following day There was a monster party that evening, in which a good number of the ship's officers joined in for a change. At 10 o'clock a rugger scrum developed between the Branch and the Executives and it is doubtful if either were superior. Uniforms were ripped and it was a wonder that no bones were broken. The effect of the 'morning after' resulted in a very quiet and uninteresting day on the 18th, but we needed to sober up because the pipe went round that we were due to sail the following day.

At 1030 hrs on the 19th *Indomitable*, flying the flag of Rear Admiral Moody, led a force out of harbour, consisting of HMS *Victorious*, the battleship HMS *Howe*, two cruisers, *Kenya* and *Ceylon*, and five 'R' Class destroyers. From 1200 hrs onwards four Hellcats were standing by on deck just in case.

It was sometime before land disappeared completely out of sight as the fleet made two turns into wind to allow *Victorious* to send off flights of Corsairs on Combat Air Patrols (CAPs), then land on the remains of her squadrons. Once completed the carriers formed up in line astern with escorts either side protecting our flanks. We quickly picked up speed until all the ships were moving at a fast cruising rate. Once away from land briefings began – the targets and our specific roles in the attack.

Once committed to a course of action our nerves began to steady a little and we let our training take over. But even with our strong sense of purpose and understanding of the risks we faced there was still a certain amount of lethargy in some people's behaviour and basic mistakes were made.

There was a bad error on somebody's part on the 20th. At first light Hellcats should have been ranged on deck ready to scramble to protect the fleet if radar picked up signs of an enemy approaching. But nothing appeared until eight o'clock, two hours after sunrise. At 12 noon *Vic's* Corsairs took over and she made a great show launching four fighters on the dot although there wasn't a suspicion of a raid. And so the day passed fairly uneventfully.

The briefings continued in the wardroom on the 21st and it transpired that 1839 and 1844 would provide fleet cover throughout the strike, while Corsairs escorted the Barracudas into the attack. The target was to be a big cement works near Padang, but at the last minute the operation was postponed for 24 hours for reasons that weren't made clear.

Early the next morning we rendezvoused with RFA *Teesdale* and our destroyers immediately left so that they could refuel, followed by the cruisers. This took up most of the day and at dusk the fleet, being as close to the enemy coast as was possible without arousing their suspicions, cruised back and forth hoping to avoid detection.

And with this the aircrew settled down for the night, most avoiding the wardroom or messes, except to eat as much as nervous stomachs would allow. If anybody drank it was simply to quench their thirst in the August heat, there wasn't time or inclination to party in a ship at action stations and under the tightest discipline. Some walked on the blacked-out flight deck, where only the moon could light their path, but with aircraft being spotted ready for the operation it wasn't the place to find a moment's peace. Many retired to their cabins to write letters and others simply tried to read the many Penguin books in circulation. But during the hours before your first operation it was difficult to concentrate and tension soon found outlet in the ships 'heads'.

After hours of inactivity many were up and dressed long before dawn and had made their way onto the flight deck to check their aircraft and talk to the riggers and fitters:

Everyone had an early breakfast and got right on the ball. The first strike which consisted of 20 Barracudas, 10 from *Vic* and the escort of 20 Corsairs, started up in semi-darkness and at 0550 hrs commenced take-off. At the same time four Hellcats led by Mac [Keith McLennan, a New Zealander from Wellington], of the odds and sods flight took off to fly CAP over the fleet. The first attack went in as the islands west of Padang showed up on the horizon. At 0650 hrs the second strike got away with nine Barras from 815 Squadron, three from *Vic* and 12 Corsairs as escort, with one crashing shortly after take-off, with the pilot being picked up safely. At 0820 hrs six Hellcats took off to relieve Mac's flight. An hour later aircraft from both strikes were down safely, leaving Val (Valentine) from 1839 and Shaggers (Godfrey) from 1844 to run over with their PRU Hellcats to photograph the target and report on the damage inflicted. The Hellcat CAPs went on throughout the day as the fleet steamed westwards back to Trincomalee. Later when all the aircrew had been debriefed we discovered what had happened.

The first strike had had no problem finding the target and it was estimated that only one bomb fell outside the target area. When last seen the whole cement works was covered by a pall of black smoke and cement dust that rose 3,000 or more feet into the air and remained there for some time. Whilst this was going on Barracudas dropped propaganda leaflets and Corsairs strafed targets of opportunity. One Corsair failed to return (S/Lt T A Cutter of 1834 Squadron, who was shot down and killed by flak), which was surprising given the absence of enemy aircraft and the lightness of the enemy's anti-aircraft fire. His luck just ran out. Very sad because I seem to recollect he had taken part in the squadron's attacks on the German battleship *Tirpitz* earlier in the year, so was no novice.

The second strike hit shipping and harbour installations around Emmahaven. They easily found the target and hits were scored on coaling wharves, workshops and other harbour installations, whilst a sloop was shot up and damaged. All the aircraft returned safely, except a Barracuda which suddenly flicked over and dived into the sea when waiting to land on. No one was picked up.

Our 'umbrella' had sweet FA to do all day although one flight almost shot down 'Shaggers' as he returned from his PR mission. A snooper was reported by HMS *Howe* at 1600 hrs, but nothing appeared on the plot so no interception was necessary. (John Hawkins)

The sense of anti-climax on *Indomitable* was palpable, having been so keyed up for this first operation. But *Victorious'* aircraft had been given the lead role because of their recent experience with *Tirpitz* and then a series of strikes against the Japanese with *Illustrious* a few weeks earlier. *Indomitable's* fighter wing was seen as the junior, less experienced partner so took a supporting role. Things would change rapidly, but in the meantime the Hellcat pilots had to put up with some leg pulling as Noel Mitchell relates:

Our job had been dull and uninteresting. On our return to Trinco we came in for much ribbing from the Barra and Corsair boys, especially when a newspaper cutting circulated which stated that, 'I'll bet the only cement produced at Padang in the few months will be what's swept up from the surrounding countryside'. Compared to the part we played, this somewhat hurt our feelings.

But others saw things differently and, using a sporting cliché, described this period as a time to 'play ourselves in before the fast bowlers resumed with the new ball'. Terribly timeworn, but true nonetheless.

Embarked and Making Ready For Action

Indomitable at speed in the Indian Ocean whilst working up before operations begin again. (DM)

A constant feature of life within the wing were regular briefs and de-briefs – here being carried out by Tommy Harrington (centre without shirt) in the lee of a multi-barrelled anti-aircraft gun mounting. (DM)

Once in the operational area, combat air patrols (CAPs) and remaining at readiness became a part of daily life. These duties could be long and boring, with the monotony only broken by the occasional mad rush to meet apparent threats plotted by radar. (DM)

Circling the fleet carrying a drop tank which extended the time aircraft could stay overhead until relieved. (JN)

The operational cycle. Even without the enemy interfering there were numerous dangers in carrier operations that regularly claimed lives. (DM)

CHAPTER FOUR

Into the Cauldron

The fleet returned to Trincomalee on 27 August and Rear Admiral Moody began a review of their performance. The targets had been fairly soft ones – having been chosen for that reason. The conflict against the Japanese would be very different to the war in the Atlantic and Mediterranean, as the Americans had quickly discovered, and new tactics had to evolve, be understood and rehearsed if success were to be achieved. It was an island-hopping battle against a hard-fighting enemy still equipped with a potent navy, air force and army. They were also well 'dug in' on the land and islands they had conquered and, for the most part, would die before surrendering. The Royal Navy, and its Air Arm in particular, could not afford to be anything less than lethal in striking the enemy. In due course they would also be serving alongside the huge American fleets in the Pacific, who would expect nothing but the best from their allies. Moody would have seen many shortcomings in the way his ships and squadrons had operated during these early operations and looked for significant improvement in the months that lay ahead.

During late 1943 the Fleet Air Arm had begun to experiment with the concept of wing leaders. It was idea the Germans had developed in 1917 and which the RAF began to copy towards the end of the Battle of Britain. The plan was a simple one. A number of squadrons operating as a single unit each with their own commander, but with an overall head who could watch and direct the battle. In 1917 the Germans developed their 'Flying Circuses', as they became known by the British, to help achieve local mastery of the air, driving away enemy reconnaissance, bombing or fighter aircraft. In 1940 the RAF employed this tactic, but this time to break up massed German formations in daytime bombing raids over London. The following year, with Hitler's forces invading the Soviet Union, big RAF fighter wings did sweeps over France more with the intention of making a show than achieving any great gain. Very quickly in the Pacific War this leader concept found favour and proved successful when employed by the Americans and Japanese on their carriers. HMS *Illustrious* was the first fleet carrier to be deployed to the Far East, as this new striking force began to be formed, and Dickie Cork, now a lieutenant commander, was appointed wing leader to its Corsair squadrons. Sadly, he was killed in a flying accident when landing at China Bay on 14 April 1944, but by that time he had firmly established the principle and rehearsed it to some effect. By September the idea had been approved for wider use and the Hellcats on *Indomitable* gained a wing leader in the shape of Tommy Harrington. With Fraser Shotton now in command of 1839, 1844 needed a new commander and this paved the way for Lt Cdr Mike 'Gammy' Godson's appointment. He quickly made his mark, in the air and on the ground, not to mention the wardroom, as Lionel Godfrey later recalled:

> Gammy settled in quickly and soon had a prolific collection of pin ups adorning the walls of his quarters, all featuring shapely legs and other attractions. His irrepressible personality soon made its mark on the squadron and the wing. He seemed to know everybody and get the best from people, whether officers or other ranks.

In the few days between Harrington taking over the wing and this force of nature's arrival, Lionel Godfrey held nominal command of 1844. During this period the two squadrons flew on more practice missions with varying degrees of success. But aircraft serviceability was proving to be a problem and on one exercise alone three out of four Hellcats stuttered and failed when about to be launched. These sorts of failures were becoming too common and all the aircraft were carefully checked over to try and identify the faults and the causes. After much work and head scratching it was found that water had found its way into the petrol tanks. This in turn had caused corrosion in the fuel pumps, which impeded the smooth flow of petrol. Over the next few days all the aircraft were stripped down and repaired, with greater care then being shown in protecting the aircraft from the elements.

Danger lies in so many aspects of life on board a fighting ship at war, not all of them linked solely to combat. Accidents continued to slowly drain men away, the lucky to hospital, the unlucky to a cemetery or the sea. Whilst at anchor in Trincomalee, on 28 August, one of 1839's armourers walked into the open void created by a descending lift. Guard rails hadn't been raised to protect the unwary and the young man fell to his death. Most of the off-duty men in his squadron attended a very sad ceremony the following morning in a small cemetery near China Bay, where he was buried adjacent to Dickie Cork.

But in the bustle to be ready for the next operation these tragic moments couldn't be allowed to dampen spirits for too long. Being kept busy can often be the best way of coping with the loss of a ship mate and the programme they faced was forcefully pursued by the two new squadron commanders. But despite the constant practice, mistakes were still being made in training. Shortly after Godson arrived the wing were flying escort to Barracudas whilst they attacked the fleet off the coast of Ceylon. Other fighters, including some RAF Spitfires, were providing protection to the ships, but in heavy cloud all the aircraft got mixed up, the Hellcats lost their bombers and confusion reigned for a time. It seemed that no matter how hard they tried the final polish escaped them. Sometimes it was bad luck, at other times it was poor maintenance and unserviceability issues, then there was the question of flying ability. Did the pilots have what it takes to be truly effective on operations? And, if not, what needed to be done – transfers in and out seemed the only way this might be achieved. Shotton's promotion and Godson's arrival gave them excellent leaders and this was supplemented by other new arrivals. But 1839's new leader was convinced that the men who had been with the squadrons since late 1943 were, for the most part, ready for combat. All they needed was a little more polishing and a few missions under their belts. The next mission was soon in coming, preceded by much speculation and many rumours, as John Hawkins recalled:

No more definite news and the chief cook still had most to say in the majority of rumours. HMS *Victorious* arrived in the afternoon and that really set the tongues wagging. By general agreement it seemed that we were going out on Thursday with the whole of the fleet and attacking either Java, Rangoon or Sumatra. On the 13th, Thursday was confirmed for sailing and all the aircraft were given a good working over and a run up, but no flying. During the day two new Hellcats were received one being for the new wing leader.

We sailed on the 14th with practically the same formation as on the cement works job – *Victorious*, *Howe*, *Kenya*, *Cumberland* and five R Class destroyers. But still nothing about the target, except that it was expected to last two days, not one, this time.

At just after 1400 hrs Dick Mackie landed on from China Bay and the wing was complete in aircraft, although two pilots were still missing somewhere in Ceylon – Shaggers (Godfrey) and Val (Valentine). We steamed merrily in a south-easterly direction, with four Hellcats ranged on stand-by, for a few hours so that any spotters on land would report this misleading course, then turned about. No more news overnight or briefings, which suggested some uncertainty on the part of the 'planners'.

Much the same on the 15th but the four Hellcats had to be moved around the deck quite a lot to enable Barracuda to take off and land as part of gunnery exercises. Finally, a flying programme for the wing was exhibited outside the wardroom, confirming that Sunday was D Day and there was to be a fighter sweep at dawn. Umbrella operations were to be carried out for the rest of the day. D+1 was an attack by the Barras, escorted by Corsairs and Hellcats and then home.

At 1400 hrs the aircrew were briefed more fully by the captain and Big F Commander (Flying). Twenty-four Corsairs to take off at dawn to strafe the aerodromes at Medan and Bindjai, whilst 12 Hellcats will attack harbour installations at Belawan-Deli on the east coast of Sumatra. If the destroyer escort can hold out with the fuel they're carrying, there being no chance of replenishment, the Barras would follow up with a strike on the Northern tip of Sumatra, if not its straight back to Trincomalee.

After a number of poorly performed exercises and operations this attack, codenamed 'Light A', seemed to take a much more measured approach, with lower expectations of the aircrew, particularly the fighters. Rear Admiral Moody later commented that, 'it was clear that the boys needed to get a whiff of gunpowder, but not on an operation cluttered up with a too complex a strike plan. The targets were expected to be lightly defended, and slightly easier for that reason, giving the pilots a chance to iron out some of the faults'.

Just in case the primary targets couldn't be reached for some reason there was a 'Light B' option, which due to very bad weather conditions on 17th was brought in to play. The fleet reached its new flying-off position the following morning in time to launch a dawn strike against rail yards at Sigli in Sumatra. But once again the early stages of the operation were marred by a very slow build-up, caused by mechanical failures and a Barracuda ditching soon after take-off, with the loss of its pilot. This was followed by three Corsairs turning back to *Victorious* once in the air due to technical problems. The form up was finally completed after 40 minutes of circling round the fleet, much to Moody's obvious frustration. Dick Mackie described the scene on *Indomitable*'s deck:

We were all up by 0400 hrs for breakfast then briefing, though only eight Hellcats would be involved – four led by the Wing Leader and four by Gammy. These aircraft hadn't been ranged on deck overnight because of the problems we'd faced with water getting into the works, although four fighters on standby had been left up there during the dark hours. At 0545 hrs the order to start up was given by Commander (F) over the loudspeaker, but at this stage the Barracuda wing leader's aircraft (Lt Cdr Britain) developed a problem, wouldn't start and had to be struck down on the forward lift, delaying take-off. More panic followed because the escort couldn't get airborne, still being in the hangar delayed by the need to get a replacement Barra up on deck for their wing leader. There was a problem with the lift which seemed to pop up and down several times in some confusion. Then, finally, the Hellcats gradually emerged then took off and joined the waiting bombers.

The whole force consisting of 19 Barracudas (there should have been 20), 16 Corsairs (there should have been 20) and eight Hellcats, eventually set course, well behind schedule in fairly good conditions. In the meantime, Mac's section were stooging back and forth over the fleet as air cover, getting increasingly bored, and four PR aircraft, flown by Jackie, Junior, Mitch and Felix Rankin were ranged on deck. At just before 0700 hrs three took off, but the starter on the fourth jammed and only got going when whacked with a lump hammer. Jackie raced off 15 minutes late, just as Lt Cdr Shotton's Flight took off to relieve Mac.

At 0900 hrs those that had remained on *Indomitable* watched from the 'Goofers' platform as the strike aircraft returned, the Barracudas landing first. One pranged as the pilot came in too low, despite the batsman waving furiously, and hit the round down and came to a shuddering halt just before hitting the barriers. Then the fighters came down, followed by the PR boys, having gathered their information and photographs. On *Victorious* things were slightly worse, with a Barracuda going into the barrier on landing, whilst a Corsair had earlier caught fire and spewed out burning petrol from its slip tank on the deck when landing. The show seen quite clearly through binoculars from *Indom's* bridge.

For the remainder of the day flight after flight of Hellcats and Corsairs took off and patrolled overhead as the fleet left the coast of Sumatra and headed to Trincomalee. There were two suspected snoopers picked up by radar, Corsairs flew off to check the first but had to turn back when someone realised they'd been fitted with empty drop tanks. Then Lt Cdr Godson's flight pursued a second plot without any success. And so the day ended with de-briefings and photo analysis."

Once the aircraft had left the fleet the weather had grown steadily worse until over Sigli swirling winds, heavy rain and low cloud intervened making the run in very difficult, even though there were no enemy fighters and very light flak. And the aircrew let themselves down with poor R/T discipline, whilst the 16 Barracudas that found their targets bombed with little or no accuracy. For *Victorious'* bombers this was even more disappointing because they had reached a peak of efficiency only three months earlier when attacking the *Tirpitz*, so seemed to be going backwards, not forwards.

When returning to the carriers these problems were exacerbated by poor ship recognition when a Barracuda and Hellcat from *Indomitable* attacked HM Submarine *Spirit*, which was on the surface rescuing the crew of another Barracuda that had ditched nearby. They did little or no damage, which said much for their skills, though it was probably better not have sunk a friend to prove their accuracy with bomb or bullet!

Despite several tongue in cheek signals the general message imparted by Rear Admiral Moody and Captain Eccles was 'must do a great deal better'. So, over the next few weeks we exercised continuously, with much hard criticism when we fell short. (Dick Mackie)

Whilst the Royal Navy gradually built up their strength and rehearsed for the time when they would fight in the unrelenting war in the Pacific, they read about the operations going on there and wondered what might lay ahead. In June there had been a major battle in the Philippine Sea between the American and Japanese fleets. Losses were huge on both sides, but American carrier-borne aircraft had decimated their enemy in a combat later called the 'Great Marianas Turkey Shoot'. The final figures are unclear, but it seems that more than 600 enemy aircraft were destroyed, five ships sunk, including three carriers, and some 3,000 men lost. The Americans had one battleship damaged, lost 123 aircraft and 109 men. And so, the pursuit continued, with the Japanese resisting strongly, with their seaborne forces diminishing rapidly, then introducing the kamikaze tactic to try and stem the flood.

Then in October, as the British continued with their pin prick attacks, there was the battle of Leyte Gulf, another large fleet-to-fleet encounter, which virtually ended the Japanese Navy's role in the war. They lost 28 warships, including four carriers and three battleships, some 300 aircraft and 12,500 men, whilst the Americans suffered the loss of 3,000 men, 200-plus aircraft and three light carriers and three destroyers. But the kamikaze attacks had begun in earnest and this bode ill for the future. Reports also began to be received from the occupied territories, about the way recently captured aircrew were being treated when picked up. Just as in Europe where the Nazis summarily murdered any captured commandoes, so the Japanese took the same approach with some airmen who came down, beheading them without thought or mercy. These reports do not appear to have been suppressed in any way and were widely known on board the British carriers, as Dick Mackie later recalled:

> Just when we thought that the horrors of this war couldn't get any worse we received this news with very heavy hearts. Capture was something we all sought to avoid at any cost, but now even more so. It also began changing our attitude towards the enemy, which was also profoundly affected when word of kamikaze attacks spread. Kill or be killed was unavoidable if you were to survive and win, but now there was no mercy shown in air to air combat or when ground strafing: something that would soon become commonplace. No one voiced any concerns over this, though later I did think deeply about what we had to do and why. We live by the rule of law and discard it at our peril. But in this case the enemy was so callous and brutal that we couldn't afford the luxury of compassion, let them escape and, perhaps, strike us again. There was also the issue of time in combat, where only split seconds to fire and disable an enemy aircraft existed. To be sure of destroying the enemy you fired at the pilot, hoping to kill him instantly, particularly if he was a kamikaze.

Lionel Godfrey later described how these reports changed the practicalities of their day-to-day life:

> The rescued crew of a downed Barracuda were picked up by a sub and had to remain on board for 10 days, until she reached port. When they returned they were subdued and much thinner. However, as someone in the wardroom remarked, '… better to be an encumbrance to a sub for a while than be a prisoner of the Japanese'. I heartily agreed, possibly because the only time I'd ever carried a side arm – a cumbersome .45 service revolver kept in a trouser pocket – whilst in the air was when we fought the Japanese. The revolver wasn't issued to shoot the Japs, but to be used for self-destruction in case you were forced down in enemy territory and were unable to avoid being captured. It was commonly thought, and reluctantly accepted, that to shoot oneself in such circumstances meant a swifter and less painful end than being captured, tortured and beheaded.

With the American attack on Leyte due to take place during the third week of October, the Eastern Fleet were given the task of a diversionary strike to try and draw Japanese forces away from the main battle area. This seemed unlikely, but was executed nonetheless. The Nicobar Islands, in the Andaman Sea, north-west of Sumatra, were chosen for this attack, with targets deemed to be plentiful and important, the Japanese wishing to defend these strategically important islands. Codenamed Operation *Millet* the attacks would be spread over three days, meaning it would be the first time in this campaign that the fleet would stay in the battle zone for a prolonged period and launch a number of strikes. Moody didn't record any particular concerns over his aircrew's ability to do this successfully, but with so many problems recently he must have had some doubts.

The fleet sailed on 15 October, this time with the carriers' escorted by the rebuilt World War I battlecruiser, HMS *Renown*, four cruisers, 11 destroyers and other support ships. Passage took two days and at 0600 hrs on 17th the two carriers were detached from the main force and steamed at full speed to the north-east where they would launch the first strike. The plan was for *Victorious* to despatch 19 Barracudas to attack airfields, with eight Corsairs as escort. At the same time *Indomitable* would launch 10 bombers and eight Hellcats to assault any ships in Nancowry Harbour or 'targets of opportunity' that appeared. All went well, and the enemy were caught by surprise allowing the aircraft time to aim more accurately and hit the few targets that presented themselves. But after a while the flak built up and enemy fighters appeared resulting in the loss of two Corsairs near Malacca, and one Barracuda.

Next on deck were six more Hellcat to 'spot' for a coastal bombardment by the big gun warships, but two failed before take-off and had to be repaired, while Stan Farquhar had to turn back when a fire developed in his cockpit. He landed safely, but a little singed, much to his amused relief, which he shared many years later:

> A small electrical fire started as I climbed away from *Indomitable*'s deck. I tried to stop it spreading, thinking of all the fuel I was sitting on, and the open canopy, which was locked back for take-off, letting in air which fanned the flames. I quickly shut it and put on my oxygen mask, so didn't have to breathe in fumes, whilst still trying to smother the fire, with some success. I quickly brought the aircraft around, radioed the ship and requested an immediate landing. Big F didn't waste time and signalled me to come down. I didn't wait but turned in quickly and put her down catching the first wire. I released my belt before coming to a halt and scampered out onto the wing and fell to the deck, my flying kit smouldering and my hands very sore. Once the goofers saw that I was OK there was much gentle ribbing and laughter. It was a near thing, but the doc gave me a clean bill of health and I was back flying later in the day.

And Lionel Godfrey, after completing two PR missions, volunteered to fly a CAP over the fleet as the day drew to a close, but came to grief:

On returning with A Flight after 1¾ hours circling the fleet I crashed over the port side of the carrier whilst attempting to land on. With the huge, red tropical sun setting on the horizon and the carrier steaming due west to catch whatever wind there was across the deck I saw the other three Hellcats of my flight down safely before coming into land myself. I misjudged height and direction badly before plunging over the port-side of the flight deck. By sheer good luck I had caught an arrestor wire with my hook, which prevented me from finishing up in the sea, and I came to rest hanging almost vertically against the armoured flanks of the carrier with the nose of my aircraft about 10 feet above the surface of the ocean. On the way over the side I saw out of the corner of my eye the hurried evacuation of a Bofor gun's crew as my aeroplane demolished their gun platform before I was left to gaze hypnotically at the water gushing past my windscreen. It took quite a while to haul my aircraft up and back onto the flight deck and to extricate me from the battered cockpit, and it wasn't until I attempted to stand on my own two feet that I realised how badly my back had been strained by the crash. Despite being in pain, as well as suffering the acute embarrassment over such a woeful deck landing, I'd still to render my A25 report to Commander Flying.

The ship's doctors cared for me and made sure I laid flat on my back for some days. I stayed with the ship until she arrived in Bombay, where I was told I wouldn't be fit to fly for three months or more, provided I behaved sensibly. In December I was shipped back to Britain, my war over.

But one pilot, S/Lt D M 'Jock' MacKenzie, a young New Zealander, wasn't so lucky when returning from the strike earlier in the day. He landed too heavily, the port wheel detached and the hook failed, slewing his aircraft sharply to the deck's edge and into the sea. He may have been knocked unconscious by the impact and made no apparent move to escape. The Hellcat quickly filled with water and sank before any help could reach him and he drowned.

Once all the other aircraft had been recovered the fleet retired to the south-west to prepare for more strikes over the next two days. But the weather closed in on the 18th making operations all but impossible, leaving the 19th to complete the diversionary raid, as Dick Mackie again relates:

The Barracuda strike with its Hellcat escort was off soon after dawn, the targets being the same as on the 17th. The three pilots – Gavin, Stan and Frankie – who had bad luck two days earlier with problem aircraft, got away this time and did the spotting for the day's bombardment. Unfortunately, Frankie ran into some Japs on the way back and was shot down. In the meantime, the enemy made an appearance over the fleet, but were met by our Hellcats and the *Vic*'s Corsairs. The Corsairs shot down four and the Hellcats three, all Oscars [the Nakajima Ki 43 single-engine fighter]. Tug Wilson destroyed two and Smithwick one. They were flying with Bing (Hawkins) and Claude, who was just about to press the 'tit' when Tug nipped in before him and shot it down. Bing got on a Jap, but his electrics failed so his guns failed to fire. At last the wing had done something really useful.

But there were losses that day other than Frank Grinham. Two Corsairs went down with their pilots and a Barracuda had crashed into the sea on take-off, with its crew being rescued. Later on two Corsairs went over the side when trying to land, but, again, both pilots survived. With that the fleet set course for Ceylon and departed at high speed:

> As we neared Trincomalee 15 Hellcats were flown off to China Bay. The wing is going to disembark while the ship goes on to Bombay. The people who flew ashore returned on board in the evening and a big party took place in the wardroom to celebrate the operation and Tug and Smithwick's claims. (1839 Squadron Diary, JN)

After each period of operations there would be the inevitable inquests and reviews, followed by more practice and dress rehearsals. But there was also the more sombre business of making good losses to men and machines. Death and injuries were becoming commonplace, though they had not lost their power to shock or sadden those left behind. The attrition rate throughout training had been high, but now they were facing the full rigours of life at sea and the enemy, and casualty figures rose still higher. One pilot later commented that in a normal naval fighter wing, operating in the Far East, a third, or more, would lose their lives to enemy action or accident. He added that it was a rate that reflected British casualty figures on the Somme in 1916 and Passchendaele a year later, and would probably have made even the Great War's callous generals blanch.

And so, with growing regularity newcomers were absorbed into the squadrons, quickly learning from the veterans the lessons of survival, as Bill Foster later recalled, having been posted to 1844 Squadron:

> I don't think there was a deliberate attempt to assign someone to watch over you, to help acclimatisation, and, of course, you had the squadron commander and your section leader to guide you. But you couldn't always go to them for simple, friendly advice, without being thought a pest. And it was here that one or two of the others showed enormous understanding and compassion for the inexperienced newcomer. In my case Bing Hawkins proved to be a blessing. I think it helped that we were similar in temperament and both had a strong sense of privacy. In those early, very difficult months Bing was always on hand to offer advice, answer my many questions and listen to my concerns, usually during a quiet walk on the flight deck. With great friendliness and patience, he helped and guided me and, I'm sure, probably saved my life as I learnt to fight and survive. I will always be grateful to him for this.

The newcomers would have a few weeks to settle in before the next round of operations began. Leave was taken, the carrier underwent some essential maintenance and the squadrons began the process of working up at China Bay and Colombo. But now there was the added pressure of transit to the Pacific to fight alongside the Americans, whose campaign was rolling relentlessly towards the Japanese homeland. The closer they got, the more difficult and murderous became the fighting.

During October and November, the future of the Eastern Fleet came under close scrutiny. With the invasion of mainland Europe now well established and the Soviets advancing steadily towards Germany's eastern borders, the war in the Atlantic and Mediterranean were all but over. Britain's large force of carriers and battleships could now be safely deployed to the Indian and Pacific Oceans to help destroy Japanese resistance. the British Pacific Fleet was born from discussions in London, and ships began being assigned to that theatre of war. With them came Rear-Admiral Sir Phillip Vian, to replace Rear Admiral Moody, who returned to the UK. In due course Vian would make *Indomitable* his flagship, just as Moody had done, and lead a force with the title 1st Aircraft Carrier Squadron.

Oblivious of these debates and decisions, those who would fight these battles enjoyed their brief rest, as only the young can. John Hawkins wrote:

> During the next 10 days everyone had a most enjoyable leave spending most of the time golfing, dancing and, what is more important, 'popsylating' [flirting]. Some were lucky, others were not, whilst others were too drunk to care either way. But on 7th November we returned to the grindstone at China Bay and a most amazing spectacle – everyone in their blues. It was so bloody cold that the boys were shivering all day and praying for hot water in the showers. The troops got on the ball with the aircraft and a flying programme was ready for the following day.
>
> Next morning twelve of the wing's aircraft took off for squadron drill, but two came back with undercarriage failure. The rest of us carried on and had a melee with some Spits.
>
> The wing welcomed some new pilots – Lt Schwenk, S/Lt Foster, S/Lt Northeast, S/Lt Smith and Major Williams, RM, our new Wing Army Liaison Officer. After this we got down to hard work and listened to the rumours spread by the chief cook, the usual source of all information.

This short break ended on 1 December when the wing flew out to join *Indomitable* again. But there was one important change. The Barracudas were no longer in evidence, having been replaced with Grumman Avengers. The feeling had grown that these TBR aircraft lacked the performance and punch needed for service in the Pacific. The American aircraft were deemed to be substantially better, with the added bonus that replacements were more readily available through the supply chain supporting the US Navy. So, 815 and 817 Squadrons left *Indomitable* to be replaced by 857, which had been enlarged beyond normal squadron size and had a complement of 21 aircraft.

> No one was sad to see the Barracudas go. We missed their aircrew, who were a fine bunch, but not the constant drag of having to protect these underpowered and vulnerable aircraft.

The Avengers were much better and certainly looked more war like. 857 soon settled in with their CO, L/Cdr 'Doc' Stuart leading the way. He and Gammy Godson were old friends apparently. (Dick Mackie)

Once at sea Vian began to make his presence felt, which surprised few in his new command. He was a veteran of the battle of Jutland, who by 1939 had risen to the rank of captain, and who had been constantly in action since the start of war. In the fjords of Norway his 4th Destroyer Flotilla audaciously captured the German supply ship *Altmark*, and rescued some 300 men taken prisoner during the *Graf Spee*'s foray into the South Atlantic and Indian Ocean in late 1939. Then his flotilla had attacked the *Bismarck* with torpedoes during the night before the battleship's demise in May 1941. With his record of aggression and success he was promoted to rear-admiral two months later, then saw service in the increasingly violent Mediterranean campaign during late 1941 and 1942 with the 15th Cruiser Squadron. Despite serious illness, which threatened to end his sea-going career, he recovered sufficiently to take command of an escort carrier group which saw action during the Salerno landings in September 1943. The following year he led the Eastern Task Force as it supported the D-Day landings in Normandy. With the sea war in the Far East beginning to take precedence it was natural for this fighting admiral to follow the action. In November he joined his flagship, the newly built carrier HMS *Indefatigable*, as it prepared to sail for Ceylon, as part of the 1st Aircraft Carrier Squadron.

Vian touched on some of the political issues behind British participation in the Pacific War and the substantial logistical problems they faced in his book *Action This Day* and in correspondence with John Winton:

The American Commander-in-Chief Ernest King was by no means enthusiastic over British participation. He felt they would best employed against Japanese oil supplies in the islands bordering the Indian Ocean. If they joined the Pacific War, they should operate in General MacArthur's South West Area.

Admiral King's attitude has sometimes been ascribed to Anglo-phobia. This is not altogether true. Certainly his loyalty was given wholeheartedly to the Navy he served. It was a feeling that also led him to look upon the United States Army and Air Force as little better than doubtful allies. Now, when the USN was poised to deliver, unaided, decisive defeat on the Japanese Fleet, it was understandable that King should want no one else to share the laurels. There was, however, another and better reason why Admiral King was opposed to the Royal Navy joining in the Pacific War. The RN had been trained and equipped for the relatively short-range warfare encountered in the Mediterranean, Home Waters and the Atlantic. But an entirely new form of warfare was evolving in the vast expanse of the Pacific. Operating thousands of miles from the nearest permanent base, the Americans had developed a logistic system and organisation of unimagined size and complexity. Their Fleet was supplied and replenished at sea, where it would remain, often for many weeks, without returning even to the temporary, advanced bases set up in the island groups.

King and the CinC (Pacific), Admiral Chester Nimitz, doubted whether the British Fleet could develop, within a useful time, a similar system…. If our Fleet was to join forces, it must be self-supporting.

The date by which our Fleet could be moved to the Pacific was governed by the time required to establish the main base (in this case Sydney some 2,000 miles away from the Fleet's planned area of operations), huge stocks of stores and equipment and manpower. For operations it depended on how soon supply arrangements could be made for the forward areas – known as the Fleet Train. This would consist of repair ships, stores carriers, freighting carriers, amenity ships, harbour service craft; most of the services, in fact, which we had previously looked to our bases to provide.

The number of merchant ships required for the Fleet Train in itself presented a daunting problem. The situation was aggravated by the worn out condition of many fleet auxiliaries and merchant ships, which had endured 5 years of war…. When the Americans inflicted a crushing defeat on the Japanese Fleet (at Leyte in October 1944) the distance for our Fleet from Sydney increased to 3,500 miles. Still more merchant ships and auxiliaries would therefore be required.

Meanwhile, in August 1944, Admiral Sir Bruce Fraser had relieved Sir James Sommerville in command of the Far East Fleet, from which the new Fleet was to be formed. In November, Admiral Fraser assumed the title CinC, British Pacific Fleet… He would be too senior to command his Fleet afloat, when it joined the US Pacific Fleet. Vice-Admiral H B Rawlings was therefore appointed to fulfil this function at sea, whilst the CinC would make his base in Australia.

Fraser, Rawlings and Vian faced a daunting task in making the BPF ready for service in the Pacific and had much to prove if they were to achieve acceptance. But despite the logistics nightmare they faced, their main problem was forging the carriers, and their air groups, into a cohesive fighting force. During 1944 this had proved elusive despite the best endeavours of the squadrons involved, even when the targets were poorly defended and of low priority. Now there would be four fleet carriers working together, with two more due to arrive. If there had been command and control problems before they would surely get worse now, if Vian and his captains didn't stamp their authority on the men under their command.

With Christmas imminent, and the next phase of the Pacific campaign due to start early in the New Year, time was fast approaching when the BPF would see action with their American allies. The main base in Australia would be ready for service in February 1945 and the fleet train existed, though still needed many more ships and a great deal of exercising before being deemed effective. But the enlarged carrier group needed to get to sea and prove itself capable of striking as one, before this major step could be deemed a realistic possibility. *Victorious* and *Indomitable* had been on station for some months and *Illustrious*, having just completed a maintenance period in South Africa, appeared in Ceylon in early November. *Indefatigable* arrived in early December, with its Seafire, Avenger and Firefly squadrons, to complete the group.

Practice and more practice were the order of the day and, until the main base was ready, Fraser agreed with Nimitz that the BPF would operate in the Indian Ocean and attack the strategically important oil refineries in Sumatra. Vian described the thinking behind this plan:

> They were of great value to the Japanese and an attack would hurt them in a sensitive spot, and at the same time it would give our aircraft carriers the experience they needed.
>
> There were three of these oil refineries, the two largest serving the important fields centred on Palembang, in southern Sumatra, the third being at Pangkalan Brandan, at the other end of the island. Refineries at the same time were particularly suitable targets for precision dive-bombing by naval aircraft, as opposed to area bombing by high flying heavy bombers.
>
> The refineries at Palembang – Pladjoe and Soengei Gerong – were the largest in the Far East, and were therefore our chief objective. But in order to gain experience, it was decided to use Pangkalan Brandan for two rehearsal attacks (using only *Indomitable* and *Illustrious*). Vice-Admiral Rawlings had been struck down before my arrival by a severe illness, which was to keep him out of action until our arrival in Australia. Upon myself, therefore devolved command.

It is difficult to say who would bear ultimate responsibility for the attacks that followed. But Vian was an aggressive and ambitious leader who rarely showed discretion 'in laying himself alongside the enemy', to quote Admiral Hawke in 1759. When the *Altmark* was captured and boarded in a Norwegian fjord in early 1940 he had breached international law by entering the sovereign waters of a country not yet at war. His reasons for doing so were sound and reflected German tactics, but it demonstrated a ruthless side to his personality that might lead him and his fleet into taking unnecessary risk. In 1944/45 some of his officers believed that the battles soon to be fought over Sumatra, as the fleet made its way to Sydney and the real war, were unnecessary and might prove far too costly for any gain made – strategically or operationally. Better to have waited and 'kept their powder dry'.

Undoubtedly both Fraser and Rawlings would have debated these issues with Vian before committing this new force to the attack, but there is a suspicion amongst his men that he was the prime mover in what happened and may have driven them too aggressively as two of his pilots recalled:

> *Indefatigable* was new to this sort of war and was having problems with her Seafires –a problem that would only get worse when flying in combat. *Illustrious*, though having operated in the Indian Ocean before refit in South Africa, needed to get back into the swing of things, which meant a lot of hard work in a very short time. Added to this the Fighter Wings on *Victorious* and *Indomitable* hadn't exactly covered themselves in glory in their first operations and still needed sorting out. Then there were the new Avenger squadrons. Good aircraft and

much better than the Barras but their crews needed more time to get used to them when flying from carriers. And over all this were the problems associated with co-ordinating so many aeroplanes in the air when attacking the enemy. Our early efforts had so often nearly come to grief through lack of central control, as well as poor R/T discipline and naivety over tactics. Palembang came just too soon for all concerned and we paid a heavy price which we could ill-afford at that stage. (Gordon Aitken, S/Lt (A) RNVR)

On paper we looked a strong fleet, but we were not fully worked up and had many novice squadrons. The Seafires were essentially designed to operate from land and fly short interceptor missions, so lacked the ruggedness and endurance for carrier-borne operations. As a result, *Indefatigable* would lose many aircraft in deck-landing accidents. They would improve but it would take a lot of time and effort to do so and many in the other fighter squadrons saw them as a liability, only good for flying CAPs over the fleet. And this placed an added burden on the Corsairs and Hellcats when flying on strikes

Vian, I think, was determined to make a show of Palembang and impress the Americans with our prowess. But we weren't ready and it was a costly mistake. In any case the USN only ever regarded us as a minor player in this game, possibly even a liability. (Dick Mackie)

In war, taking risks and incurring casualties is inevitable, but all commanders have to balance the likely gain with the likely losses and be sure that their tactics were correct and their men trained appropriately for the combat ahead. Throughout the Great War British commanders grossly misjudged the strength of the opposition, the depth of their defences, their resolution, the state of terrain and the true capabilities of newly developed weapons such as tanks and aircraft. At the same time their men received training more suited to 1815 not 1915 and only belatedly introduced better tactics when the Germans were becoming a spent force in the latter part of 1918. The result – slaughter. Fraser, Rawlings and Vian were in danger of committing some of these basic mistakes, but on a much smaller scale, simply to impress a reluctant ally. Small wonder that the pilots, who in many cases were the children of Great War survivors, were concerned. But the will of the admirals, with the support of Churchill and his government, prevailed and the campaign commenced, with the attack on Pangkalan Brandan just before Christmas. John Hawkins takes up the story:

On 13th December there was more air firing practice with very mixed results. Some of the pilots although trying hard weren't improving that much. Buzzes during the day concluded that the new RAA (Vian) was about to shake things up etc etc. But next day air firing was postponed and the aircraft were made ready to be taken by lighter out to the carrier for loading on board. Something big was coming off but no one knew what it might be.

The admiral arrived on board and for the rest of the day everyone was giving their opinion of him. A big conference was held later and so it was obvious that something was in the wind. All the following day the troops worked like mad to get all the aircraft serviceable, working long into the night without break.

At 1330 hrs on the 17th the ship set sail, with four Hellcats range on deck as standby The fleet consisted of ourselves, HMS *Illustrious*, the cruisers *Newcastle*, *Argonaut* and *Black*

Prince with five escorting destroyers. At 1430 hours the target was finally revealed in the first briefing – the big oil refinery at Pangkalan Brandan on the east coast of Sumatra. To get there the fleet was to go between the Nicobars and Sabang and so to the entrance of the Malacca Straits.

The next day was very calm and peaceful and by lunchtime we had rendezvoused with a tanker and her escort, two destroyers. She refuelled the cruisers and destroyers and was then left unescorted to await our return. Late in the afternoon 1839 did a radar calibration run back and forth over the Fleet. Up early on the 18th and from 0800 hrs two Hellcats were airborne throughout the day as ASP (Anti Snooper Patrol), except for a break over lunch when the Corsairs took over. At 1930 hrs the fleet was due south of the Nicobars and there were last minute briefings lasting for two hours covering all aspects of the strike. Everyone disappeared to their cabins very early, but few if any managed any sleep. Before turning in I wandered to the hangar deck and checked my aircraft over and chatted to my hard-working and ever faithful crew.

December 20th – D Day – Operation *Robson*. The weather was poor and the take-off was delayed until 0635 hrs. The strike force consisted of 12 Avengers from us and 16 from *Illustrious*, each with four 500-lb bombs. They were escorted by 16 Hellcats and 16 Corsairs. Four of these were carrying 500 lb too. Two flights from 1839 were providing close cover and two flights from 1844 were flying top cover. Jack Ruffin and Junior were in each flight carrying cameras to take photos of the bombing. At 0835 hrs Gavin's flight took off to patrol over the fleet and watched as the strike aircraft returned two hours later, carefully counting the numbers and looking for anyone in distress. But all seemed OK.

The main target had been covered in cloud and the secondary objective – the port installations around Belawan Deli – were attacked instead, with little obvious damage done. The weather was foul and several aircraft became separated, including Mac and Tug who came across an oil storage tank, in a break in the cloud, and beat it up from low level. It went straight up and they then found an engine which was last seen belching smoke and steam. Meanwhile Bryan Hicks and Taylor tracked a Sally just taking off and sent it down to crash into a house. Apart from this the fighters had nothing to report.

Late in the afternoon – and to our great surprise – Rear-Admiral Vian decided to send eight Hellcats and eight Corsairs on a strafing mission. Needless to say everyone was keen to go. But the final selection was the wing leader with the remainder of Gavin's Flight and Jenks leading a mixed bunch from '39 and '44 – those who hadn't flown in the strike earlier. At 1640 hrs they took a hurried departure, each having dived into the nearest aircraft, and streaked off to Sabang. They overtook the Corsairs on the way and forged ahead.

As we reached the coast at very low level the aircraft did a quick pull up and right ahead was a jetty and a small harbour, with several barges and junks. All had a good squirt and experienced no flak. At this point in the proceedings I experienced finger trouble and lost the rest of the flight, who carried on to the aerodrome. Here they blew dispersal huts to pieces and also flattened the canteen manager and his cobbers. I had a little session on my own and destroyed a Rising Sun emblem on the way out. A little flak came our way, but did no damage and everyone returned to the fleet as darkness fell. Foster had to make an emergency landing with a fire in his cockpit, but got out safely, with assistance. The final CAPs landed on both carriers at 1800 hrs with difficulty, the carriers showing little light being so close to the enemy coast. So ended another none too successful day. Captain Eccles was heard to remark 'Hmmm – the boys will do more damage in the wardroom when they get back than they've done over Sumatra today!' We heard nothing from Vian. It was an ominous silence.

Noel Mitchell added a humorous footnote that seemed to sum up the day's debacle when recalling that:

> Gavin Torrance had been so busy shooting up some Japanese soldiers, running for their lives across the airfield, that he flew through a dead tree and arrived back on board with branches in his radiator and engine cowling. This pleased the wing's ratings so much that they painted a large tree on the side of the aircraft.

And so the fleet returned to Ceylon for Christmas. It had been a difficult work-up period, with losses to bear and stress to absorb, and the New Year promised an even more difficult time. Even though they hadn't had confirmation of their passage to the Pacific, few were in any doubt about their destination and the likely outcome. The reports they read in the press, which were toned down by censorship, still pulled few punches.

And, of course, the Navy Intelligence Branch briefings they received painted an even gloomier picture. It wasn't that the Americans weren't pushing the Japanese back, it was the sheer cost of doing so in men and material. Also, as 1945 dawned, the menace of the kamikaze was becoming only too apparent. So, it was a Christmas to be enjoyed, but one that would be the last for many then celebrating, be they airmen or ship's crew.

Into Action (August–December 1944)

The dawn CAP prepares to depart on the run into the strike area. The imposing figure of the Flight Deck Officer commanding all around him. (DM)

On strike day the deck would be crowded with aircraft with many well forward to boosted off by the ship's single port side catapult. Here the pilots mount their aircraft ready to depart. The absence of bombs suggest these Hellcats from *Indomitable* will be flying escort to the bombers. (DM)

Post strike the photo-reconnaissance pilots compare notes before submitting their reports (Lionel Godfrey second from the right). (LG)

In late October 1944 the Admiralty issued a press release with this photo. It read: '22 October. Left to right: S/Lt E. J. Hawkins, RNVR, aged 21 of Cambridge; S/Lt E. T. Wilson, SANF(V), aged 21 of Johannesburg, who accounted for two of the enemy; Lt R. C. Westfield, RNVR, aged 21 of Sunbury-on-Thames, who led the successful flight, and S/Lt J. D. S. Smithwick, RNVR, aged 21, of Liverpool, who accounted for the third enemy fighter. It was his first action.' (DM)

Some lived – Lionel Godfrey went over the side but was saved, albeit with a back injury. (LG)

Some died – 'Jock' Mackenzie landed too heavily, his hook failed and he went over the side and drowned. (DM)

Some just 'pranged' with embarrassing results – an 1844 Hellcat and Barracuda get entangled. (DM)

Between operations pilots could spend a considerable amount of time on standby, often taking their meals in the cockpit as demonstrated here by John Hawkins. (DM)

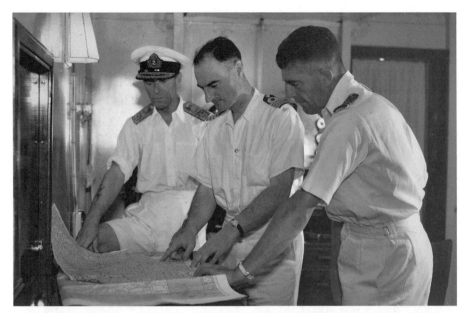

Indomitable was Rear-Admiral Vian's flagship for a prolonged period, which placed a heavy burden on the ship's captain, who might be subjected to back-seat driving to an unpleasant degree. But this doesn't seem to have been the case. Here Vian (left), Captain J. Wright, his Chief Staff Officer (middle) and Captain J. A. S. Eccles pose for this official photograph in Eccles' quarters. (DM)

After Pangkalan Brandan the fleet returned to China Bay to enjoy Christmas, sending squadron cards to friends and family at home. Celebrations on the ship were measured but soon degenerated into drink-fuelled fun allowing tense nerves to 'blow off' before a return to action. The pilots' games were studiously ignored by senior officers, most of the time anyway. (JN)

Christmas '44 seemed to involve a great deal of swimming with or without uniform. John Haberfield (above) recorded the high jinks in letters home to his family in New Zealand. A month later he was lost presumed killed over Palembang. (KM)

As *Indomitable* left the combat zone the crew could begin to relax. In this case, with a makeshift football. Three Hellcats are spotted aft, with drop tanks, in case any enemy aircraft are observed. (DM)

CHAPTER FIVE

Into the Fire

25-12-44

Christmas Day in the Tropics! I want to go home!

This is the first Christmas I have spent on board one of our HM ships and I must say they make a pretty good job of it. A lot of work was done decorating the ship trying to capture the festive atmosphere. Our Fighter Wing was given the job of producing a tree for the troops. So a working party of officers was sent ashore armed with spades, hammers, saws and hatchets and returned many hours later looking 'fair worn out', but triumphantly carrying an enormous tree. This we rigged up on the forward lift, decorated with lights, balloons and presents. During the evening, just as it was getting dark we ranged the tree onto the flight deck complete with Marine Band and while the ship's company sang carols, officers of No 5 Wing danced around the tree dressed as fairies and distributed such presents as soap, razor blades and packets of cigarettes to the troops – it was a great success.

In the wardroom we had our dinner at lunch time, preceded by a rather hectic gin session, in the middle of which the Admiral popped in to wish us a Merry Christmas. At dinner therefore, spirits were very high and the great Gammy Godson produced several rolls of lavatory paper and a magnificent chain was produced, each member of the mess taking the roll in turn, passing a loop round his waste and solemnly passing it to his neighbour who repeated the performance. Remarkable though it may seem, this chain went right round the wardroom without being broken, which only goes to show how well naval officers can hold their gin!

I feel I cannot mention anything about the inter ship parties that were organised before and after Christmas. One cannot remember much about them anyway, so maybe they are best forgotten. I have vivid memories, however, of gaily leaping over the side of *Illustrious* at 2am on Christmas Day and calmly swimming around in full 'Red Sea Rig'. One hears dreadful stories of a party of mad Sub Lts (A) raiding the *King George V* and heaving the Officer of the Watch into the drink and pinching all the ship's boats......

1-1-45

The New Year started for us in a very business-like fashion as, about mid-day we sailed in company with *Victorious* and *Indefatigable*. The Admiral had given us our Christmas in harbour and now we were to finish of the job we had started about a fortnight ago. (Douglas Smith, Sub Lt (A) RNVR – Diary entry)

This time the fleet would be joined by a film unit from Gaumont Pictures, Hugh McWhinnie, a journalist working for the *Illustrated* magazine, and the photographer Reuben Saidman. Throughout the war the armed forces tried to encourage constructive stories, even though the material the War Office produced often flew in the face of reports emanating from journalists working in the front line, which seemed to record only defeats and set-backs. But if they couldn't deflect bad news they could, at least, illustrate the day-to-day lives of servicemen and -women and those working and surviving on the Home Front. And so a great number of articles and booklets appeared, each helping produce a microcosm of life in a world at war. To some these publications were simply propaganda, whilst for others they provided some reassurance. Either way, they helped lift a veil on worlds shrouded in secrecy and mystery, allowing them to glimpse the reality of the lives of their loved ones.

The *Illustrated* had been in the forefront of this reporting and McWhinnie and Saidman had become trusted advocates of the RN in particular. As a result they were given the exclusive privilege of joining the British Pacific Fleet to see them in action. Saidman sailed east on HMS *Indefatigable*, and before joining *Indomitable* had already begun putting together an extensive portfolio of work that captured the essence of life on carriers. Meanwhile McWhinnie took a quicker route, flying out east in a series of transport aircraft, stopping en route several times to report on different aspects of the war effort

McWhinnie, who was born in 1906, the son of a Liverpool journalist, worked for the *Daily Herald* and gained a reputation for sound and accurate reporting. It is therefore unsurprising that the War Office approved this, and other commissions by him during the war and after it. Saidman, his *Daily Herald* collaborator, was the third son of émigré parents, George and Bailey, who had arrived in Britain from Russia at the turn of the century and set up a photographic business in Blackpool. They had five sons in all and four, Mendle, Maurice, Reuben and Israel, all trained as photographers in their parents' studio and later worked as journalists. The fifth son, Solomon died aged when only four.

For some reason, now lost to time, the pictures taken by the brothers were often simply stamped 'Saidman', demonstrating an amazing sense of unity in such a competitive field. But, for this reason, it is not always possible to confirm who took what with any certainty.

Dick Mackie later recalled the very determined photographer:

> Who joined us in the Wardroom and, when pressed, described his many assignments, both funny and serious. He had a very easy way with people and only took pictures with our agreement. When we had just returned from a strike wasn't the time and he respected our privacy, only taking pictures of aircraft taking off or landing, and only then if there were no mishaps. He and McWhinnie made an interesting pair. Both were good men and

very professional in their approach, with any copy they wished to print carefully prepared so that the Admiral and his staff had no need to censor it. In the months that followed, Saidman, very generously, sent copies of his photos and negatives to a few on board the ship who had requested them. In April I received a parcel with 25 or more prints and many negatives, plus a personal note, just signed 'Saidman', hoping that I was well and surviving the rigours of war.

The article, when it appeared in February 1945, entitled 'Tropical Sea War Is Unending Turkish Bath', proved very popular on-board ship and with the relatives of those involved. Some pilots and their crew simply cut out pictures or adverts to adorn their log books or journals, often with comments added, some funny, whilst others reflected their wish to be at home and in a peacetime world.

To see this magazine now is to visit a world long gone, a world with which direct contact – through veterans – is coming to an end. To read it now is to step back in time and sense their wartime world and the direction of a society grown tired of all the killing. The hope for peace is palpable, though there was still some way to go before it would end and between times there would be the revelation of Nazi concentration camps and more horrors 'out East' to bear. But, in January at least, the Allies were making huge gains in all theatres of war. So, some sensed that the end might not be far away, though the group of young men on *Indomitable*, who were soon to face another trial by fire, were unlikely to share their optimism. The danger was far too close for that.

The Gaumont cameramen, who were producing films to appear in Pathé News, were less restricted in what they filmed. It would be weeks before their work appeared at British cinemas and in that time the War Office censors would cut and paste each piece of film so that anything less than a positive image would end up on the cutting room floor. The Government's aim was to show fighting men in a calm light, where death and destruction might be hinted at but were largely hidden from view. Reality, of a type, certainly, but only a superficial, heavily sanitised version for public consumption. The offcuts weren't lost and much later would appear and these, when spliced into the footage released during the war, would help paint a more vivid picture of brave men facing an uncertain future and the possibility of death.

The Royal Navy's American cousins were rather more open in what they released to the public and whilst not allowing a completely transparent picture to emerge they came much closer. They, of course, had the benefit of the Hollywood film industry to help portray the lives of their fighting men, without recourse to the phoniness of a two-hour fictionalised feature, though there were plenty of these as well. With such talent available and an openness to present an honest and frank picture, the USN and Hollywood came together to produce *The Fighting Lady*. It was directed by Edward Steichen, the photographer, film director and painter, for 20th Century Fox, and followed the carrier USS *Yorktown* in 1943 and 1944, during some hard fighting at Truk and in the Marianas. It showed actual combat footage, in full technicolour, and portrayed tragedy and loss in a fairly open way, all the time with a slightly gung ho! commentary that reflected the period, but still conveyed the feeling of life close to a precipice. Such openness was refreshing and treated the audience in an adult way, which they responded to positively and with lasting effect.

In 1945 it won the Academy Award for Best Documentary and became compulsive viewing for Fleet Air Arm pilots so recently in the front line and those about to enter the fray, as my father recalled:

> We saw it first in Canada, at a special showing as though it was an instructional film. These were usually very matter of fact and prescriptive in nature, ideal for general education on flying matters – how to get out of a spin, don't try to turn if your engine fails and so on – though little else. But suddenly we saw in a graphic way the end result of all our training. It caught my breath, as it did my friends, and brought home to us exactly what we might be facing in the near future. It did give me an added sense of purpose, but would, undoubtedly, have worried my mother a great deal if she had seen it. It was released on video in the late 1980s and it still profoundly affected me.

Pathé News had no such freedom and produced films stripped of real impact. When copies were shown on *Indomitable*, most pilots thought it fun to see themselves and their comrades, but, as Noel Mitchell related:

> It had little impact and could simply have been a film of a training exercise for all the use it was. The reality couldn't have been more different. What we were doing deserved far better than this. I remember seeing the 1916 Battle of the Somme documentary, which was given a wide public viewing during the Great War, at a cinema in the 1930s. It pulled no punches and I thought should have been copied in 1944 and '45.

And so, with these brief distractions over, the carriers returned to war to strike again at Pangkalan Brandan and, hopefully, complete what they'd started on 20 December.

Undoubtedly Vian and his captains were hoping for much more, in terms of hitting the target, but also in the fleet's general performance, from the speed and effectiveness of replenishment to R/T discipline and the aircrew's ability to get airborne and form up quickly. All had been deficient the previous year. The success of Operation *Lentil*, as it was codenamed, was of the greatest importance.

Little time was wasted in putting to sea after the Christmas celebrations and the fleet sailed on the 1st, this time with *Indefatigable* and a fully restored *Victorious* joining *Indomitable*. *Illustrious* would stay 'at home' undergoing maintenance.

By the 3rd the Task Group was nearing its flying-off position and paused to refuel the destroyer escort and cruisers; *Suffolk*, *Ceylon*, *Black Prince* and *Argonaut*. Meanwhile, *Indefatigable*'s Fireflies patrolled overhead all day, leaving the Hellcat and Corsair squadrons to rest and prepare.

As they approached Sumatra on the 4th Douglas Smith thought about what lay ahead and later wrote in his diary:

> We arrived in perfect weather. The coastline looked very imposing – sheer forest-clad cliffs running down to the surf and not a sign of human habitation anywhere. I was destined to escort the bombers on this occasion and I think I really experienced an 'operational twitch' for the first time.

John Hawkins takes up the story:

> January 4th – D-Day. At 0610 hrs eight Hellcats, Lt Cdr Shotton and Gavin Torrance's flights, took off and joined eight Corsairs from *Victorious*. They set off on sweeps of the aerodromes in the Medan area to destroy any enemy aircraft and disrupt any defences, airborne or otherwise. The Seafires, whose reputation for endurance and landing problems were now well known, flew CAPs over the Fleet during the operation and generally kept out of the way. At 0650 hrs the main strike force began taking off with 32 Avengers, 12 Fireflies, 16 Corsairs and 16 Hellcats, but took an hour to form up before setting course for the oil refinery at Pangkalan Brandan.
>
> Meanwhile the sweep boys were enjoying themselves beating up anything military that they saw. Two trains were claimed, with our shells riddling their boilers, which sent up clouds of steam, and several aircraft were destroyed on the ground. Gavin hit a tree again, but stayed airborne.

Meanwhile Douglas Smith hovered above the bombers searching the skies ahead for any signs of enemy aircraft:

> We crossed the coast with a cloudless blue sky above and there below, thickly covering a range of jagged mountains rearing up to 10,000 feet, was one of the best jungles that Sumatra could produce. Just sheer hills and deep valleys completely coated with dense tropical jungle!!! 'Twitch' – an engine failure here would have meant weeks and weeks of close association with snakes and mosquitoes. Even then after miles of tramping your only prospect was that of being captured by the Japanese. Not a pleasant prospect!
>
> The target looked very peaceful and I believe their first inkling of our presence was the tell-tale whistles of our 500-pounders crashing amongst their refining plants and oil tanks. Fires started straight away and when we left a thick column of smoke was drifting lazily upwards to 27,000 feet. There were only a few Oscars around so most of us went down for a good strafe. Dick Neal, Bill Foster, Tug Wilson and Keith McLennan stayed up aloft and hacked down four of them. The boys were literally queuing up to take a poke at them.

Noel Mitchell, who was following the attack ready to photograph the results, watched this air combat take place and listened to the various shouts and screams over his radio:

> Once again R/T discipline was abysmal, but it was rather amusing when four or five Hellcats and a couple of Corsairs were all chasing one Japanese aircraft, who led a charmed life for three or four minutes. But it all became rather dangerous because as one was firing another arrived to fire before the other had finished. One Corsair tried to cut in front of Tug Wilson, who shouted, 'Get out of the way you bastard'.

Richard Neal (a Sub/Lt with 1839 Squadron) described his combat in a letter to the author in 1996:

> I was flying escort to the Avengers. Whilst I was weaving about over the target, watching my tail as much as much as possible, I had a nasty premonition about underneath. I inverted my Hellcat (JV 100) and saw about 100 feet below me, and oblivious, an Oscar in browny green dress. I could see the pilot's arms and legs. I rolled up and climbed like mad and then dropped on him. I set him on fire and still have a rather gruesome print from my gun camera.
>
> I thought I better give him another burst and as I did so another Hellcat (Jack Haberfield) swam into my sights from underneath. The gun camera saw him as I fired and I had to lift off. The Oscar was struck again and crashed, but I later felt raw that I was given a ½! Had I not been quick I should have had to claim a Hellcat.

Later in the day, after being debriefed, John Hawkins wrote:

> The strike was a very successful one – the Fireflies went in first firing their rockets to good effect, closely followed by the Avengers with their 4x500lb bombs. Columns of smoke were observed at 15,000 feet and still climbing as they left the target area. During the bombing our fighters were busy with a number of Oscars, six of which were hacked down. Mac got one, Tug and Foster shared another and Dick Neal and Habers got a third between them. Several other people also claimed another one. Whether or not this was confirmed is unclear at the moment. All our Hellcats returned safely and on the whole it was a bloody good show!
>
> Late in the afternoon there was great panic caused by a signal from RAA indicating that a repeat performance might be necessary on the 5th. But once all the PRU boys had returned and their pictures been developed and analysed the Admiral seemed satisfied and flashed to the fleet 'Operation completed'. This news was received with loud cheers from everyone.
>
> CAPs were kept up with Hellcats and Corsairs taking turns over the fleet throughout the day. And only once were they called into action when radar picked up a possible snooper, thought to be a Zeke 32, at 30,000 feet. The Corsairs scurried after it, but the EA [enemy aircraft] was long gone.
>
> There were no losses of aircrew on all three carriers apparently, although an Avenger from 857 Squadron was badly mauled by an Oscar and the air gunner seriously wounded. He is now on the 'improving' list. One Firefly was forced to ditch when it ran out of fuel just astern of *Indefatigable* and the crew were picked up none the worse for their adventure."

Post-strike reports didn't share the confident views expressed by some of the pilots, who, in most cases, were simply glad to get back alive, with success being measured by survival and the optimism of greatly relieved minds. Their performance had certainly improved, but Vian and his staff still noted worrying deficiencies. The Avenger crews felt that their escort had been inadequate, with both Corsairs and Hellcats seeming to wander off en masse to chase enemy aircraft. R/T discipline was still poor and the strike seemed to lack coordination between fighters and bombers. With the Japanese offering only a minimal defence this didn't present a problem, but against a determined and aggressive force the consequences could have been more serious.

In reality, bombers were only too keen to have their escort close by where they could see them. This had proved the case for the Royal Flying Corps in World War I, the Luftwaffe during the Battle of Britain, and the USAAF when flying daylight bombing raids over Germany. But, as most fighter pilots were quick to reply, they could only do their job when free to roam and intercept at will. Staying close to bombers, though reassuring to their crews, robbed the fighters of their greatest assets – speed, height, manoeuvrability and surprise. The experience of many battles proved this to be true. But the success of this tactic did depend on experience and great discipline. Just haring off, shouting into their radio transmitters as they went, was not necessarily the most effective way of meeting and removing a threat. But on 4 January the fighters did at least knock down enemy aircraft as they tried to intercede, and so proved the point.

In one case some 12 enemy fighters were engaged as they closed in and Corsair pilots claimed five destroyed, with others driven down, one, unusually taking to his parachute:

> His cockpit seemed to glow red as I hit him with a long burst. I could see bullets hitting all around the aircraft's nose. He lost attitude before levelling off, then began a climbing right hand turn to try and escape. He came up into my sights and I fired again. He then rolled over and fell or jumped out. I watched as he landed in the water, but he seemed to be dead. As I climbed away I didn't observe any movement. (S/Lt D Sheppard RCNVR 1836 Squadron, from a letter to the author in 1993)

And the fighters conducting the initial sweep also achieved some success. Seven out of 25 aircraft were destroyed on the ground as the fighters roared in at very low level – a tactic that would become increasingly important as the enemy grew better at defending their 'territory' with flak. In due course they would claim the lives of many pilots, particularly those who didn't go low enough or returned for another pass. But for the moment this new risk was in the future, as were the kamikazes.

Of those conducting the sweep, Lt Durno and S/Lt Richards, from 1834 Squadron, distinguished themselves particularly. At the end of their run they came across a Dinah twin-engine reconnaissance aircraft and a Sally bomber in the landing circuit. Both were destroyed in seconds.

Although no aircraft were lost to enemy fire during the operation, an Avenger ditched 12 miles from the fleet following engine failure. But, as with the Firefly which came down near *Indefatigable*, its crew were picked up, this time by a destroyer that rushed to the scene. Apart from these two incidents, all the other aircraft landed on safely, leaving the photo reconnaissance aircraft to do their work as Noel Mitchell wrote later:

> We had followed the strike and saw the escort fighters taking on enemy aircraft, performing manoeuvres that one would never normally do. All this took place in a matter of seconds – split seconds when the pilots knew no fear. It was just before and just afterwards, when things calmed down that fear crept in and you remembered the swift glimpse of one of your enemy going down in flames, but luckily even then one never had much time to relax and think.
>
> As the strike formed up and returned towards base Felix Rankin and I followed up from opposite directions from a distance of 80 miles from the oil refinery and began by photographing airfields. Navigation was easy – we just flew towards the huge column of black smoke. Our Hellcats had no guns and were therefore superior in speed and we flew over our targets at 20,000–25,000 feet. We were allowed to photograph the airfields within 4 or 5 miles of the oil installation without interruption, but the very moment we poked our noses over them we were met with the biggest barrage I had met to date. I immediately opened my throttle to its maximum and climbed up to 27,000 feet.

With the last PR aircraft and CAPs down the task group was heading towards Ceylon, the need for a second strike having come to nothing. By comparison to earlier strikes this effort was judged a qualified success. Any shortcomings being marked down to inexperience, rather than any fundamental problems with men or machines. With this in mind, Fraser felt able to approve their move to Australia and operations in the Pacific, but on route they would have one more go at the oil installations on Sumatra – a much bigger effort involving all four carriers.

In many ways, having seen both Corsairs and Seafires in action, 5th Wing pilots felt themselves lucky to be flying Hellcats, although by this stage of the war they were beginning to be superseded by the Chance Vought fighter. Tommy Harrington summed up Hellcat's benefits:

> One of the main points I recall was their extreme reliability as well as their great flexibility for attacking anything on a high CAP right through the machinations of ground attack by gun and rocket, up to their usefulness as both night-fighter without radar and a camera-carrying vehicle for photo reconnaissance work.
>
> Because of their wonderfully docile flying qualities our accident rate on the deck was extremely small. They were particularly adept at landing regularly in a very short space of time. Another comforting feature of this splendid aircraft was that it was ruggedly built and

would absorb a great deal of enemy fire from astern. This our excellent ratings were able to repair much more quickly than any other aircraft types engaged in this particular war.

The only drawback the Hellcat had was that its wings had to be spread manually and this rather knocked points off our ability to get into the air quickly.

In his correspondence with John Winton, Philip Vian reflected on this operation and concluded that:

> We were now ready to tackle the larger objective, now that our technique was rapidly improving. We were pleased with our American type aircraft – Avengers, Corsairs and Hellcats. Their robustness, reliability and long endurance showed up in marked contrast to our own types, particularly the Seafires which still formed the main outfit on *Indefatigable*.
>
> The full effect of the years during which the Fleet Air Arm had to rely upon adaptions of RAF machines, designed for short-range operations, was now to be felt. Seafires had an hour less endurance than the Hellcats and Corsairs, and this was to be an acute embarrassment when we joined the American fleet. Their crash rate was also high by comparison to the American types. This, too, was to be a source of trouble in the time to come.

When Vian wrote these words, 14 years later, he'd had sufficient time to weigh many matters and choose his words carefully. His words are very dry, which is surprising considering all that he had done and seen, and it tends to gloss over issues that were not so clear cut at the time. One of these concerned the need for the strikes authorised in the 'Outflank' programme, especially on the eve of the fleet's passage into the Pacific. Operations *Robson* and *Lentil* had achieved mixed success without significant loss and had given the carriers a chance to prepare for what lay ahead. But two more attacks were planned and Fraser decided they would take place, en route to Australia, towards the end of January, despite doubts over their validity.

We might be forgiven for thinking that this decision had universal agreement. But in the Admiralty, and amongst the CinC's own staff, there were dissenting voices. Having spent a long time building up a precious resource, with a fairly limited reserve to make good the losses, some thought it shouldn't be squandered in this way before the main battle was joined.

They had been relatively lucky so far, but the last two planned attacks on Sumatra's oil installations might be tempting providence once too often. If these targets were that important might they not be better tackled by submarine operations against tankers taking the oil to Japan? Alternatively, these installations were ideal targets for America's high-flying, fully pressurised Super Fortresses. Although proving marginally successful against *Tirpitz* and Pangkalan Brandan, carrier-borne aircraft were an expensive and not particularly effective way of hitting these large strategic targets. High-level heavy bombers could saturate such defences as the Japanese possessed in Sumatra, then quickly and accurately lay waste to these facilities in a single operation, or so the argument went. The RAF had proved, in November 1944, that a difficult target such as *Tirpitz* was more effectively destroyed by Lancasters, with their 'Tall Boy' bombs, than low-level attacks by masses of carrier-borne aircraft, which had failed to achieve this essential aim, leaving it as a threat, albeit a damaged one.

It was for raids against such targets as Sumatra that the airfield at China Bay had been massively developed at great cost by the Americans, in late 1943 and early 1944. By the summer it was capable of handling a large fleet of Super Forts that could range across the Indian Ocean and bomb suitable targets at will. But victories in the Pacific had given these aircraft bases from which they could begin bombing the Japanese home islands from October onwards. So, China Bay became an expensive, but largely unused backwater. Nevertheless, these bombers could have had other targets injected into their programme, leaving the British Pacific Fleet free to join the Americans with their experienced aircrew intact. But here inter-service rivalry came into play. As Vian had observed, the USN and USAAF both promoted their strike potential as war winners, so, in simplistic terms, they saw the other service as an interloper trying to steal their glory. As a result, a strong coordinated attack fell victim to the selfish whims of intransigent commanders

Also, by this stage of the war, both Allied air forces were convinced, in the face of experience, that an enemy could be forced into submission by area bombing alone, although battlefield support was deemed more effective by many commanders. The Americans had also experimented with daylight precision bombing over Europe with very mixed results and very heavy casualties. By late 1944 they, like the RAF before them, had begun to shed this tactic, even when effective long-range fighters came into service, offering the bombers greater protection from enemy aircraft to and from their targets. Area bombing of cities became the panacea of choice, though it would singularly fail to drive an enemy towards defeat by itself. The USAAF would do it all over again – this time against Japan – leaving other important targets to one side. With the Army Air Force attacking Japan in hopes of driving its leaders to the negotiating table, strategic attacks and the island-hopping assaults would fall to the American Navy, supported by the Royal Navy. Which meant that once again Vian's fleet would attack the oil installations on Sumatra, no matter how poor were the arguments for doing so.

There were also problems with the proposed targets themselves around Palembang. These attacks would involve a long dangerous flight over Sumatra and they would face an enemy that would surely have strengthened its defences considerably following the earlier strikes. Heavy losses were predicted in a force still learning its trade and to some this was unacceptable. But counter-arguments failed to convince or deflect Fraser or Vian, who strongly believed that the value of the targets outweighed these other considerations. As Fraser later said, 'Eventually everyone at headquarters gives in, when the man on the spot insists', and in this he appears to have had Admiral Nimitz's tacit agreement. But in some quarters a huge doubt remained, the tactics continued to be questioned and a costly disaster was gloomily predicted. Meanwhile the task group sat at anchor in Ceylon or exercised close to the coast with its men waiting for news, largely oblivious of the debates taking place at a higher level.

The routine was well established now as John Hawkins recalled:

> A slack day only spoilt by a rumour that proved correct that tomorrow there would be a mock battle, with *Indefatigable*, a cruiser and three destroyers playing the enemy. And with that they quickly disappeared over the horizon. At first light the following morning five Avengers took off to search for them. At the same time a strike and escort group were ranged on deck, with others on Vic. While sitting there 'hostile' Fireflies turned up having flown in under the radar, or so it seemed, attacked the fleet and rendered our aircraft useless, in war game terms. Nevertheless, undeterred by this 'destruction', we took off and proceeded to sink *Indefatigable* and her escort. Meanwhile some Hellcats flew CAPs throughout the day, but saw nothing, although they were vectored out to search for an Avenger which was reported missing. It had in fact landed on the 'enemy' carrier having got into trouble.
>
> The day's exercise proved costlier than the attack on the 4th. One Avenger shot through both barriers and was badly damaged. Shortly afterwards another came in without flaps, due to hydraulic trouble, and broke its tail wheel when hitting the round down. Later on Chas [Lavender] bounced badly on landing and went into the barriers. All told it was another unnecessary 'Fred Karno' day's work. Everyone was wondering who to blame?
>
> In Trincomalee, lunchtime came with the recommencement of the usual sessions and many modest lines were again shot and various rumours discussed. In the afternoon there was bathing or getting one's head down as a prelude to more good work at the bar. The CO (Gammy Godson) was last seen heading in the direction of a lovely young Wren. How fortunate life is for some!!!
>
> As many of our aircraft were getting tired and battered Tommy Harrington and Gavin Torrance went ashore to select and test a row of new ones lined up at China Bay. The best of them then came on board having been brought out on lighters. One was slightly damaged during a rather clumsy lift. During the evening many took to the bottle and had to be put to bed.
>
> Next morning we were visited by the Supremo, Lord Louis Mountbatten himself, so we knew that operations were to begin again soon! He gave the assembled officers and troops a farewell pep talk. Then, later on, he was introduced to Tug, amongst others, who figured he was a nice guy. Certainly, his talk was interesting. And with that briefings began in earnest.

Drinking was deeply imbedded in naval culture, as it still is now. For many it softened the blow and made life on board a ship of war tolerable. But its benefits were short term and did little to hide the effects of combat fatigue or, for that matter, the rigours of being at sea, which could itself be a very hostile environment. Douglas Smith, who would later qualify as a doctor, observed all this and wrote in his diary about these issues and the way the Navy tried to cope with men under extreme stress:

> There is an air of tension going about at the moment. I wish to God they would hurry up about it though!
>
> Puttalam (on Ceylon) is rapidly becoming known as 'Parishes Mad House'. Lt Cdr Parish is 'wings' of the medical facility there and if anyone is round the bend he most certainly is. He is an excellent type and in spite of his slapdash air and mannerisms is very popular and gets his job done. Here we have an ever-growing group of pilots known as the 'clapped-out brigade' or the 'twitchers'. They consist mostly of chaps who have lost interest in flying owing to nerves. Some are genuine, but others are only making out that they have the twitch so that they can get sent home on the first possible occasion.

In his diary Douglas Smith's insights are honest, but only hint at what he and others were feeling. In many ways they were an inscrutable, tough, self-deprecating generation who would rarely if ever let the mask slip. Even fifty or more years after these events, few if any chose to express themselves on these issues, yet the fear of failure or breakdown probably inhabited all of them to some degree. In 1944 and 1945 they chose fortitude and reticence as a shelter, with the sedating effect of alcohol to deaden any anguish they may have felt, and some continued to do so for the rest of their lives. Some did speak a little of these things, often in the third person to deflect attention:

> Old ...... had just had too much and kept bursting into tears each time he flew, much to our embarrassment. I was always worried it might become infectious and affect the younger pilots. Even though it left us one short Commander F and Captain Eccles agreed to take him off flying and quickly shifted him home. I saw him a few months later and he seemed OK, but it was clear that he wouldn't fly again. (Barry Nation, Lt Cdr (A) RN)

To this Dick Mackie added a personal note:

> My nerves held up fairly well, though before Palembang I was convinced my number was up and this made life difficult for a while. Before a strike most suffered from nerves and the 'heads' on board were kept busy! But after Pangkalan Brandan most would have gladly taken a long leave away from the carrier and flying. I certainly had the 'twitch', but kept quiet, didn't see the Doc and tried to keep myself busy as a distraction. The dark hours were worst for all of us, and nightmares, usually consisting of crashing in flames, were quite common. Once in the air our training and the task at hand took over. But you could only 'go to the well' so many times before exhaustion set in and you became careless or had a breakdown. I'm sure many died because of this, whilst the lucky ones were taken off flying by astute Commanding Officers before it happened. I held up pretty well but was relieved when the war ended, bolstered in the meantime by leave and the occasional breaks from operational flying.

Rugged Construction of the U. S. Navy's Grumman
Hellcat Helped Bring This Pilot Back to Fight Again

Grumman

AIRCRAFT ENGINEERING CORPORATION, Bethpage, L. I., N. Y.

More than 12,000 Hellcats were built between 1942 and 1945, with 1263 being supplied to the Fleet Air Arm. Such was its success that Grumman's advertising campaign contained no idle boasts (THG).

It seems that young men destined to fly the Hellcat were all pleased to have done so and, in many cases, owed their lives to this exceptional fighter. (THG)

A MK 1 Hellcat being test flown in the USA before delivery to the Fleet Air Arm showing the colour scheme adopted by that service in 1943. By the end of the war new production aircraft were painted in overall dark blue as used by the USN. (DM)

Accurate weather forecasts were essential when planning operations and each ship had to be self reliant in producing this information. Here *Indomitable's* 'weatherman' gathers material before the fleet's aircraft strike the oil refineries at Palembang. This photograph graced the front cover of *Illustrated* magazine. (DM)

The caption of this evocative photo, taken by Reuben Saidman in January 1945, is '5th Wing pilots at rest between ops'. Dick Mackie, who appears lost in a Penguin paperback, recalled the day, adding 'we look far too relaxed for the picture to have been taken before an operation. That was never the case before a mission'. The pilots (left to right) are Tim Schwenk, Gammy Godson, David Jenkins, Felix Rankin, Dick Mackie, Sammy Langdon, John Smithwick and Fraser Shotton. Three of these young men – Godson, Langdon and Smithwick – would be dead by the end of May. (DM)

An Avenger on *Indomitable* being loaded with bombs with a 5th Fighter Wing Hellcat in the background. The leisurely pace of the work suggests that the carrier is still some way from the strike area. (DM)

The flight deck party enjoy a tot of rum. Working conditions above or below decks in the tropics were described as challenging, unhealthy and inherently unsafe with many men falling victim to heatstroke and a variety of other illnesses. Then there was the real enemy to deal with! (DM)

They also serve. Without the support of men from many trades the aircraft could not have flown. It took at least five of these unsung heroes to support each Hellcat – in the hangar and in deck parties. Their relationship with each pilot was a very close one and memories were treasured as though formed in the confessional; a secret world of mutual trust, only understood by those involved. It was these men who truly witnessed the terrible effects of combat on those who flew and were the first to give aid and clean the cockpits. (DM)

Noel Mitchell of 1839 Squadron happily poses for Saidman. This very experienced pilot excelled in night flying and was reported by Dick Mackie as having exceptional eyesight, seeing things in the dark that most others missed. He survived the war to live out his days in the Manchester area. (DM)

Charles Lavender who hailed from Enfield, North London, was one of the original members of 1844 Squadron and remained with them until April 1945, returning home on HMS *Illustrious*. (DM)

Pilots not on duty tended to gather together on *Indomitable's* 'goofers' platform to watch their fellow pilots in action. Here a mixture of Hellcats and Avengers set off on Combat Air Patrols (CAP) and anti-submarine duties as the ship transits to the strike area in January 1945. (DM)

In many histories of the Pacific War, Japanese servicemen come across as unthinking, violent automatons. Most Allied servicemen didn't see beyond this stereotype, as they daily lived with stories of the enemy's vicious excesses and the reality of kamikaze attacks and reports of executions. But in the years following the war many pilots in the 5th Wing thought deeply about these issues, Japanese culture and the nature of their war. They came to a more sympathetic understanding of their adversaries and some even made contact with them, with friendships developing. But as Dick Mackie recalled 'they were a tough bunch who gave no quarter and we learnt to do the same'. It is a feeling summed up, in many ways, by this photo of a Japanese fighter pilot, which Dick kept as a souvenir. (DM)

When the kamikazes struck death and destruction were inevitable, with little remaining of the pilots or their aircraft to show they had ever existed. When *Indomitable* was struck on 4 May 1945, the pilot's wallet washed up on the deck. These notes and coins are reputed to have been kept as a souvenir of the occasion. (PG)

For many who died there was no known grave and grieving families had no certain knowledge of their fate or a place they could visit to lay flowers. This was particularly important for the 'Palembang Nine', who were executed by the Japanese when the war was over. To provide some focus for their loss, memorials were eventually erected, including this one for John Haberfield, late of 1839 Squadron. (KM)

Bill Foster was, perhaps, more forthcoming when he described flying in combat and the emotional consequences, during a conversation in 1997:

> It was very easy to become blasé about the rigours of combat flying, but it was always a case of diminishing returns. The longer you went on the harder it became to hide the effects. In the beginning inexperience and fear of the unknown made you very nervous. I remember clearly being sick in the cockpit after my first action against the Japanese. Luckily the ratings had seen this many times before and carefully helped me out of my straps then down on to the deck. I was unable to stand unaided for a while my knees were shaking so much. This only lasted a few seconds though it seemed like an eternity before my senses returned to normal and I felt more confident. Bing Hawkins, who was always a rock in these circumstances, turned and waited for me as we walked to the wardroom to begin making our reports, offering encouraging words along the way. As time passed I grew in confidence and the nervous effects induced by combat flying, though never disappearing, did lessen. I remember Gammy Godson calling this the 'veteran stage' of a pilot's existence. But the longer you went on without a rest so weariness and combat fatigue crept in. Those affected seemed to glow with self-confidence at times, even become overly aggressive during combat. And this soon turned to risk taking, as though any sense of self-preservation had gone.
>
> Even if you survived intact the effects never left you. Even now, while sleeping, I can be taken back and dream of a violent death by fire or going down from a great height trapped in the cockpit, unable to escape. Yet, at the same time, I'm glad that I was able to take part as a fighter pilot. I gained much more than I lost. But occasionally I wonder what it would have been like to be that eighteen-year-old boy again and live a life not burdened by war.

Whatever the cause or the effects the days following Panglakan Brandan were tense with expectation. All the aircrew knew that these operations had been a prelude and within days the main event would begin in earnest. It is little wonder that Mountbatten, as Supreme Allied Commander in the South East Asia Theatre, visited the fleet and wished them well. He knew better than most the cost of war and the expectations that rested on so many young shoulders. He also knew the responsibilities of command when ordering men to fight and die and, as brave men do, he wished to look them in the eye.

On *Indomitable* the Hellcat pilots made ready for departure, with the ship a hive of activity around them. Stores were loaded in large quantities, new aircraft brought on board, checked and struck down into the hangars. Men came and went busily doing a multitude of tasks or simply grabbing time ashore to enjoy life before the serious business began. New pilots arrived, such as the Canadian Bill Atkinson, Alex Macrae from New Zealand and Bill Fenwick-Smith from England, whilst others departed, their time expired or recognised as being too tired to continue. A warship in such a state is always a scene of controlled pandemonium and in these few days bedlam existed on each vessel soon to sail away as part of the BPF. Most were not unhappy to see the back of Ceylon, having grown tired of its uncertain attractions. The expected pleasures of Sydney and Australia seemed much more alluring by comparison. For the many New Zealand aircrew on board they would be nearer homes they hadn't seen for far too long – two or three years in some cases. But first more attacks on Sumatra had to be endured.

John Northeast described their day of departure:

> 16th January – A big day as the BPF raised their anchors and left Trincomalee Harbour, leaving other ships behind to form the new East Indies Fleet. Australia was our destination but we hoped to do some damage to the enemy on the way. *Illustrious* had re-joined the fleet after missing the last attack on Pangkalan Brandan and so we had a full complement of carriers; *Indomitable* as flagship, followed by *Vic* and *Indefat*. The *KGV* passed amongst us looking very regal and powerful. She was probably more suited to Jutland than any sea battle in 1945, but her array of guns did give us confidence – she could put an awful lot of flak up if the fleet were attacked by kamikazes. *KGV*'s sister ship, HMS *Howe*, didn't sail with us having gone ahead to Sydney, with the CinC, so missing the 'treat'.
>
> Nobody seemed very sad at leaving Ceylon except the skipper (Harrington) and Mitch, who had their wives there, and a few others with girlfriends amongst the Wrennery.
>
> The following day we carried out an exercise with eight Hellcats and 10 Avengers, one of which had to make an emergency landing, whilst I had to return with a serious hydraulic leak. Claude also returned with a technical problem, as did Bill Foster. The two of them competed for the heaviest landing of the day, with Bill winning by a long way.
>
> During the afternoon, with Ceylon a long way behind us, briefings began.

Noel Mitchell takes up the story:

> With the coastline falling behind us, the captain made his usual announcement telling us where we were bound for. But initially he didn't tell us what we would be striking, in case we had to return once more to Trinco due to bad weather. But with conditions set fair, detailed briefings began and we were given full details of the targets and what we faced.

The targets for the next attacks were the two oil refineries around Palembang, situated on the north bank of the Musi River, 40 or so miles inland from the sea. There were two targets on Sumatra – and these lay 5 miles south of the town, where the Komerine River meets the Musi. The aircrew studied models, maps and photographs of the major oil refineries there – one at Plagjoe, the other at Soengei Gerong. Then the detailed briefs began, with special emphasis being given to the defensive measures the Japanese might have in place to deter attack. The intelligence, secretly gathered by 'watchers' on the ground or through radio intercepts, had established how heavily defended these targets would be.

The 9th Air Division on Sumatra were reported as having six fighter squadrons and one reconnaissance unit in January, though it was suspected that the number was increased after the 4 January raid. The enemy fighters were single-engine Oscars and twin-engined Nicks (the Kawasaki Ki-45 twin-engined two-seater fighter). Intelligence reports suggested that the quality of the pilots had dropped significantly due to their losses in the Pacific against the Americans, but those on Sumatra might contain a number of instructors and other veterans so could present far tougher opposition. Ground defences around the refineries and airfields were believed to be very strong, with many barrage balloons over the targets adding another hazard.

Douglas Smith recorded his thoughts that evening in his diary:

> Once again the atmosphere of tension on board was very noticeable. This time we are going to flatten an important but well defended target in south-east Sumatra and, if necessary, stay there for a week until our task is completed.
>
> The usual briefings started straight away, and it soon became apparent that we are to meet the dreaded Jap 'Togo' fighters over the target. As this machine has a performance superior to ours we are naturally apprehensive as to our chances of returning in one piece!

And with a sense of impending doom the pilots talked about attacks and then returned to their cabins to begin a process of preparation that no one would enjoy, as Dick Mackie recalled:

> Each person prepared themselves in their own particular way. Some tried to find a distraction, but reading or writing were difficult in the circumstances because your mind was full of thoughts about what lay ahead. Excessive drinking in the wardroom was out, although many kept private supplies and may have hit them pretty hard. Others took to walking up and down the flight deck or busied themselves with various duties. And some wrote 'last letters' to be delivered to relatives in the event of them not returning. Very few of us had good appetites during those days, even though the food was good and the cooks and stewards tried their best to tempt us. Our maintenance crew could see the stress levels rising and to a man would jolly us along, with gentle banter and wonderfully dirty jokes that certainly brought laughter and a brief respite.

D-Day was set for 21 January, but had to be postponed for three days due to poor weather over the targets. The cloud and rain cleared during the evening of the 23rd and the first attack was set for the following day. Few slept soundly that night.

Hugh McWhinnie and Reuben Saidman sailed with *Indomitable*, observing all around them, but both were loathe to write or photograph the realities of what they saw. Each of them would be deeply affected and, within the limits imposed by censorship, would try to give even a vague impression of this reality. They didn't succeed, but Saidman's photographs, or at least the ones he later sent to Dick Mackie, do capture the strange, haunting beauty of a carrier at war. After seeking permission, he took a series of more intimate pictures of those soon to fly in combat and those who returned. But these have yet to emerge – they may have been suppressed by the War Office or the *Illustrated*'s own editors. If they do ever appear they will add much to our understanding of what these young men endured.

Pangkalan Brandan, 4 January 1945

On 4 January, the wing was part of the attack mounted on the oil refinery at Pangkalan Brandan on the east coast of Sumatra (Operation *Robson*). For this attack *Indomitable*'s Barracudas were replaced with the much more effective Grumman Avengers. Here one of the Hellcats due to fly escort is prepared. (DM)

A busy and dangerous environment as Hellcats and Avengers make ready to depart. (RN)

'Coming unstuck' as it was called would often see nerves stretched to breaking point suddenly relax as the mission begins. The unexpected remained but the pilot had 'gone over the top' and was committed to battle. (DM)

The target is already being struck by bombs as more Avengers prepare to attack. (DM)

One of *Indomitable's* PR Hellcats captures details of the attack before passing over the area to record the extent of the damage. (NM)

Hellcat pilots safely down on deck watch other aircraft landing on with professional interest. (DM)

The deck crowded with aircraft ready to be 'struck down' after the raid. Returning aircrew discuss recent events with the deck party. (DM)

CHAPTER SIX

Meridian

Before any major operation an 'order of battle' is published. Tradition and practicality come together in a document one could imagine being broadcast with grandeur and to great fanfare by Nelson before Trafalgar and Wellington before Waterloo. The statement is clear – these are our numbers, this is who we are and this is how we will fight. A declaration of intent. But it is part of a chess game where the opposition's pieces are unseen, only to appear when you have committed your forces and your tactics have been revealed. When this type of battle is joined, there is the vastness and fluidity of a three-dimensional battlefield spread over hundreds of square miles of sky with elements of sun, cloud, rain and wind to be understood and exploited. The side defending always has the greatest advantage, unless the attackers can exert overwhelming force and in January 1945, over Sumatra, this wasn't the case. With insufficient numbers, a multitude of tasks to complete, the need to escort the bombers and a degree of inexperience, even naivety amongst its aircew, the strike force struggled against an enemy using hit and run tactics. Havoc could have been wreaked, but, as it was, the British squadrons were sorely pressed and took casualties they could ill afford, or so many thought at the time.

In addition to the aircraft included in the order of battle, there would again be Hellcats assigned to photo reconnaissance missions, two Walrus seaplanes on *Illustrious* for air sea rescue duties and *Indefatigable*'s Seafires flying CAPs over the fleet. Vian and his staff had so little faith in the durability and ruggedness of these fighters that they wouldn't commit them to the strike on Palembang. This attitude was understandable, but as fighters their performance was far better than either the Hellcats and Corsairs and in time they would prove themselves. On the 24th their speed and dog-fighting capabilities were missed.

Lt Col Hay's role as air coordinator was an interesting one. During 1944, as the fleet's multi-carrier role developed, the need to have someone in overall charge of each large strike groups seemed imperative. Each carrier had their wing leaders for fighter and TBR squadrons, but they tended to be committed to specific tasks and would, possibly, only see part of the battle. Hay's role was seen as crucial to the whole operation and his background made him ideal for the task.

Order of Battle

Meridian One

Air Coordinator: A/Lt Col R. C. Hay,
Royal Marines (*Victorious*)

Strike: No I Bomber Wing:

11 Avengers from *Indomitable* (857 Squadron: Lt Cdr Stuart, RNVR, **Strike Leader**)
12 Avengers from *Victorious* (849 Squadron: Lt Cdr D. R. Foster, RNVR.
12 Avengers from *Illustrious* (854 Squadron: Lt Cdr W. J. Mainprice, RN.
12 Avengers from *Indefatigable* (820 Squadron: Lt F. L. Jones, RNVR.
All Avengers to be armed with four 500-lb bombs

Escort: Top Cover:

16 Corsairs from *Victorious* (1834 and 1836 Squadrons: Lt Cdr C. C. Tomkinson, RNVR, **Top Cover Leader**)

Middle Cover:

8 Corsairs from *Illustrious* (1830 Squadron: Lt P. S. Cole, Senior Pilot)
16 Hellcats from *Indomitable* (1839 Squadron; Lt Cdr M. S. Godson, RN, and 1844 Squadron: Lt Cdr T. W. Harrington, **Middle Cover Leader**)

Strike and Bow Close Escort:

12 Fireflies from *Indefatigable* (1770 Squadron: Major V. B. G. Cheeseman, RM)
Armed with eight 60-lb rocket projectiles each.

Stern Close Escort:

8 Corsairs from *Illustrious* (1833 Squadron: Lt Cdr N. S. Hanson, RNVR, **Close Escort Leader**)

Mana Strike and Escort:

5 Avengers of 857 Squadron and 4 Hellcats of 1844 Squadron, all from *Indomitable*.

Fighter Ramrod Sweeps 'X Ray' and 'Yoke':

12 Corsairs from *Illustrious* (1830/1833 Squadrons: Lt Cdr A. M. Tritton, RNVR, **'X Ray' Leader**)
12 Corsairs from *Victorious* (1834/1836 Squadrons: Lt Cdr R. D. B. Hopkins, RN, **'Yoke' Leader**)

Born in Perth on 4 October 1916, one of five children, Hay joined the Royal Marines in 1935 and began pilot training in 1938. Over the next few years he would be in the thick of the action, seeing combat over Dunkirk in May 1940, then as a Fulmar pilot during the Battle of Britain, flying from Wick in West Sussex. As the daylight raids over England ended his squadron, 808, joined HMS *Ark Royal* and he would remain with the ship until it was torpedoed and sunk on 13 November 1941. During this period he was credited with the destruction of four enemy aircraft and took part in the sinking of the German battleship *Bismarck*. A period ashore then followed as an instructor with 759 and 760 Squadrons, before being posted to command 809 Squadron on HMS *Victorious* during which it supported landings in North Africa.

Promotion to the rank of major and a posting to China Bay, in May 1943, followed, where he was appointed senior RN representative in a hierarchy dominated by the RAF. It was an unhappy combination, especially when the RN began deploying large numbers of aircraft and carriers there from early 1944. Fleet Air Arm pilots complained, with some bitterness, that they were treated as second-class citizens even when their flying needs dominated activity on the airfield. It was a situation which reached rock bottom when RAF incompetence led to the death of two Corsair pilots in a collision on 14 April 1944. One was Mudge Anderson, a young New Zealander, and the other Lt Cdr Richard Cork DSO, DSC RN, the new fleet's most gifted and experienced wing leader and fighter pilot. Ronnie Hay was called upon to investigate the 'accident', which senior RAF officers wished to be marked down as pilot error and not failures on the ground by their men. Hay, caught in the middle of this nasty shambles, erred on the side of the living.

There is little doubt that Cork, with his vast experience of fighter tactics, whilst serving with the Fleet Air Arm, and on secondment to the RAF, would have become air coordinator and been very successful at this task. He had already demonstrated a keen grasp of these tactics and had an all-seeing eye, as Mike Tritton, a fellow pilot, put it when describing his ability to observe all that was going on in the sky around him, whilst still fighting. By an odd twist of fate Ronnie Hay inherited this mantle and would, in time, find himself faced with many issues over which he could exercise little control, problems he'd already witnessed first hand, as he recalled in a letter to the author in 1994:

> I would fly with my flight of Corsairs high above the battle area and observe and direct operations as the attack developed. All well and good if the weather was clear and R/T discipline was maintained, but this always seemed to break down and became an embarrassment. At the first sign of an enemy aircraft the escort pilots started shouting and began tearing off all over the place, leaving the bombers to survive as best they could. A few of the more sensible souls hung around but they were often quite small in number. It was

little wonder that the Avenger crews complained bitterly about this ill-discipline and the lack of protection.

It is a fairly natural reaction for any bomber pilot to feel that he is the only aircraft in the sky – seldom can you fly in neat, regular formations with the escort flying on your wingtip as a morale booster. But the fighters did stretch this point to the limit at times.

The sky is never so empty as when you're flying and you appear to be on your own with the enemy. The more so, if some of the escorting fighter pilots and their COs are inexperienced. There was a strong temptation to take my flight down and intervene, but I had a clear role to play and tried to maintain some discipline.

It didn't help if other attacks – such as ground-strafing 'Ramrods' – were ineffective. They were supposed to stop hostile aircraft taking off and disrupt the enemy's ground defences, but often arrived too late to do so. I had no control over this, much to my great frustration.

Noel Mitchell recalled the build up to the first operation against the oil refineries at Palembang, codenamed *Meridian One*:

We attended briefing after briefing until we had learnt everything by heart – such as the best way back to the West Coast, the dates and places we would be picked up by submarines or the two Walruses if we were forced down. Most of us scribbled this down and jammed the notes into pockets in our trousers. We were given practice interrogations if made POWs, which made you realise how easy it was to make a slip and give something away. Basically say nothing but name and number and hope they don't torture and execute you!

In our kits we carried revolvers, water bottles, hatchets, mirrors, razor blades, silk maps, energy pills, chewing gum, chocolate and twenty gold sovereigns for bribing our way back to the coast, first aid kits and anything else we thought fit. One or two jokingly asked for cyanide pills. At 0430 we were awakened and went down to eat our operational breakfast, which was the best part of the whole operation, as it always meant a real egg. Despite this the meal was difficult to eat and some left theirs untouched. Whilst we sat there no one spoke or if they did it was simply to ask someone to pass the tea or jam or butter. If anyone did try to make conversation they were ignored. We then had final briefings and as dawn broke we gathered our belongings and made our way on to the deck to check over our aircraft, which had been ranged in position, with their wings back or up, during the night. Once strapped in I went through my cockpit drill, had one more check and awaited the order to start up. The sea was fairly calm and it looked as though it would be a fine day, with some cloud still hanging around the fleet. Over the last few days we had been shrouded in mist and rain, with high humidity, which had made life below deck very uncomfortable.

Finally over the flight deck loud speaker the familiar voice of Commander Flying ordered, 'Start up your engines'. And with this each engine coughed as the propellers started to turn, slowly at first, then suddenly, as the engines sprang into life, they raced into invisibility. One or two hesitated momentarily, ejected a few angry bursts of pale smoke from their exhausts and then they to settled down to a smooth roar.

I busied myself with the controls and listened to the engine beat to make sure all was well. My thoughts were always the same at this moment – would I see my young wife again and live to old age with her? I'm sure everyone probably had similar thoughts, but these were quickly put aside as take-off approached.

When all was ready Admiral Vian signalled the whole fleet to swing into wind and suddenly you could feel your aircraft shudder as the turn was completed and a gale sped down the deck.

That evening Douglas Smith wrote in his diary:

> Groping my way around the ship at 0400 hrs in pitch blackness, with breakfast always a very difficult proposition to cope with when flying, but under action conditions almost impossible. Every mouthful had to be washed down with a swig of tea owing to a strange dryness in the mouth.
>
> Onto the flight deck where the grey mountain shapes of the aircraft are just beginning to take form in the ever-increasing light of dawn. You find your own machine with the fitter busily doing a final check on the engine, and the rigger polishing away at the already spotless cockpit cover. With a few words to both men you climb in and go through the difficult process of getting properly strapped in and with that the men disappeared and you are all alone waiting for the word to go. You sit there looking at your watch and listening to the tempo in the throb of the ship's engines which will tell you that she is gathering speed for the fly off. It's almost light now and you can see most of the instruments in the cockpit, when suddenly Commander Flying's deep voice booms out and you automatically start your engine. The world around you is turned into a roaring, vibrating hell.
>
> You run up your engine, check the cockpit and after a few minutes of stifling heat and fumes from the aircraft in front, the whole fleet swings into wind.

Having brought themselves to this crescendo of activity and with so much going on in such pressured environment events could move very quickly in any direction, with trouble never far away. On *Indefatigable* an Avenger taxied too quickly and collided with an aircraft nearby. Both were damaged, but more seriously this incident delayed the remainder of the launch for some 20 minutes, with the remaining 10 aircraft finally getting away at 0638 hrs. On *Victorious* an Avenger became unserviceable and had to be scratched, whilst a second returned shortly after take-off with a mechanical fault, soon followed by three others. It was later discovered that these problems were probably caused by water ingress while the machines had been parked on deck for a prolonged period. But with so many aircraft failing the loss of five bombers would be felt later on.

Meanwhile *Indomitable* and *Illustrious* had successfully launched all their Avengers by 0619 hrs, with Hellcats and Corsairs joining them by 0636 hrs, their aircrew slowly settling down ready for the other carriers to launch. By the time the problems had been sorted out the full strike force wasn't ready to depart until just after 0700 hrs, nine minutes behind schedule. Ronnie Hay looked on with a growing sense of frustration, especially as the second range of aircraft from *Indefatigable* were again delayed. Major Cheeseman's Firefly, at the head of the line, could not lower its flaps and had to be quickly repaired and 1770 finally got airborne at 0710 hrs and only caught up because the main strike force was still flying around the fleet waiting to depart. The 24 Corsairs that would fly the Ramrod mission had no problems and overtook the main force very quickly. The Fireflies were slightly slower but still managed to arrive and to do their job before the main attack started.

> After what seemed like an interminable age, the strike force sorted itself out into a uniform pattern, collected together and we were away, heading for the dark outline of the coast. In the distance we could just make out the rugged, unfriendly mountains which we had to cross.
>
> Suddenly we found ourselves climbing up into a clear, blue sky with the bombers below in a compact solid mass, with the fighters circling around me with the sun glinting on their wings as they twist and turn in pretty zig-zag patterns.
>
> Then you know that your job has really begun and you start the tiring business of escorting them in earnest. Your head is never still, your neck aches and your eyes feel strained as you search the sky seeking those tiny black specks which will tell you that an enemy fighter is approaching. Beneath you the country rolls slowly by, with the gaunt forest-clad mountains now well astern and below are marshes and a few isolated villages on stilts, but mainly marshes and more marshes.
>
> In the distance I can see the balloons floating high above the unsuspecting target and as they grow larger so the rhythm of the weaving fighters quickens and the bombers speed up until everyone is watchfully jinking around the sky at full combat readiness. The R/T crackles into life with cries of, 'Flight break right', 'Watch your tail' and 'There he goes. I'll get the blighter' and there are also screams. All this telling us that the boys ahead are mixing it with the Japs, fighting and dying. (Douglas Smith)

The strike force crossed the coast at 4,500 feet and quickly began climbing to 12,000 feet to get over the mountains. A very low incursion would have been preferred on the way there, to have masked their approach from enemy radar or the enemy's early morning patrols. But the terrain made this impossible and dropping down to a lower level after this was of little value or so the strike leader believed; a move which confused their escort somewhat. They pressed on in excellent visibility, with the Komerine and Musi Rivers clearly visible in the distance marking their aiming point.

The incoming raid had been detected by the Japanese warning system soon after it crossed the coast. Fighters – a mixture of Nicks and Tojos (a single-seater Nakajima Ki 44 fighter) – which were already circling at between 15,000 and 30,000 feet south-west of Palembang, screamed down with the sun behind them, and quickly sliced through Top then Middle Cover and attacked the bombers, with Hellcats following them down.

Ahead of the main force the Ramrod Corsairs were doing their work, but found many of the airfields they strafed had already launched their aircraft and – forewarned of the incoming attack – the ground defences were on full alert, meeting the fighters with a heavy and accurate barrage of fire. Five were shot down, but their efforts seem to have kept other aircraft from taking off to attack the main strike force or the distant fleet.

The Fireflies, meanwhile, deploying just ahead of the Avengers, launched their rocket attack on the refinery, following up with cannon fire. However, the strike leader, seeing many balloons hanging over the target, sought to direct the Fireflies to destroy them, but this message wasn't received and they continued to drift at 2,000 feet and then quickly ascend as they drew closer. This was a Japanese tactic that proved to be particularly successful against a force seeking to bomb a target at low altitude, with great precision.

The Avengers weren't far behind them and were met with fighters coming down from above and others coming up from below. Pulled in many directions Corsairs and Hellcats were soon involved in running fights that pulled the escort apart, leaving only eight Corsairs from Close Escort to protect the large force of Avengers into the target. As they drew closer the bombers were quickly submerged in a sea of flak from the mass of guns around this key target. It was into this maelstrom that the Avengers dived.

Eric Beeny, flying one of *Indomitable*'s Avengers, described the problems he faced as they attacked, in a letter to John Winton in 1968:

> During briefing we were told that R/T silence would be observed until we reached the target, and that we would bomb at about 3,000 feet. If a balloon barrage was spotted the CO would issue new instructions about bombing. I didn't hear a sound over the radio and it wasn't until later that I learned that it was unserviceable.
>
> As we approached the target at about 12,000 feet we could see a carpet of bursting shells 2,000 feet below us. We saw the CO begin his dive and followed. When we were down to 7,000 feet we were somewhat alarmed to see four 500lb bombs whizz by just in front of our nose. It was the Senior Pilot letting go his bomb. Apparently they had been told over the radio not to go lower. Knowing nothing of these altered plans we continued down, only to see a couple of balloon cables flashing by. Down to 3,000 feet now, we spotted our target and pressed the tit to release the bombs, only to discover we had a hang up. Preparing to go round again, the air gunner warned me that an enemy fighter was approaching. Taking evasive action and trying to find some cloud and being several thousand feet below our formation, we were on our own. The Tojo was attacking and the air gunner thinking at last he had him in his sights, pressed the button and the guns jammed. Fortunately, for us, the CO of one of the fighter escort squadrons (Tommy Harrington) had spotted us and the Tojo, and had given him a good burst and winged him. But the Jap wasn't quite finished yet and tried to ram us and was actually flying level with us when his tank caught fire and he rolled over and crashed near his own aerodrome.
>
> We made our way safely back after that to land with our bombs still on board.

Tommy Harrington later recalled:

> I made two passes at the Jap fighter as it attacked one of our Avengers. I always insisted that we carry a special cocktail of ammunition made up of 5 ball, one armour piercing and one tracer. With this load we could tackle any sort of target and the tracer provided a visual effect on the enemy and ensured he knew he was under fire, which generally resulted in

him making a turn, thus enabling us to close the range. On this occasion it had the desired effect and he went down in flames and crashed.

Jack Ruffin (Sub Lt later Lt RNZNVR) of 1844 Squadron, who was flying in Middle Cover, takes up the story:

Before launching the strike we didn't know that the whole area was protected with Barrage Balloons. As we quickly discovered they effectively stop dive bombing and, on this occasion, kept the bombers at a height where the flak is more effective.

Attacking a relatively small target area at speed a pilot hasn't much time to make up his mind what to do. So most of the Avengers had no alternative but to jettison their bombs at too great a height and this made precision bombing a great deal more difficult. As they dived into the attack most of the enemy fighters had been driven off or shot down so I was able to circle the target and observe, whilst protecting my own skin. I remember as though it was yesterday the bombers moving into the area. The first one ignored the balloons and dived down through them. The second hesitated for a moment then did the same. I remember shouting to myself 'Hell No!!!!'. The others dropped their bombs as best they could from above the balloons at various heights, some as high as 8,000 or so feet.

At this stage I noticed a Hellcat go into a spin and knew the pilot was a write-off and later realised this had probably been Jack Haberfield, who was the only wing pilot not to return. I didn't see him crash so presume he bailed out at low level.

Fortunately there were enough Avengers and enough bombs to scatter about to make a fairly good impact. Another thing we didn't know was that their storage tanks were about 10 miles further up the coast. As we turned to go home another fighter and myself (I think it was John Hawkins) made a detour to strafe the tanks. We made only one run at treetop level and hit a tank each. But the ground fire was a bit intense and our aircraft were both hit. However, on looking back I was really pleased to see we had started fires and smoke was billowing skywards. We then climbed up and found other Hellcats and formed up in some semblance of order.

Heading homewards I spotted Dick Mackie. His aircraft had been hit in the motor and was losing oil and speed. I broke from the formation to follow him and mark the spot should he bail out or ditch. Our course, on the way back, passed over Lake Raau, so that anyone damaged or felt they couldn't make the sea could ditch there and possibly be picked up later by those daring boys in a Walrus. Luckily Dick's aircraft held together and we were the last ones home.

Dick Mackie remembered this incident only too well:

I was the luckiest pilot ever. A Tojo hit me first in a head-on attack. He went down, I was told later, hit by my return fire. My engine was holed and there was oil everywhere. I quickly headed for home about an hour away, with my engine coughing and missing all the way. I didn't know whether to bail out and pulled back the canopy just in case I needed to get out quickly. But oil just poured in covering my face and flying kit, so I shut it again and hoped that there wouldn't be a fire and the wind might clear the screen a little bit so I could see what I was doing. Meanwhile Jack Ruffin sat on my wing offering encouragement and never wavered for a second. Despite my predicament I felt confident that I could make it and land on. When about 30 miles out, and slowly losing height, I asked for an emergency landing and duly arrived over the fleet and a couple of Seafires came down for a look. As I lined up to land the batsman signalled 'as usual', but I couldn't see a bloody thing through the windscreen, came in too high and fast, hitting the deck rather hard but took a wire. Breathing deeply, having held my breath whilst landing, I taxied forward over the barrier and the engine just gave up! It was a remarkable aircraft to have survived all that.

As I walked slowly to the wardroom I saw Claude Westfield, with blood all over his face and flying kit, receiving first aid. He didn't seem too perplexed by his injuries. He just smiled and said a bullet had hit his canopy and splinters had shot into his face and through his goggles into his eyes. It's a wonder he managed get back and land safely. But he couldn't fly for a while and Gavin Torrance took over his flight until he had recovered.

Douglas Smith, greatly relieved to have survived the ordeal, stayed with the bombers and watched as the survivors formed up below:

> I weaved around some of the stragglers until they were safely attached to the main body. Looking back I could see the fires raging and great columns of black smoke drifting lazily across the sky – an occasional, silent explosion adding to the conflagration. Flak still drifts up, but no longer seems harmful. Then back to the job of escorting the bombers back to the waiting fleet. Even more vigilance is needed now as there may still be wily Jap fighters in the clouds ready to pounce on a lame duck.
>
> Back over the marshes and the mountains until we see the friendly sight of our ships steaming peacefully below. The weaving tentacles of the fighters are retracted into organised groups again and the various striking forces split up and circle their respective carriers to await their turn to land on. You feel great relief as you proceed to the waiting position knowing your job is completed and the fighter 'umbrella' over the Fleet is watching and protecting you. I steel myself once more during my approach to the ship, eyes glued to the batsman, and an occasional glance at the deck so that I can judge my turn in correctly. A little more motor and then a bang, and I'm down safely on the deck. Taxi forward, switch off and climb stiffly out of the cockpit as the wings are folded back. The fitter and rigger busily inspect the aircraft for flak holes, look up and say, 'Did you get anything Air 7?' to which I replied, 'No, but you should have seen.........'. Then you are down in the wardroom, inhaling deeply from that much-longed-for cigarette, thirstily consuming cups of tea and shooting lines with the rest of the guys. The operation is over. I'm still alive and quite normal. Thank God!!!

For those who had survived there was only a short time to sit and think about these events before debriefing began. Confused, excited minds had to be brought gently back to earth so that a picture of the attack could be formed for the admiral and his staff to consider – Did we hit the target? What are our losses? What opposition did we meet? What could have been done better? – with many more questions to follow. Waiting in the wings the ship's doctors and 'sky pilots' looked on, trying to gauge how well each man was coping with the strain. Then there were the dead to mourn and the missing to lament and hope for. But this came later in the quiet of their cabins, where thoughts could no longer be constrained or held back.

There would always be casualties to absorb and a slightly callous attitude was often displayed by survivors to these losses. Bravado, perhaps, but it was a protective shield that served an essential purpose. But each loss served to remind these young men, with a sense of invincibility stitched into their DNA, that it might be their turn soon. Older, but wiser often meant greater susceptibility to stress and with it slower recovery. For most pilots in the 5th Wing two or more years of war were taking their toll. But with many more major operations still to come there would be little respite for months to come. Dick Mackie summed this attitude up when he wrote:

> It was the loss of Jack Haberfield on the 24th that hit me hardest and made me more aware of my own mortality. If such an experienced fighter pilot could be hacked down – and we thought he was killed that day – what chance did the rest of us have. Having only just made it back on board I certainly looked at the future in a more negative way. For a time it looked very bleak.

And so the day came to an end. CAPs were flown until dusk with some fighters landing on in near darkness, including Douglas Smith who nearly came to grief as he hit the deck far too hard and bounced a bit before coming safely to rest. Reports were completed and, as John Hawkins later recalled, 'we all felt that the Butcher's Bill was far too long for what we had achieved'. But Vian recorded a slightly different view once intelligence had been gathered and analysed:

> Our aircraft were unmolested until they had almost reached their objective. The attack completed – and later it was known that the productive capacity of the refinery had been reduced by half – the Avengers made their rendezvous, fifteen miles to the west of Palembang.
>
> Fighters and bombers were handled cleverly, and there were many examples of exceptional skill and courage. Our losses were not light – six Corsairs, two Avengers and one Hellcat failing to return. Nevertheless it had been a shrewd and successful blow at the Japanese in a vital spot, and we planned to repeat it.

As the day drew to a close Vian's staff issued a press release. Within 24 hours the signal had been flashed to the Admiralty and would appear as a brief article in newspapers two days later, even before telegrams had arrived at the homes of the missing. Meanwhile on board *Indomitable*, McWhinnie and Saidman continued preparing their article for the *Illustrated* having witnessed the day's events first hand. As experienced journalists they would have undoubtedly have wished to present a truer, more detailed picture of all they had seen and photographed on board. But even if they had, the censors would never have sanctioned its release and probably have restricted any access they might have in the future. The war was being won, but too much reality was still frowned upon. Not so the Americans who allowed much more graphic pictures of war to emerge. Once victory had been secured, and the full horrors of concentration camps were exposed, journalists were allowed greater freedom in reporting what they had seen. But this never happened in the Far East, where British and Empire forces fought hard and successfully, in almost total anonymity. It is small wonder that they believed themselves to be the 'Forgotten Army' or 'Forgotten Fleet'.

As always in the cut and thrust of combat the destruction of enemy aircraft was sometimes hard to establish with any certainty. Three people firing on one target might each claim it as a 'victory' or an experienced enemy pilot might simply have pretended to go down, but pull out near the ground and escape. Either way it seemed to be a rule of thumb that dividing these 'successes' by two or three gave intelligence staff a far more accurate picture of what had happened. Propaganda, of course, needed no such reassessment. But nine aircraft missing presented only a partial picture of losses. None of the aircrew would be seen again – some died quickly, but others would die far more slowly at the hands of interrogators. Then there was the loss of other aircraft – damaged or ditched – to consider. The fleet carried a small reserve of men and machines, but at this rate the squadrons might soon struggle to muster a sufficient complement of either. As the second Meridian attack was prepared there was a nagging doubt in many minds that attrition rates were far too high. But the spirit of the offensive wouldn't be purged from Vian's mind no matter what the cost, or so it seemed to his young pilots.

The fleet sailed away from the Sumatran coast as the pilots tried to rest after their efforts on the 24th. Apart from the losses in combat the perennial problem for the fleet remained – lack of fuel. Such a large group of warships, operating at speed in the combat area, consumed vast amounts, but the number of supply ships and reserve stocks close at hand was inadequate. Vian understood this only too well and planned a two-day replenishment period, hoping that this would be sufficient for their needs:

> During the 26th and 27th January the force refuelled at sea. We then had sufficient oil for one more attack on Palembang, before proceeding to Sydney (a third, 'mopping up', strike had been planned but this would have stretched our meagre reserves too much). As a result of experience gained in the previous operation, we revised our plans. Fighters to dominate the air above the two main enemy airfields were to proceed in two sections, timed to arrive simultaneously over their targets in the hope of taking them by surprise. The route for the bombers also changed, to avoid the bad areas of flak that had had been observed on the 24th.
>
> This time, too, a further precaution was taken. It had to be assumed that the Japanese, by now alive to the presence of a carrier squadron in the vicinity, would react by mounting air attacks on the fleet. We therefore greatly increased the standing patrols over the ships.

Replenishment proved to be a slow process, with hoses parting and poor station keeping causing many delays. When refuelling at sea the ships involved have to steam on a straight course, virtually in line astern, with little or no deviation and this makes them vulnerable to attack. These operating principles had to be exercised effectively by the task group, especially when they would soon be operating in the Pacific, where the enemy would be far less obliging in leaving them to re-supply in peace. The longer it took, the greater the dangers and on the 26th and 27th the delays and inefficiencies severely tested Vian's patience. But, at least, this long pause gave his staff and the squadrons time to prepare their plans and get the maximum number of aircraft ready for service.

Whilst they refuelled, rumours came from the Pacific, often started by Japanese radio broadcasts, that American task groups were being destroyed by wave after wave of kamikaze attacks. The thought that men might dive at you and eviscerate themselves willingly, with no thought for their own safety, had an inhuman quality hard to rationalise. A diary kept by some of 1839 Squadron pilots gave voice to these fears, but also chided enemy propaganda:

> The Jap news announces the Pladgoe raid. They shot down 78 British aircraft for the loss of 14 Japs!!! Oiling all day, the ship creeping along at 2 or 3 knots. Awfully hot. A rumour is spreading that US Battleship *Iowa* has been sunk by 90 'Divine Winds' – the Hari Kiri boys. Big twitch about 'Divine Wind' and what they might do.

After the usual briefings and fevered preparations Vian ordered his fleet back to Sumatra to begin the second attack. As they did so few pilots managed to rest, as Dick Mackie recalled:

> There was a certain amount of nervousness and foreboding. If you hadn't slept much before the Pladjoe strike you got even less this time. After my near miss I had begun to believe that I was pushing my luck a bit. I had flown CAPs in the meantime and this helped, but I didn't sleep at all and it was a relief to get up and have breakfast, which I forced down despite feeling nausea.

Jack Ruffin remembered this feeling only too well and the way others reacted to it:

> I shared a cabin with Wilson, Lavender and McLennan. Tug, who was known for his sang froid, just slept peacefully and woke ready to do battle with the enemy as always. Charlie, Mac and I just slept as best we could, which wasn't much. Charlie had one of those portable gramophones in a black leather case that was old fashioned even then, but did the job. He only had about six records – all classical – while I had one of the 'Warsaw Concerto', which I used to carry in my tin hat box – in which it fitted perfectly. We played these seven records throughout the night, quite quietly, and this seemed to help.
>
> When it came time to take off my nerves left me completely and all my attention was focussed on the job in hand. I remember the veterans from the First War describing the moments before 'going over the top' – the panic, sickness and fear – and the release they felt when they had climbed out of the trench and were making for the enemy front line. It was just the same for me.

The weather on the 29th was poor. The deck had been swept by heavy rain and wind throughout the night and with dawn approaching a low cloud ceiling hung over the ships. But through breaks in the overcast sky and between downpours the mountains to the east could occasionally be glimpsed, so it was hoped that conditions overland might be better.

Order of Battle

Meridian Two

Air Coordinator: A/Lt Col R. C. Hay, Royal Marines (*Victorious*)

Strike: No 1 Bomber Wing:

12 Avengers from *Indomitable* (857 Squadron: Lt Cdr W. Stuart, RNVR)
12 Avengers from *Victorious* (849 Squadron: Lt Cdr D. R. Foster, RNVR)
12 Avengers from *Illustrious* (854 Squadron: Lt Cdr W. J. Mainprice, RN)
12 Avengers from *Indefatigable* (820 Squadron: Lt F. L. Jones, RNVR)
All Avengers to be armed with four 500-lb bombs

Escort: Top Cover:

12 Corsairs from *Illustrious* (1830 and 1833 Squadron: Lt P. S. Cole RN, **Top Cover Leader**, in place of Lt Cdr N. S. Hanson who was recovering from the effects of a ditching in the sea on the 24th)

Middle Cover:

16 Hellcats from *Indomitable* (1839 and 1844 Squadron: Lt Cdr T. W. Harrington, **Middle Cover Leader**)

Close Escort:

12 Corsairs from *Victorious* (1836 Squadron: Lt Cdr C. C. Tomkinson, **Close Escort Leader**)
10 Fireflies from *Indefatigable* (1770 Squadron: Major V. B. Cheeseman)

Ramrod 'X Ray' (Talangbetoetoe):

12 Corsairs from *Illustrious* (1830 and 1833 Squadron: Lt Cdr A. M. Tritton)

Ramrod 'Yoke' (Lembak):

12 Corsairs from *Victorious* (1834 Squadron: Lt Cdr R. D. B. Hopkins)

Armed Reconnaissance (Mana):

2 Fireflies from *Indefatigable*.

Photo Reconnaissance:

2 Hellcats from *Indomitable*

Air Sea Rescue:

2 Walrus

The strike was due to launch at 0615 hrs but was delayed by 25 minutes to see if the visibility might improve still further, which it did. Squalls still occasionally appeared, but didn't hinder take off too much, though forming up in such changeable conditions was more challenging. All aircraft took off safely, but an Avenger from *Indomitable* ran into problems and had to ditch, its crew being picked up safely by the U Class destroyer HMS *Undine*.

By the time all the strike and escort aircraft were in the air the strike leader decided that another circuit of the fleet was necessary. It was an action that Ronnie Hay, who was circling above with his flight, thought pointless and later wrote:

> The result of this extra, unnecessary circuit was that three Avenger squadrons were hopelessly out of position and the fighter escort was all jumbled up. I felt that this made aviation in the area extremely hazardous.

And yet photographs suggest that the force, when it departed, did so in fairly good shape and that visibility had improved considerably over Sumatra in the meantime – the delay proved beneficial, even though it appeared to test Ronnie Hay's patience.

The main Strike Force were overtaken by the fighter Ramrods, which attacked their targets shortly before the Avengers reached the oil refinery at Soengei Gerong, losing one of their number in the process, Lt Durno, who bailed out and wasn't seen again. But they had limited success, many Japanese aircraft having taken off at dawn to patrol to the south-west of the refineries directly in the Avengers' line of flight. The 24 Ramrod Corsairs strafed any target presenting itself – aircraft around the airfields and other ground targets – but may have been better employed adding weight to the escort trying to protect the Avengers.

Before long three Avengers and four Corsairs had turned back to their ships with mechanical problems, although Mike Tritton, for one, thought that strung-out nerves may have played a part in this high return rate. Aircraft had been ranged on decks overnight in rain and wind, and so may have been affected by these adverse conditions. It wasn't an unknown problem, but whatever the cause the attacking force was seriously depleted by the loss, especially the Corsairs, which were sorely needed especially with the enemy on high alert.

Japanese aircraft soon made contact with the incoming raid as it came over the mountains. The strike leader had taken the Avengers up to 10,000 feet and continued climbing. This forced their escorts, then weaving above preparing to tackle incoming fighters, higher still where they were soon immersed in cloud, making their job even more difficult. Tommy Harrington, losing his patience, made Stuart aware of this in no uncertain terms, but to no avail and even Ronnie Hay couldn't make them understand.

The first enemy fighters made contact at 0814 hrs, when the Avengers still had 50 miles or so to run to the target, but Percy Cole, leading 12 Corsairs from *Illustrious* soon dispersed them, with Winnie Churchill, another New Zealander, destroying a Tojo (a single-seater Nakajima Ki 44 fighter). Meanwhile the Hellcats stayed in position and didn't feel the need to hare off, which had been a strong temptation on earlier missions. But in doing so they were targeted by anti-aircraft fire as they drew closer to Soengei Gerong, as Jack Ruffin recalled:

> The enemy were putting up a 'lot of filth', more than on the 24th, or so I thought. We could see distant specks that soon became Jap fighters climbing up from below and some diving down having escaped the attention of the Corsairs. We soon broke away seeking targets, though sticking in pairs to guard each other's tails. I shot at several Tojos but didn't see any results, though the CO and Dick Mackie were luckier, sharing an Oscar. All the while R/T discipline was again appalling, making it useless as a means of controlling what was happening. Occasionally you could hear the Air Controller screaming 'Bloody well shut up all of you!' but to no avail. No matter how hard they tried the COs didn't seem able to improve things. And, of course, the Japs were listening in and gathering intelligence.

Richard Neal also saw enemy aircraft climbing up to attack the bombers:

> Whilst we were weaving at high speed I spotted a silver Jap fighter below. I felt I had to clobber it at once, waggled my wings at David Jenkins and dived like mad to cut him out. I was about 5,000 above it and wanted to use speed to get right up under its tail. But it climbed like a rocket and, to my dismay, my closing speed dropped off.
>
> I fired at 450 yards from about 5–10 degrees to port. I saw the whole of the port side of the plane being stitched and torn up. I closed right up to 75 yards and fired at point blank range. It didn't look like a Zero (the Mitsubishi A6M single-seater fighter) – I thought it was more bulky. It flicked over, belched smoke and dived vertically at huge speed into the balloons and smoke.

John Hawkins felt that the enemy 'attacked with great determination and seemed oblivious of their own flak and the balloons hanging over the target. They weren't kamikazes but fighter pilots determined to drive the bombers away, or, at least, make aiming difficult'.

Despite these attacks the Avengers pressed on with great determination and dived down to less than 2,000 feet, through the barrage of shells and enemy fire, seemingly oblivious of the balloons hanging over the target ahead. Mainprice, 845 Squadron's leader, and his wingman, Armstrong, paid a heavy price for this bravery when their aircraft were torn open by the cables. They went down, all six men killed. At such a low height the chances of bailing out were slight. As the other aircraft followed them they were shot up and damaged. But they passed through this hell and headed for the rendezvous point, to the south of the refineries, though few escorts were still in touch with them, having been called upon to tackle the enemy fighters which still sought combat above. John Hawkins described the scene as being 'a complete muddle, with the lighter more agile Japanese fighters twisting and turning away from us making it very difficult to get them in our sights, but they weren't fast enough to get away and just kept turning in and frustrating our aim'.

And as they climbed away, more Tojos, Hamps (Mitsubishi A6M3-32 single-seater fighter, later codenamed the Zeke 32) and Oscars tore into the Avengers sending two more down – flown by S/Lt Burrenston and S/Lt Lintern from 849 Squadron. A Firefly from 1770 tried to intervene and its pilot, Lt Levitt, destroyed an Oscar before he was hit by an enemy aircraft that had closed in unobserved under his tail. But the Fireflies were being flown aggressively and they destroyed two more opponents, a Hamp and another Oscar. But relieved of their bombs the Avengers ceased to be 'sitting ducks' and fought back as though fighters, using their forward firing guns to good effect. They would later claim two Tojos shot down, such was the strength of their defence. Gradually the Strike Force extricated themselves and flew back above the plains and then over the mountains to home, their numbers greatly depleted. But behind them huge fires raged in the refinery and smoke again billowed up to immense heights.

Richard Neal, having spiralled down during combat, found himself near the balloons over the refinery. Quickly climbing away and gaining height he came across an Avenger and recalled that:

> It had been badly hit and had an undercarriage leg hanging down. I escorted it all the way back to the fleet where it ditched. It only scraped back over the mountains. The pilot was S/Lt F Stovin-Bradford. Later on my fiancee met and talked to him in Sydney and was able to tell him who had escorted him home.

As the surviving Avengers and fighters made their way out over the sea to the carriers, damaged aircraft were forced to ditch near the fleet. Six bombers came down with 18 crew members saved, although one died later of his injuries. Elsewhere the fighters landed on without serious mishap, with the PR Hellcats setting down at 1030 hrs to complete the strike. But it soon became clear that the Japanese were trying to track the fleet's movements so that they could launch their own attack with the few aircraft they could muster.

As early as 0917 hrs a flight of Seafires spotted a Tojo seeking out the fleet, but it dived into cloud and made its escape as the CAP approached. Then at 0930 hrs a Seafire, flown by S/Lt J. W. Hayes, stalked then attacked a group of enemy aircraft, destroying a Mitsubishi Ki 21 twin-engined bomber in the process. Its escort then overwhelmed him and his Seafire crashed into the sea. Hayes took to his parachute and was later picked up by HMS *Undine*. But still the enemy continued their search with Seafires, Corsairs and Hellcats patrolling in force, being vectored out to any suspected raid. During one of these S/Lt S. G. Maynard, of 1836 Squadron went missing.

With the fleet steaming away from the coast at speed the chances of the Japanese finding then attacking the task group was slowly diminishing, but the danger hadn't disappeared and became a reality just before noon. A number of enemy aircraft, believed to be from the Shichisi Mitate Tokubetsu Kogeki Tai Unit led by Major Hitoyuki Kata of the Special Attack Corps (a kamikaze detachment), approached the fleet. They were spotted 14 miles away at low level, clearly hoping to come in under the radar, and deployed for an attack. The British fleet was on high alert and Corsairs from *Illustrious* dived to attack, as the ships turned at speed to the north-west to present a more difficult target.

One Sally was 'splashed' by a Corsair at the same time as *Indomitable* was readying to launch four Hellcats – Keith McClennan and Bill Foster being the first two in line. But only the first aircraft was up quickly enough to engage the enemy and he rapidly sent two down into the sea. The battleship *King George V* was firing at the same time and managed to pepper both friend and foe with shot, the captain later claiming the credit for one aircraft, on his gunner's behalf.

Despite the fact that the ship was under attack, some pilots watched the combat from the 'Goofers' platform, including Jack Ruffin, Noel Mitchell and Douglas Smith:

I'd known Keith, who was from Wellington, for some years and we had become good friends. He always seemed unruffled and was never seen without a pipe in his mouth. He was a good, reliable pilot who seemed to take most things in his stride, but he had very quick reactions and always achieved high scores in gunnery exercises. On the 29th these skills served him well. Ranged on deck, to support the CAPs already flying around the fleet, with his engine idling, he quickly took off when the enemy were sighted, even though the carrier hadn't turned into wind. Our main armaments were firing at the time which must have added to the speed of his take-off. Even before his wheels had retracted he turned sharply towards the enemy and, with tracers flashing passed from various ships, opened fire as the range quickly closed. The first, a Sally I think, was hit and went straight into the sea, then exploded, and a few seconds later it was joined by another. Now with wheels up and with a little height he and a Seafire, also braving the fleet's gunfire, brought down a third. Bill Foster also took off and began chasing another bomber before getting his wheels up but it crashed before he could open fire. (Jack Ruffin)

An air raid warning 'red' was flashed at the fleet and immediately six dots on the horizon were seen coming from different directions. They were flying low on the water and the fleet put up the noisiest barrage I've ever heard. Hellcats and Seafires came in amid our own fire to achieve certain kills. One, two, three, four, it was almost as quick as that. One got within 100 yards of the *Illustrious*, dropped something, pulled up, sprayed the deck with machine-gun fire and went into the sea in a mass of flames just ahead of the ship. Keith McClennan, who took off amidst all the gunfire, and was at the time putting his wheels up, shot down two Japs in seconds, one of which was attacking *KGV*. When he returned to the ship afterwards his aircraft was riddled with bullet holes, hence Vian's signal to *KGV* reading, 'Our ace S/Lt McClennan reports your fire very accurate.'

This all happened and was all over in about three minutes, and was the most thrilling three minutes yet experienced. No one had a moment to think of personal danger. (Noel Mitchell)

Unfortunately my old aircraft, the faithful 5H, was standing on deck at the time and the blast from the guns blew her across the deck and twisted the airframe. She is a complete wreck and will never fly again. I feel quite sorry as she has carried me safely through four operations and I had become quite attached to her. My rigger cried when he saw the mess the old girl was in. (Douglas Smith, diary entry)

The Japanese attack stood little chance and all the aircraft were quickly despatched. The number and types reported by all who witnessed these events varied from five to 10, and included Ki 21s, Ki 48s and G4M bombers. But later the number was assessed as seven and the G4Ms were dropped from the reports. Although they pressed their attack with great determination in the face of heavy odds the bombers did no damage. However, in all the excitement *Illustrious* was hit by shellfire, around the bridge and flight deck, from the cruiser HMS *Euryalus*, her crew unable to 'check' its guns in time and 12 men died and another 21 were injured in this tragic case of friendly fire.

For the rest of the day the task group steamed away, with the fighters flying a strengthened series of CAPs, just in case the enemy returned. Radar picked up distant echoes but they came to nothing and the fighters were ordered to return without making contact. Richard Neal, who would spend more than six hours that day flying combat missions remembered that:

I flew as CAP leader on the withdrawal. Colin Keay sent us off to chase something which was at about 35,000 feet. We gave up. The sun was very low when Colin called, 'Come on down for tea Dicky!' We were circling the ship in a minute or two and I well remember this, my last land on. A huge red sun was directly forward of the carrier, making it a black silhouette with oily smoke wafting from the funnel. Dead tired and anxious to get down before dark, I dragged JV100 along at deck level, hopping over the round-down and gratefully plopping down on about the 2nd wire.

I developed vertigo the next day due to an inner ear haemorrhage. I was lucky to get down.

And so ended the 'Outflank' raids, although Vian wished to continue. He later wrote:

> It was unfortunate that shortage of oil prevented a further assault on Palembang, to complete the task of destruction. The stage was set for a final raid. Fighter opposition was largely overcome, the enemy's special Army Attack Corps had been rendered innocuous, the weather was reasonable, and the position of the Fleet was still unknown to the enemy. But our small tanker force had gone back, empty. There was only enough fuel in our tanks to get us to Freemantle, en route to Sydney.
>
> Darkness brought the end of an air battle which could be accounted a great success for our airmen. Besides the heavy damage to the refinery, at least 30 Japanese aircraft had been shot down, and another 38 destroyed on the ground.
>
> On the other hand our losses were heavy. Sixteen aircraft had been shot down, and another twenty-five lost from other causes. Thirty-two of our airmen were missing at the end of the day. The fate of the majority remained unknown to us.

To this he could have added the wounded and those rendered unfit to fly following their recent experiences. In reality he had just lost 16 per cent of his aircraft, with more than 50 others in need of major maintenance, with 12 per cent of his aircrew dead or captured, including many experienced men who he could ill afford to lose. Even 'Bomber' Harris with his numerous and costly raids over Germany thought that 5 per cent losses were unacceptable and unsustainable. Vian exceeded this limit with ease. To this could be added the effects of stresses and strains on many others, plus physical wounds which required time to heal. But he felt himself to be another Nelson and drew the threads together of great endeavour to deter any criticism of the losses before they had even begun their main campaign in the Pacific. In his official report he wrote:

> Into the execution of the plan, the squadrons put the limit of human endeavour. That they achieved so great a measure of success against a not easily accessible and heavily defended target justified an outlook of high promise for the future, besides being most creditable to the officers and men involved.

Whatever else Vian may have thought, one thing was certain – the aircrew needed time to rest and recuperate. New men would have to be absorbed and trained by the surviving veterans and there would be goodbyes for some very tired and damaged men being posted home to recover. To all of them Australia became a beacon and their voyage across the Indian Ocean saw their spirits lift; the promise of leave and the need for normal lives, at least for a time, were impossible to ignore. The pleasures of Sydney, and a world where reminders of the war were minimal, would act to calm the senses and revive the spirits. There would also be time for thought and time for privacy; a commodity hard to come by on a carrier packed with 2,000 or more men.

For the New Zealanders on board their homes were also tantalisingly close and they hoped to make the 'short hop' across the Tasman Sea to see their loved ones.

The voyage to Freemantle then Sydney passed slowly. At 0800 hrs on 10 February, *Indomitable* entered harbour, but not without incident. After two Hellcats were flown off at dawn so that their pilots, Dick Mackie and A. R. 'Junior' Andrews, could pick up a flight to New Zealand, a Seafire from *Indefatigable* took off and crashed into sea killing its pilot. Even so far from the combat area, lives continued to be claimed with a terrible regularity.

Soon port routine started and the pilots could begin to relax or let off steam, as each saw fit. John Hawkins recorded how the time passed:

> Not many up early, although Tommy had everyone in his cabin drinking gin. Junior Andrews and Dick Mackie went home, but Alex Macrae was disappointed after being told he was going and had already packed.
>
> Next morning everyone but me, as duty boy, pushed off on leave. The quiet types went to the country the others to try their luck in Sydney. But Claude, having headed for the bright lights, was taken seriously ill with a stomach complaint and joined Dick Neal, who was being treated for an eye complaint, in hospital. Both were in a rather sorry state when we visited them.
>
> We began doing some night-flying exercises from Nowra, while the others were on leave, and this proved very successful. The Hellcat being so stable was an ideal aircraft for this sort of work. But all good things come to an end and everyone had returned by the 26th ready to begin work again. There was good news. Tug Wilson was awarded a DSC and Smithwich a 'Mention in Despatches'.
>
> We were out at sea on the 28th so that eight new Hellcats and some Avengers could be flown on. Other fighters had been loaded alongside in Sydney, so the wing was pretty well up to strength. Losses of pilots to one cause or another were made good by the transfer of eight men from 1840 Squadron (including three Dutchmen – Mocke, Twysle and Naire). Luckily some of them are quite experienced.
>
> During our time in Sydney we were visited by Betty Nesbit, a journalist working for the *Australian Womens Weekly* magazine. She was eager to write about life on board the carriers. As duty boy I accompanied her around the ship, which was by then pretty quiet, but she wanted to see everything, and spent many hours doing so with a break for drinks then lunch in the wardroom. The article didn't appear until June, but copies found their way to us, including my brief comment in reply to her observation that the flight deck seemed huge. It was a pleasant day after a month of operations.

And with this, and the completion of essential maintenance work on the ships, the fleet began the process of working up their crew and squadrons again. Flying began in earnest and on 2 March the wing put most aircraft up in the air to rehearse tactics and get the new men used to squadron routines. But the day was marred by two accidents. Jenkins hit the round-down, his arrestor hook came away and he flew headlong into the barriers writing off his machine.

Then Noel Mitchell, having made a good landing, also went into the barriers, but this time, at least, the aircraft was repairable. The next evening Smithwick misjudged his landing, went over the side and, as Noel Mitchell related:

> He moved very quickly to get out of the cockpit and swim away before his aircraft sank. He was apparently unaffected by the crash and was picked up by the duty destroyer, having been plied with gin by his saviours. He returned to us sporting a marvellous black eye.

At this rate it began to seem that the reserve of aircraft built up in Australia might not last very long, and the fleet hadn't even set sail to join the Americans yet.

Palembang (24–29 January 1945)

Hugh McWinnie, the journalist (left), and Reuben Saidman, the photographer (right, figure with moustache), joined *Indomitable* in time for operations in January 1945. (DM)

Avenger crew from 854 Squadron being briefed by their CO, Lt Cdr 'Charlie' Mainprice, before one of the raids. (DM)

A meal before a mission was essential in providing energy but was a difficult tense time for the aircrew. (DM)

The strike forms up and departs. (DM)

Strike photos taken during *Meridian One*, on the 24th (above) and *Meridian Two* on the 29th (below). (NM)

Safely home but not all were so lucky, the two raids cost 16 aircraft shot down, another 25 written off, with 32 airmen (or 12% of the force) missing when the fleet sailed into Sydney Harbour on 10th February. (RN and DM)

CHAPTER SEVEN

A Long Day's Journey into Night

1945 would be a tumultuous year, and as the New Year dawned there was little certainty about the future. The Japanese and Germans were being pushed back on all fronts but the resistance they offered was intense even when faced by overwhelming force. Germany, being landlocked and surrounded, would surrender in May, but the Japanese, as an island race, had the inconstant sea to help repel their enemy. If they were to be defeated the Allies would have to approach their homeland island by island, fighting a war of great violence and excessive casualties. It was also a war that tended to favour the defender, who, in this case, was well prepared and driven by a suicidal level of patriotism. Yet despite this they couldn't hope to hold out indefinitely when faced by the industrial might and endless resources of an enemy still smarting over the attack on Pearl Harbor. As one American war correspondent put it, 'They're defeated but don't know it yet. They'll be taken to hell and back before it's over'.

And in the absence of any meaningful signs that Japanese leaders were considering surrender, all the Allies could do was press on, force a decision and hope that each defeat might instil a need for peace in a regime seemingly set on self-immolation. In February 1945 the weapons to send a barbarous enemy to a barbaric end were being constructed and gathered. In the islands to the south of Japan the USAAF were mustering a massive force of bombers that would soon devastate their cities. At sea a naval armada of unparalleled power was continuing to move northwards, with an amphibious force capable of taking any island. In the States the Manhattan Project would soon produce the most devastating weapon of all, with Allied leaders beginning to contemplate its use if surrender wasn't soon forthcoming. Yet despite all this the Japanese still gave no quarter. This madness, and a growing belief that an invasion of Japan could lead to millions of casualties on both sides, was pushing the war to an inevitable atomic conclusion.

In Australia men of the British Pacific Fleet sat on the periphery looking in and wondering what their future held. To add to their growing concerns were more reports of kamikaze attacks, the continued strength of enemy resistance and their treatment of prisoners. Vian believed that this: '... not only made casualties particularly hard to bear, but led to our aircrews being kept ignorant of details of operations other than the particular sortie on which they were engaged. This could not but affect morale to some extent.'

It was probably the suicide attacks that created most apprehension, although the way the fleet had despatched the raid on 28 May have given some reason to believe that they could survive more of these in the future. Yet the signs were not good – intelligence gatherers increasingly believed that these attacks would grow in intensity as the Allied fleets approached Japan. Some agencies predicted that the enemy's changing tactics might make the attacks in late 1944 pale into insignificance by comparison.

At Leyte in October the newly formed Special Attack Force had sunk five ships and severely damaged 23 more, including the fleet carrier *Hancock*, and the escort carriers *Franklin* and the *Belleau Wood*. Then the *Intrepid* was hit on 30 October and again on 25 November, along with the *Essex* and the *Cabot*, killing or wounding over 100 men. After that, during January, the escort carriers *Manila Bay* and *Salamaua* were hit, followed by the fleet carrier *Ticonderoga* on 21 January 1945. Two kamikazes struck *Ticonderoga*, killing 143 and injuring another 202 men, inflicting damage that kept it out of service for four months. In February, as the British Pacific Fleet made ready to leave Australia, the veteran carrier *Saratoga* was put out of action for four months by kamikazes, with the escort carrier *Bismarck Sea* sunk and its sister ship, *Lunga Point*, torpedoed in the same action.

Amongst those shortly to face this onslaught there were many who wondered what sort of men they were facing and why they would contemplate sacrificing themselves when Japan faced almost certain defeat. Logic and reason provided no answers and few understood the different cultures or appreciated the standards by which others lived. In an age where the world has grown so small, with the internet and rapid global news, it is hard to understand how lacking in knowledge of other civilisations and their traditions most people were in the 1940s. Before the war it was commonly thought in Britain and America that the Japanese were a physically weaker race with poor eyesight and lack of fighting ability. On the other hand, many Japanese people often only saw the West's excesses and decadence. Exactly why these beliefs should have taken root in the 1930s is difficult to understand now, but they did and would cost both sides dear in the years to come. The invasion of China, and that people's brutal subjugation, should have rung alarm bells in the West, but it took Pearl Harbor, and the sweeping victories that followed, to convince the Allies of their enemy's strength. Equally so, the Japanese would underestimate their enemies' resolve, their sheer industrial muscle and their ability to fight and sacrifice when necessary. By 1945 reality was beginning to dawn on both sides that a negotiated peace was an impossibility, and so the conflict descended into rounds of thrust and counter-thrust without clemency or mercy shown by either side. Yet there was an obvious dichotomy; both sides shared many common values and beliefs – amongst them religious principles, order, and honour.

The Japanese Navy was also a fearsome adversary, with evidence of its capability to be seen even before the Great War when they had destroyed a Russian fleet in 1905 during the war between the two nations. In the intervening years Japan had invested heavily in new and better ships and an air arm of immense strength and advanced technology. While during the 1930s the Royal Navy acquired aircraft barely more advanced than those used in World War I, the Japanese sought quality and quantity. By 1941 they probably had the most advanced carriers, flying some of the best fighters and bombers in the world, with aircrew of the highest quality. It was a force that, until the battle of Midway, was probably better than anything the US could muster.

As with all navies though, there were factions who believed in different strategies, squandering their strength in wasteful and distracting projects. Some clearly saw the future belonging to aircraft, but others still saw big gun battleships as the only way to fight wars. So the huge investment in battleships continued even though aviation soon exposed them for what they were; dinosaurs from a bygone era only surviving if given protection from the air. It would have been better had the Japanese had focussed much more on their carriers. But this was a situation echoed in Britain and Germany and to a lesser extent in America.

With so many fronts on which to fight and an enemy growing ever stronger, the Japanese air arms were a dissipated force by 1945, unable to keep up with the pace of losses. But despite this they were still capable of wreaking destruction. However, by this stage the quality of its aircrew had greatly diminished and there was little time to make good the losses. The kamikaze offered one solution. New pilots could be given minimal training and still hit a target with devastating consequences. Many young Japanese men believed in sacrificing themselves for their emperor and country and gladly went to their deaths.

John Northeast later meditated on the way Japan had fought and the feelings many had as they prepared to face the kamikaze:

> In Sydney we were able to catch up with the news and see newsreels at local cinemas. There was some footage of suicide attacks on carriers and other warships. The Americans seemed less restrained in showing this sort of thing, whereas our government would have slapped a censor's notice on it, fearing for our morale. But they would have been wrong to do so, because it helped steel us for the battles ahead and, when the moment came, to hit the enemy as hard as possible.
>
> In the 1940s we knew little about Japan and its society. It was as though hidden behind a bamboo curtain, made worse by all the atrocity stories that began to emerge during the war, so making us think of them as vermin. It wasn't propaganda that did this. By 1945 we were pretty well inured to that, but a natural response to what we saw or heard from those who were in the front line. Bing Hawkins, for one, had personal experience of this having already lost a brother to them. But there were many other examples.
>
> It wasn't until much later in life, through TV documentaries, that I began to understand Japanese society more clearly. I read widely on the subject and began to form a much clearer picture, supplemented by biographies written by fellow pilots and surviving POWs.
>
> But the more I read the deeper became the contradiction. How could such an orderly society, run on so many civilised principles, descend into such barbarity, to be bolstered by unquestioning self-sacrifice, when enlightened alternatives were available? The truth is that nationalism is inevitably fanned by racial prejudice and a sense of superiority. It happened in Hitler's Germany and it happens everywhere else to a lesser or greater extent even now. My country right or wrong is not an edifying prospect or a mantra to be valued.
>
> Yet when facing the enemy, although feeling a degree of consternation over the kamikazes, I could still admire their bravery in the face of impossible odds. I would have liked to have met them after the war because I feel that we would have had much in common. And it didn't take a leap of the imagination to see that our pilots might have done the same in 1940 if Hitler's forces had invaded and defeat stared us in the face. I well remember reading how some RAF boys deliberately flew into enemy bombers when their ammunition was spent. It was only a small step for these attacks to become more deliberate and frequent, though I hope for us it would have remained a matter of personal choice, not a military strategy calling upon some arcane Bushido or Samurai beliefs to reinforce it.
>
> Many years later I came across a poem written by Admiral Takijiro Onishi, who was one of the founders of the Special Action Force. He had tried to give voice to their beliefs by conjuring up the Samurai symbolism contained in the depiction of cherry blossom:
>
> > 'In blossom today, then scattered;
> > Life is so like a delicate flower,
> > How can one expect the fragrance
> > To last forever?'
>
> I hoped to find some explanation for their actions, but didn't discover any real meaning in these words. The contrast between what they did and these gentle expressions was too great.

In their last few days before sailing, the BPF continued exercising, with emphasis on deck landings at night as Noel Mitchell recalled:

We landed eight new aircraft on in the afternoon, only to learn that in the evening we were to practise night landings. We were all twitched up a little and it was rather like the first time you landed on a carrier. You were scared out of your wits for half an hour before you were due off, but when you came to do it you were so busy doing things that it was over before you'd actually done it. Gavin and Fraser did three each and they looked all right. I went off to try one and felt particularly guilty when after my first attempt they stopped flying for the evening. But I was greatly relieved that in my intense anxiety I had not noticed the weather deteriorating.

My own impression was that it was much easier at night than in the daylight. In the light there were so many things to distract your attention, such as being able to see the entire ship, which makes you less inclined to watch the batsman. But at night you can only see a row of lights down either side of the deck and the batsman's illuminated paddles. I followed every movement of his muscles because there was nothing else to see for guidance.

Joe Brough, who was as good a batsman as you could get, always maintained that it was a waste of time batting me in as I never looked at him anyway. I'm sure he was exaggerating because if he hadn't been there I would have ended up in the barriers more often than I did. However, I only owed the Admiralty about two thousand pounds for deck crashes, but one or two of the other boys went for it in a big way, finally owing our Lords the Commissioners about a quarter of a million quid each.

The next day we sailed for Manus in the Admiralty Islands, north of New Guinea, except for *Illustrious* which remained behind for her centre screw to be replaced. During the voyage we flew every day and attended lectures on procedures in the Pacific, helped by the half dozen American liaison officers we had on board. They were a grand bunch of fellows and soon made themselves at home, giving us lectures on some of their fleet actions in the Pacific.

As we approached Manus, a Royal New Zealand Air Force Corsair Squadron made a dummy attack on the fleet. It was rather a farcical affair, as we were also using Corsairs, and after a few seconds nobody knew who was who, with attackers and defenders merging into a single force.

During January and February, the fleet's CinC, Bruce Fraser, had been trying to establish with Admirals Ernest King and Chester Nimitz the role the BPF should play. Various options had been considered with King favouring the British joining his 7th Fleet under the command of Admiral Thomas Kincaid, which was operating in support of General Douglas McArthur in the South-West Pacific. But Nimitz, realising that the main thrust of the campaign was towards Japan, believed the BPF should be attached to his 5th Fleet, under Admiral Ray Spruance. He didn't see them playing a central role, but one on the flanks, so to speak. It was a debate that took some time to resolve and tested Fraser's diplomacy skills to their limits and as they reached Manus, on 7 March, King was far from convinced that this was the best option. As Vian recorded:

We had therefore to remain at Manus until the 18th March, when Admiral King's objections were at last overcome, and when the executive order came through for the British Strike Force to form part of the 5th Fleet. We moved to Ulithi in the Caroline Islands, an advanced anchorage, where we refuelled, before sailing to join operations already in progress for the capture of Okinawa, as Task Force 57.

The delay, whilst the BPF waited at Manus, proved a testing time for the fleet. This huge anchorage was hot and humid, making life on board ships that were ill-equipped for such conditions almost unbearable. With little to do while they waited, boredom set in and incidents of ill-discipline became a problem. But most of all this waiting period increased worries over the future, leaving many to brood and fret. Fraser, ever conscious of the morale of his men, later wrote, 'The Fleet's stay at Manus was a period of most unpleasant suspense'. In his diary Douglas Smith wrote about Manus: 'I have seen some Godforsaken holes in my time, but this was the most Godforsaken.' Noel Mitchell later recalled the feelings of most on board when he wrote:

> Whilst the big shots argued, getting no nearer a solution, we sat in Manus. Conditions were appalling and things were rather grim as no boats were run to other ships and there was practically no shore leave; not that there was anything to see ashore. The Americans had installed a club on the beach where they threw a party for the officers in honour of our arrival, but apart from that there was nothing to do but sweat and suffer.
>
> Gavin Torrance had to leave with a septic leg which would not heal in the tropical heat. This was a great pity, but unavoidable, and heaven knows we were already short of pilots as it was.
>
> Once or twice things got so bad that it looked as though we might have to return to Sydney, but eventually the hotheads were shouted down by the rightful thinkers and we found ourselves en route for Ulithi, the forward American base. It was bang next door to the island of Yap, still in the hands of the dreaded Jap. We reached there as an air-raid was in progress, but this turned out to be a B29 returning from an operation without sending the correct code. There were fun and games for a while with American fighters buzzing around looking suspiciously at all newcomers.

By this time *Illustrious* had re-joined the fleet, but was only capable of a maximum speed of 24 knots, only just sufficient to operate – until a replacement arrived it would have to struggle on. With this Task Force 57 was up to strength – four carriers, two battleships, four cruisers and twelve destroyers. But its fleet train, designated Task Units 112.2.1 and 112.2.5, each protected by an escort carrier, seemed to lack sufficient numbers and certainly some of the ships lived up to the 'Fred Karno' image so beloved by some of the pilots in the 5th Wing. When replenishment at sea began they would again seem ill-prepared for the role.

Okinawa was a valuable prize in the campaign to reach Japan and it continued the American policy of island hopping towards this final target. But before this could happen there were other objectives to attack, subdue and occupy. In February, after eight months of preparation, a large amphibious force landed on the volcanic island of Iwo Jima. Fierce fighting had lasted until the end of March, allowing a B29 air base to be established there. But it proved unsuitable as a fleet anchorage or as a staging post to invade Japan itself. Okinawa then assumed added importance and the effort to be expended significantly increased, with the BPF providing a force which could help significantly, whatever doubts may have been expressed about its capabilities. If Iwo Jima was anything to go by casualties would be heavy, with intelligence reports suggesting that kamikazes would be deployed in vast numbers to repel the invaders. As John Hawkins recalled:

> The briefings we received didn't play down the risk and Gammy Godson at the end of one simply said, 'Oh bugger! All hands to the pumps', and later, in private with a large gin in his hand, added, 'Here's to a short life and a merry one'. I don't think any of us thought we would survive. Gavin Torrance's septic leg was much envied.

The attack on Okinawa was codenamed Operation *Iceberg*, with the first amphibious assault due to begin on 1 April. The invasion would be an all-American affair, with British and Empire forces providing support. Ray Spruance, possibly the most successful American admiral of this or any other war, was at the head of the 5th Fleet, with Vice-Admiral Rawlings, now restored to fitness, in command of TF 57. With them leading, the prospects were far better than many of the pilots thought possible. But even though the Allies enjoyed overwhelming superiority the Japanese were well dug in and would be defending home territory for the first time, so a hard slog was expected. As things turned out it proved far worse than the planners had thought possible.

In 1945 the Allies saw the kamikaze as an air-launched weapon. But it was a principle that reached deeply into the Japanese psyche and at Okinawa its widespread use, by all elements of society, became common. Was it an inhuman response as many believed or a natural reaction to an enemy few understood, but feared for their apparent savagery. Misconceptions spread by propaganda obviously played a part in this, and both sides would be guilty of this transgression. But at Okinawa each side had reason to see the awfulness of the other and believe the worst of what they were told. Behind it all lay the undeniable knowledge that the Japanese had treated anyone they'd conquered with savagery. The stage was set for an unrelenting, unmerciful and callous battle in which both civilians and servicemen would die in enormous numbers. When Okinawa finally succumbed, in late June, some 150,000 civilians would be dead, with 76,000 Allied and 120,000 Japanese military as casualties. It was small wonder that President Roosevelt then Truman, and their military commanders, began to believe that storming the Japanese mainland would cost millions of lives and so looked for 'cheaper' alternatives.

Spruance was the perfect leader for *Iceberg* and he would prove to be a strong ally to the BPF, seeing them as an asset in this great endeavour. He had led the American navy to victory at Midway and then in the Philippine Sea – two of the most important battles in World War II – so had a keen grasp of tactics and the need for strong, effective leadership. He also knew how to develop excellent working relationships, as did Rawlings and Fraser, and this stood his whole command in good stead at a very difficult time. With good American and British liaison officers embedded in each other's ships the level of mutual understanding quickly grew. Gammy Godson soon developed this to a higher level when befriending Lt Cdr John Ramsey USNR, who was attached to *Indomitable* as air intelligence officer. In this role he proved an invaluable support to all aircrew, but particularly the Fighter Wing, where his presence, matched with Gammy's drive and good humour, helped calm the nerves of many young men.

Task Force 57, having stored at Ulithi and then again refuelled at sea, with the usual level of delays and embarrassment, reached its operating area to the south and west of Okinawa, on 26 March. The brief was a simple one – patrol off the Sakishima Gunto and attack the heavily defended airfields there, so neutralising the threat posed by enemy fighters and bombers operating from the islands of Miyako and Ishigaki. It was feared that when the invasion of Okinawa started the Japanese would send aircraft from Formosa and Sakishima to fly kamikaze missions or simply to provide reinforcements. TF 57's role was to stop this happening and to do this it had nearly a quarter of Spruance's naval air power. So the British fleet's role wasn't an inconsequential part of the operation or even a sideshow to the main event, as Admiral Vian had suspected it might be.

Noel Mitchell recalled Captain Eccles briefing the ship's crew and the attacks that followed:

> He told us that we would be at sea for some considerable time and our job was to make all the airfields in the Sakishima permanently useless. This would render them u/s for the enemy and stop then ferrying aircraft from Formosa to Okinawa. D-Day was the 26th and as it approached we all grew accustomed to many new procedures used by the Americans. CAPs were flown by fighters from each carrier throughout the day and night. Avengers wandered off on anti-submarine patrols and the PR Hellcats flew high over the islands gathering intelligence and monitoring aircraft movements. Rawlings didn't seem too concerned that these flights might attract the Japs' attention. We speculated that he wanted them to know, so they'd be unsure where the next attack might fall and keep aircraft on the islands to guard against any eventuality.

On D-Day we were awakened for breakfast at 0430 hrs, and as dawn came up our engines kicked into life and the first raids on Miyako and Ishigaki were launched. Up to this time we had made only one strike a day before the force retired, but this time we were to strike, strike again and strike yet again. So from dawn to dusk we went on hour after hour dropping bombs on each airfield and strafing anything that moved.

Douglas Smith takes up the story:

Our Avengers bombed the six main airfields, the docks and the radio station, while the Hellcats, Corsairs, Fireflies and Spits escorted them and carried out ramrods on the dispersal areas and then there were fighter bomber sweeps usually late in the afternoon to catch the unwary. We kept this up all day, which meant doing at least seven hours flying. *Indomitable* was very lucky, we only had one casualty – Lt Macrae, RNZNVR. He was badly shot up over the target and brought his plane back and crash landed. He had lost so much blood that he was almost unconscious and had to be lifted from the cockpit and carried to sick bay.

In its official history of the naval war the New Zealand Defence Department reported this incident:

He was severely wounded when carrying out a low strafing mission on the Sakishima Gunto airfields. Though in great pain he carried out two more attacks. It wasn't until he ran out of ammunition that he told his leader that he was wounded and was returning to his ship. Encouraged by radio messages he flew back 100 miles alone, injecting morphine on the way to ease his pain. His right leg was now useless, and he was weak from loss of blood.

In 1996 Alex Macrae, in a letter to the author, wrote:

My tour on the 5th Wing stage was pretty fleeting, about 15 weeks, of which three were spent below decks in the Sick Bay being patched up. On the 26th I was Fraser Shotton's wingman, as I had been over Palembang. Indom was a great ship to have served in.

After I was hit I had faith that my job was to make the ship and there I would be patched up. Joe Brough, 'Bats', saw my predicament and guided me safely down to the deck. Surgeon Roger Lee pulled the bits together. My initial instruction was to bail out over the fleet. No way could I have survived that. A strike had just flown off so I had the carrier all to myself and Eccles called me down even though I could have messed up his deck quite badly. I was presented with these three photos as my 'going away' present from Indom.

The Hellcat with six .5" guns was a potent weapon for the ground attack role. On Sakishima the targets we attacked along the airstrip must have been in fairly predictable positions and some were dummies. The Hellcat was a truly fearsome animal and did a lot of damage. It really had a roar like thunder and a bolt to match.

Then there was the numbers game. Jenkins, Haberfield, Langdon and myself shared a cabin. Only I survived.

Dick Mackie, who was himself a most courageous man, thought Macrae's actions, 'the bravest I ever witnessed and this amongst a group of the most gallant men you could hope to meet. In pressing home his attack, despite being severely wounded, then fighting to get home with the most appalling injuries, he deserved the VC. When lifted from his aircraft the medics literally had to hold his leg together and the cockpit looked like an abattoir. He survived but it was at a terrible cost to his health and life'.

The early strikes seemed to meet little resistance and only one fighter – a Corsair – failed to return, its pilot ditching near Ishigaki, where he was spotted and picked up safely by a Walrus. But later attacks met more opposition with an Avenger from 854 Squadron being shot down and the CO from 1836 Squadron, Chris Tomkinson, forced to ditch after being hit over the target, though wasn't picked up. Captain Denny of *Victorious* reported that, 'the loss is thought to have been caused by a faulty life jacket', but privately wondered whether sharks may have killed him. The task force could ill afford to lose men of his calibre.

In a letter to his parents Gammy Godson wrote, 'I've lost another good friend. I can't help thinking about how many more will go before the enemy surrenders, as they must surely do'.

As the pace of the attacks picked up so the strain on aircrew increased. For most, life consisted of flying, fighting, eating and trying to sleep, with little time to think, let alone drink in the wardroom or socialise. In fact, most would later find it difficult to recall individual operations, with one merging into another. The single strikes over Palembang, with pauses before going again, were remembered, fifty years later, with much greater clarity. Even contemporary reports written within hours of landing became devoid of fine detail so great was the rush of activity. When catching up with his diary on the 31st, Douglas Smith, though involved in six or seven hours flying each day, including many strafing runs and escort missions, could only write:

> The 27th was an exact replica of the previous day. Air opposition was very slight owing to our successful plastering of the airfields, but the ack ack was far too accurate to be healthy. A good proportion of our aircraft got nice friendly holes in them. After that the fleet retired for a day to oil. I think I spent that day asleep and most of the other lads did likewise.

Luckily John Hawkins was more conscious than most of the passage of time and the importance of these events and felt the need to keep a more precise record of all he saw. As a result, he kept notes throughout the day and built these into a more detailed account of the first operations over Sakishima. He was a careful observer, even when stress levels were exceptionally high, and his recollections capture a true flavour of this life:

> The 26th dawned fine, but a little overcast. Sixteen Hellcats were already ranged on deck at first light and Tommy Harrington led the strike which took off at 0630 hrs. Our mission

was to sweep the island of Ishigaki. At the same time Fraser Shotton took off on a CAP. Meanwhile *Victorious* and *Illustrious* were launching 16 Corsairs apiece to hit Miyako Jima.

No airborne opposition was encountered, much to everyone's disappointment, but the flak when strafing the airfields at Hegina and Ishigaki Main was very intense. Tug Wilson took many hits and was forced to ditch about four miles from the island, where a few hours later he was picked up by a Walrus from *Illustrious*. Alex Macrae was badly wounded in the groin and thigh. He applied a tourniquet and carried on attacking, and then, in great pain and fainting through loss of blood, managed to fly back and make a perfect belly landing.

Several types when returning found holes in their aircraft and a burst of flak had hit the top of my canopy. A few inches lower would have proved fatal. Luckily we knew to fly as close to the ground as possible when attacking an airfield. Some always found this difficult and lost their heads as a result.

Next came an escort for Avengers bombing the airfields, with good results, but still no air opposition. It was strange to see a bomb explode, but hear no sound from the blast.

The day ended with eight Hellcats, four with bombs, giving some small ships a pasting and we flew away as they burnt and sank. There was little flak, but what there was proved to be accurate. There were six holes in my tail plane and four through my wings. Nothing serious though.

Altogether 184 sorties were flown from the four carriers, but this didn't include CAPs, RATCAPS or Jack patrols. Everyone just fell into bed hoping the hell we'd have a peaceful night.

We were unlucky. There was great excitement when an enemy aircraft was picked up on radar and Noel Mitchell was launched at 0400 hrs to intercept it. He was unlucky though.

At dawn eight Hellcats and 16 Corsairs were led by Tommy Harrington once again to Ishigaki for a look see, but no luck. Junior Andrews turned back before reaching the target, with a failing engine, and made it safely back to the carrier. Then the Avengers were off just before noon to bomb installations and airfields again with fair results. 857's leader, 'Doc' Stuart, was forced to ditch near a destroyer and he and his crew were safely picked up, though not returned to *Indomitable* for some time.

During the day two Seafires were seen to collide when forming up, with both going up in flames. One Corsair spun in on its approach, but was fortunate enough to recover and then get down on deck, its pilot with a broken arm.

We spent the 28th oiling and catching up with much sleep. Later in the day a typhoon was forecast and everything, including the aircraft, had to be lashed down. It proved to be a false alarm and all the preparations had been for nothing.

Noel Mitchell retained very clear memories of his attempted interception:

At 0350 hrs I was flown off to intercept the enemy. It was a beautiful night and I roared along at 600 feet thinking how peaceful everything looked. I spoke to the ship the whole time knowing that I was the only aircraft in the sky and Colin Keay kept up a continuous flow of information as he followed the plot on radar. Finally, he gave me a wonderful vector for as I peered over the side I almost flashed right over my prey, who was only 50 feet below me. I slid away to one side climbing and losing my excess speed continually watching him as a cat watches a mouse. He was a dead easy target, but as I started my attack he suddenly disappeared. He had been flying in a bright pool of moonlight and was silhouetted against the dark sea below. As I prepared to shoot he flew out of the moonlight into a jet-black shadow, produced by a bank of cloud. The effect was the same as a person leaving a brightly lit room into a black night. Colin gave me a new vector, by which time the Jap had dived for home. I pursued at maximum boost and closed the gap to 10 miles before being recalled. Reluctantly and cursing my ill-luck I abandoned the chase and returned to the fleet, which was in the process of launching the first sweep of the day.

Throughout these early operations the night fighters from *Indomitable* were learning their trade. Fraser Shotton, Noel Mitchell and Bill Foster, in particular, were beginning to excel at this form of work. But the results continued to be frustrating, as Mitchell again discovered:

It was thought that the enemy would try and attack the fleet as night fell. So the form was that Shotton's flight then mine should do the dusk patrols on alternate nights. Ten minutes before dusk we would take off just before the last CAPs of the day landed. If nothing was showing on the radar we came back and landed on in darkness, but with minimum lights showing. But invariably there was something on the screen.

One particular evening my flight was vectored to intercept a radar trace. After several changes of course directed by the plotters we saw an aircraft flying towards us 2,000 feet below. We tally-ho'd and flew into a position to dive and attack. We jettisoned our long range tanks for combat and in line astern peeled off to attack. Halfway down someone shouted over the R/T, 'It's a friendly!' But I kept on closing ready to fire and then recognised an American Liberator. I kept diving determined to frighten him for not identifying himself earlier. Closing in on his tail he began to manoeuvre madly, at the same time switching on all his cabin lights and firing recognition cartridges in all directions. I pulled up close alongside shaking my fist, then pulled away to resume our patrol.

Meanwhile Rawlings and Vian's staff were trying to make sense of all the reports prepared by tired and often confused minds. It proved difficult but the fleet needed to get a clear picture of what had happened so that future operations might be better directed. But there was also a need to prepare communiques for the Admiralty back in London and for Nimitz. All the effort expended had to be justified and Task Force 57 had to be seen as worthy addition to the fleet. Their log of events captures a broad view of each day's operations:

26th March

At 0605 hrs CAPs and one ASP were flown off, whilst HM Ships *Argonaut* and *Kempen* felt were detached to carry out picket duties. At sunrise strong fighter sweeps were flown off from a position 100 miles 180 degrees from Miyako Jima to attack the airfields at Ishigaki and Miyako; they reported little activity.

These sweeps were followed by two escorted bomber strikes and one fighter bomber strike with airfields and associated buildings as targets. Withdrawal was begun at dusk.

Throughout the day there were frequent air raid warnings, but all bogeys were eventually identified as friendly except for one Dinah. After the last aircraft had flown on, the fleet disengaged to the south eastward. The night was fine and the moon bright and an enemy attack was considered likely.

27th March

At 0245 hrs a bogey to the eastwards was contacted by radar. As it seemed the fleet was being shadowed the course was altered in an attempt to shake of the aircraft. At 0307 hrs HMS *Euryalus* was ordered to open out from the screen and fire at the enemy aircraft, which then stayed at a respectful distance for a time. A Hellcat was then flown off from *Indomitable* to intercept. At 0305 hrs Japanese ASV (aircraft radar jamming equipment) transmissions on 152 Mc/s were reported and the fleet was ordered to commence jamming.

At sunrise a fighter sweep was sent in to Ishigaki only. No increased activity was reported. Two bomber strikes were directed against radar stations, barracks and airfields, not covered on the 26th. Coasters off the islands were also attacked. Withdrawal was begun at dusk.

In the reports little mention is made of the losses, which in the circumstances were light though still significant. There was Alex Macrae, of course, safely returned but out of the war. S/Lt Peter Spreckley, of 1834 Squadron, was shot down and killed over Ishigaki, whilst Chris Tomkinson, CO of 1836, had also been lost. An Avenger from 854, flown by the squadron's CO, Freddie Nottingham, took hits over Hirara, but made it out over the sea before fire took hold and his starboard wing suddenly broke away. Only he survived, picked up later by the American submarine *Kingfish*.

The two Seafires that John Hawkins had observed in flames, took their pilots, S/Lts Tony Cooper and Sam Yarde, with them. Then there were the crash landings, ditchings and battle damage to take into account. In total Vian recorded that, 'the Task Force lost nine men and six aircraft in combat and another eleven operationally. 273 strike and 275 CAP sorties were flown. At least 23 aircraft had been destroyed (though some of these might have been decoys). The Avenger Squadrons dropped sixty-four tons of bombs, while the Fireflies fired 150 rockets'. It seemed that the airfields, if not put out of action, had at least been seriously disrupted. But the Japanese were undoubtedly aware of the forthcoming landings on Okinawa, so may have already routed as many aircraft there before Task Force 57 began their strikes. This would have left the Sakishima Gunto lightly defended, which may have accounted for the muted defence against the incoming Fleet Air Arm attacks.

Another reason for the lack of enemy aircraft may have been due to Task Force 58. The American Fast Carrier Group was attacking the enemy head-on leaving them little time to protect other targets, such as Sakishima. As early as 14 March they began raiding airfields around southern Japan. Their aim was a simple one – to destroy their air forces on the ground or lure them up and dispose of them in combat. After the Marianas 'turkey shoot', many believed this to be a realistic option and one worth pursuing. The Japanese responded strongly, sending out large formations of torpedo-bombers, fighters and kamikazes to attack the American force. The carriers *Intrepid* and *Enterprise* were lightly damaged on the 18th, but, the next day, two bombs landed on the *Franklin* causing grievous damage and killing some 700 men (though some estimates place this higher) and wounding another 265 in the process. Only good damage control saved the ship, but repairs were only completed after the war, so, in reality, it had been rendered 'hors de combat' by the enemy. But the Americans believed that enemy losses in these attacks were substantial and significantly reduced their ability to defend Okinawa, so the loss of a carrier was given some balance. Nevertheless, the damage to *Intrepid*, *Enterprise* and *Franklin* was another wake-up call for Nimitz and Spruance, who had already seen many other carriers severely damaged by aircraft, no matter how stretched the enemy force might seem to be.

Reports of these operations were soon winging their way to Rawlings and Vian, who naturally assumed that TF 57 would soon be attacked. TF 58's raids on Japan had clearly stirred up a hornet's nest and the effects would soon be felt far and wide. Vian pondered the next round of attacks while the fleet replenished. He concluded that:

> As targets the airfields proved both disappointing and dangerous. Though heavily defended by anti-aircraft guns, few seemed to be in active use. Furthermore, the runways being hewn out of coral were easily repaired during darkness, when operations ceased. As a result, not only was it necessary to repeat attacks day by day, but a large proportion of our effort had to diverted to putting the anti-aircraft defences out of action. In this, we were not altogether effective, the high-explosives bombs not being very effective against such targets.
>
> Although our bomber aircraft were disappointed by the unrewarding nature of their targets, our fighters, maintaining a Combat Air Patrol over the islands, found much to occupy them. We felt that we were, therefore, fulfilling our task of preventing air attacks on the expeditionary force lying off Okinawa.

On the 30th, TF 57 headed back towards Sakishima, this time knowing that the Americans would 'hit the beaches' on 1 April. And with pressure rising the islands' defences would, undoubtedly, be placed on full alert and increased in strength as much as possible. On *Indomitable* John Hawkins again observed the preparations and wrote:

> Tug Wilson returned to the fold this afternoon and certainly looks well. Apparently his worst fright was seeing turtles and sea snakes near his raft and the occasional shark. I'm surprised they risked getting so close!
>
> Had a general briefing during the day for the next stage of *Iceberg*. The word is that we will have a dawn sweep and if any opposition is encountered then Plan 'Peter' will go into operation. But if nothing happens we move onto Plan 'Queen'. Tommy Harrington will again lead the sweep. The two Air Group Commanders (Hay on *Victorious* and Luard on

Indomitable) will take their flights up before the Ramrods begin and spy out the land then decide which plan to adopt.

For the next two days missions were flown and the cycle of operations appeared to be going well, but on 1 April the enemy began to strike back. The first Ramrods of the day had flown off when radar began plotting an incoming raid, westwards at 8,000 feet. Forty miles out the formation began to break up; the aircraft dispersing to confuse the defenders and make separate attacks. A number of fighters were scrambled to intercept them and the Ramrods were recalled. Corsairs from *Victorious* made first contact and S/Lts Leddy and Watt attacked a Zeke and sent it down in flames.

When the Ramrods arrived on the scene, they detected the raiders down at sea level and quickly waded into them, even though they were within range of the ships' guns. A Zeke machine-gunned the decks of *King George V* in passing, then crashed into the *Indefatigable*, despite the best endeavours of Richard Reynolds flying a Seafire. Within 20 minutes he had despatched two more, then had to look on as his comrades below struggled to repair the damage done by the Zeke and its 500-lb bomb. The armoured flight deck proved its worth, although dented to a depth of three inches, but a sickbay, briefing room and both barriers were all badly damaged, with eight men killed and 16 wounded. Nevertheless, within 40 minutes the carrier was able to receive its first Seafires and remained operational.

Meanwhile Tommy Harrington and the Hellcats joined the fray as others from the wing were launched from *Indomitable*. John Hawkins, who was part of a flight scrambled from the carrier, recalled what happened:

Chaos reigned that morning. Sammy Langdon, in the dawn CAP, due to take off at 0610 hrs, had brake trouble and his propeller chewed into the tail of an Avenger and Bill Foster's wing tip. The mess was eventually cleared away to allow eight Hellcats, led by Tommy Harrington, to take off on a sweep. Halfway to the target, at 20,000 feet, they were recalled when a Jap force was reported coming in from astern of the fleet.

Meanwhile two flights of Hellcats were launched from the carrier. Within minutes all piled into the enemy – mostly Tojos and Zekes. Tommy got one, while Smith was hit by a Seafire in the confusion. Generally, everyone had fun bending their throttles, but we couldn't stop an enemy aircraft strafing *Indomitable*'s deck with machine-gun fire, killing two and wounding others, including Ken Chapman. Over on her port quarter a destroyer was damaged by a near miss before all the Jap aircraft were destroyed. For the next few hours the fleet sorted itself out and then concluded the day with a bombing raid by the Avengers on Ishigaki and a final sweep over the islands to make sure the enemy got their heads down for the night. During this attack, which I flew on Gammy Godson's wing, we destroyed several aircraft on the ground, including a large four-engine job. Apparently the other squadrons accounted for another eleven aircraft.

In a letter to John Winton, Harrington recalled this combat and pondered the nature of war over Sakishima:

> One suicide aircraft was flying just out of killing range and I carefully fired a long burst over his port wing. He very kindly obliged by executing a turn to port which enabled me to close and shoot this unhappy amateur down. This type of operation was repeated by many of my boys as well as myself on a number of occasions.
>
> The final recollection I have of the Gunto operation is the effects of the continuous offensive flying on both men and machines. I decided that the Japanese were having an even worse time than ourselves because they rarely took to the air and when this happened they were generally even sadder. In other words, the exercise of air power was being classically and successfully operated.
>
> I still have my log book and I noted that whilst in the operational area we were in our cockpits on an average of 6 hours per day; my personal record being 10½ hours.

Intelligence sources later revealed that the Japanese force, numbering some 20 aircraft, were probably part of their First Air Fleet based on Formosa. Few, if any, survived. But the day wasn't without its losses to TF 57. A Seafire diverted to land on *Victorious*, while *Indefatigable* was temporarily out of commission, crashed into the barrier and its pilot, S/Lt W. G. Gibson, of 894 Squadron, was killed. During the final sweep a Corsair flown by S/Lt H. J. H. Roberts, of 1834 Squadron, was hit when making a low pass over one of the airfields and was struck by very accurate anti-aircraft fire. He managed to reach the sea and ditched, but he couldn't be found by a searching Walrus or ships in the area and was presumed dead.

But the enemy raids were not quite over for the day, though by the standard of Japanese attacks against American ships around Okinawa their efforts against TF 57 were fairly minor. At 1730 hrs, when the fleet was being manoeuvred to starboard, a kamikaze attack developed, with two aircraft coming in very low. Hellcats were vectored to intercept and may have brought one down but the other flew in and appeared to be flying a circuit around *Victorious* as though to land. In the last few moments he pulled up and turned ready to attack, but Captain Denny, on the ship's bridge, aware of what was happening, quickly increased the rate of turn to starboard, whilst his gunners blasted away. This seemed to distract the enemy pilot sufficiently to make his aim poor and his dive ended with a wing clipping the port edge of the flight deck. With this the aircraft cartwheeled into the sea, coming to rest some 80 feet away. The bomb it was carrying exploded underwater and 'threw tons of water, a quantity of petrol and many fragments of aircraft and pilot on to the flight deck'.

Next day the task force was back on station expecting more attacks, with everyone on high alert until nightfall. But an early morning fighter sweep over the airfields saw little enemy activity and gradually the suspicion grew that the Japanese may simply have been using the islands as an overnight staging post for aircraft transiting from Formosa to Okinawa. At the same time any aeroplanes permanently based on Ishigaki or Miyako would take off before dawn to avoid being destroyed on the ground in early morning strikes, and meet the enemy head on, also taking whatever opportunity presented itself to seek out and attack TF 57. To counter any of these moves four Hellcats were flown off *Indomitable* by moonlight, with two each destined to hover over Ishigaki and Miyako to see what was happening. But the second pair suffered radio failures and returned before completing their mission. The other proceeded as planned though had nothing to report, everything being quiet on the ground. Noel Mitchell was one of the pilots assigned to Ishigaki:

> As the moon was still up we were to try a night intrusion, taking off in darkness to arrive over the island before dawn. Doug Smith and I went over, and the 30-minute flight was one of the best I ever experienced. There was something exotic about it, more like a dream that suddenly burst into reality as we arrived over the target. We flew right round the island at 200 feet as the dawn came up, but as it grew lighter we felt less and less brave and gradually increased our height. We were in loose formation at about 3,000 feet when suddenly the enemy woke up and a barrage of flak came up and soon surrounded us. Doug and I jumped in our seats, broke up and rammed our throttles fully open, zig-zagging off in different directions. At 8,000 feet where the fire was far less accurate we formed up again and resumed our patrol breathing a little more freely until relieved by other aircraft.

At 0630 hrs, a fighter Ramrod made up of Corsairs and Hellcats departed and found some Japanese fighters over Ishikagi. The combat was short and sharp, but largely inconclusive. Only S/Lt Mocke RNN, who broke away from his flight, latched onto a Japanese fighter, quickly despatching it with a full deflection shot. He later reported it as a Zeke painted in mottled colours and thought it poorly handled, as though by a novice. Another aircraft was destroyed on the ground, but apart from this the Ramrod returned without inflicting or receiving any further damage.

And with this attack TF 57's second operational period came to an end and they sailed away to join their fleet train to replenish. During their absence TF 58 detached a small carrier group to patrol the skies over Sakishima. But they had little to keep them busy, such was the state of play over Okinawa where the Japanese were at full stretch trying to stop the main Allied thrust.

That evening Vian composed a summary of his carriers' work in the first two operational periods. He wrote:

> During the period 23rd March to 2nd April inclusive our losses of aircraft were 25, compared to 47 destroyed or probably destroyed and 38 damaged on the ground. Enemy vessels sunk and damaged were – 1 lugger, 13 other smaller vessels probably sunk, and over 40 small craft damaged.

He then added some interim assessments outlining the performance of each part of his force, paying particular attention to the 5th Fighter Wing:

> Trained and led by Act Lt Cdr (A) T. F. Harrington RN, the wing has, throughout the whole course of the operation, been remarkable. Flying by day and sometimes by night, I can recollect but one barrier crash, whilst their break-up from the landing circuit and speed of landing on has been exceptional. Whilst not so fast as Corsairs, their tactical eminence has enabled them to account for their full share of what enemy aircraft have been available.

To the north-west the landings on Okinawa began well, largely because the Japanese commanding officer, General Mitsuru Ushijima, decided not to contest the beaches, keeping his men well back in fortified, camouflaged positions on the Motobu peninsula. But when the serious fighting began a war of attrition was inevitable. If the Japanese gave ground, it was only when most of the defenders were dead. Into this difficult mix the kamikaze soon appeared in greater numbers than ever before – in the air and on the sea.

As early as 26 March the Americans uncovered evidence of assault motor boats, called 'Shinyu', being constructed and made ready for suicide missions. At the same time intelligence reports suggested that the Japanese could have as many as 6,000 aircraft available to attack the Allied forces and to defend the homeland. In addition, the decimated IJN still had some capital ships left, including the giant battleship *Yamato*, which might be used to strike the invading fleet at any time.

The first kamikaze attack took place on 1 April. It was a small affair, but the battleship *West Virginia* was hit, as was an LST and transport ships. The raids continued. Two days later the escort carrier, USS *Wake Island*, was put out of commission for two months, the destroyer transport *Dickerson* was so badly damaged that it had to be scuttled and more transport ships were hit. Then the weather closed in for two days and the attacks stopped, but it proved to be the lull before the storm.

On the 6th, waves of Japanese fighters came over Okinawa to secure air superiority and allow the kamikazes to attack with less chance of facing enemy aircraft. The tactic was only partially successful and dogfights soon filled the sky, but not enough Corsairs and Hellcats were distracted to protect the 110 suicide planes as they approached the American Fleet. Destroyers initially took the main brunt of the attack, with two being sunk, for the loss of 14 aircraft. But the rest moved on to the main invasion Fleet, where radar soon picked them up and more interceptions began. Many were knocked down but sufficient remained to dive into a number of destroyers, minesweepers and LSTs, including the *Newcomb, Leutze, Defense, Witter, Morris, Howarth, Hyman* and *Mullaney*.

When the raid was finally over the Japanese escorts that had survived reported seeing 150 smoke plumes around the enemy fleet. It was undoubtedly an exaggeration, but so may have been the American claims of 486 Japanese aircraft shot down, by fighters or shipboard gunners.

Meanwhile, at Kure Naval Base, the Japanese prepared the *Yamato*, a cruiser and eight destroyers for a suicide mission of unparalleled scale. Without air protection this Surface Special Attack Force set sail on the 6th on a one-way mission to Okinawa. *Yamato's* purpose was to destroy any enemy ships it came upon, then run onto a beach and become a shore fortress using its big guns to support General Ushijima's planned counter-attack. But early next morning it was spotted by a search plane and by the early afternoon it and five of its escorts had been sunk. There was some revenge though. A kamikaze group found the main carrier force that day, one managed to evade the fighters and guns to crash on the fleet carrier *Hancock*. Some 70 men were killed and another 82 injured, while 20 aircraft were written off. *Hancock* wasn't too severely damaged and, after repair, returned to the front line in June.

It was into this cauldron that Task Force 57 returned on the 6th, after replenishment, fully expecting to face a fresh and more determined onslaught in the waters around Ishigaki and Miyako. For the next two weeks, until 20 April, TF 57 would be in and out of the battle zone with gloomy regularity. The cycle of action again became so intense that few could later recall many details, let alone gain a bigger picture of events – a common phenomenon for any military campaign. Official communiques, prepared by the admiral's staff, were inevitably a cold, simple narrative stripped of any human reactions to combat. But they do at least provide a framework to help us understand the rigours and then sense what it was like to be young men at war on *Indomitable* during these days, when the pace was unremitting and remorseless.

Four contemporary accounts have survived to describe these two weeks, written by Gammy Godson, John Hawkins, Douglas Smith and Noel Mitchell. To this can be added the words of Bill Atkinson, Bill Foster and Bill Fenwick-Smith, plus Lt Cdr Norman Hanson (from the 15th Wing on *Illustrious*) written or recorded decades later. Together their memories paint a brief and moving account of the most intense period of their lives. For many of them it would also be the last time they would fly in combat.

6th April
Back again for another couple of days. We certainly seem to be holding our own and doing a good job of work. We tend to look at it like a 'Milk Run' now. (Douglas Smith)

Four Hellcats took off at 0500 hrs and carried out intruder patrols. CAPs also flown over the islands. Northeast got a Frances on the way back, the CO and Tug got a Judy [the Yokosuka D4Y dive bomber] while doing Fleet CAP and Atkinson plus two shot down another Judy. One Divine Wind boy hit *Illustrious*, finishing up in the 'oggin'. (John Hawkins)

As we flew away from Ishigaki I saw a Yokosuka P1Y twin engine bomber flying low over the sea towards the fleet. It was weaving at high speed hoping to avoid detection. I followed for about 30 miles then dived down low and came in from the port side unobserved by its rear gunner and fired from 100 yards recording many hits. It simply flew into the sea. (John Northeast)

In all the chatter that filtered through the headset every day it was only natural that one should recognise friends' voices, particularly when they came from other carriers. A voice from somewhere – apparently young and naive – came up on the R/T, on the 6th as we were flying CAPs, asking something which I thought would be self-evident and quite elementary. Our good friend Gammy Godson appeared to be in agreement, for it was his voice which told the youngster 'not to be such a bloody fool!' (Norman Hanson)

Avengers bombed and hit Hirara runway and town, and Nobara, Sukhama and Miyara airstrips causing fires. Fighters attacked radio and radar stations, sank two junks and blew up a bowser. At about 1700 hrs bogeys were detected on the screen. Fighters intercepted and splashed one Judy. One enemy broke through in cloud and dived on *Illustrious*, who took radical avoiding action. The suicider's wingtip hit the island, spinning into the sea where the bomb exploded. Only slight damage and no casualties were caused. Ship probably hit aircraft in dive.

Most regrettably one Seafire was shot down by gunfire from the fleet during the raid; the pilot was not recovered.

Our losses for the day were the Seafire, two Corsairs damaged by bomb blast on Illustrious and one Avenger which crashed when taking off. Total enemy losses were: Destroyed – four airborne, one suicide and one on the ground. Damaged – six. (Operational Summary)

7 April
Nothing further shot down although there were probably more aircraft on the deck than usual. Bill Atkinson chewed up the deck whilst taxying fast behind some other cove. One unlucky soul succeeded in hitting the S4 pom-pom with Tommy's aircraft. He wasn't at all popular. No aircraft attacked the fleet much to the CAPs disappointment. Day's flying completed we pushed off to rendezvous with the oilers. (John Hawkins)

The plan for the day was to maintain a constant CAP over the enemy airfields, bombing and strafing when targets offered. The weather at dawn was good and the clouds higher than yesterday.

The CAPs reported little activity on the islands, but noticed that bomb craters on Ishigaki had been filled in, and that Hirara and Nobara airfields appeared serviceable. It was therefore decided to send in three bomber strikes during the day to re-crater these fields. This was successfully carried out without loss.

During the afternoon HMS *Urania* and two fighters were despatched to look for and rescue a Corsair pilot who had lost his way and ditched 70 miles from the fleet. When recovered he was found to be dead.

During the day the enemy lost three aircraft destroyed on the ground and four were damaged. We lost two to flak and four from other causes (Operational Summary).

8–10 April – Replenishment period.

Signal from COM 5th Fleet (Nimitz) (1650 hrs 8th April) 'CTF 57 cancel 10th April Sakishima operation. TG 52.1 continue neutralisation that day (over Sakishima). CTF 57 to advise if following not within capabilities. If approved by C in C Pacific, CTF 57 to strike Shinchuka and Matsuyama airfields, Formosa 11/12th April'.

This was the first intimation that a change of plan was contemplated (It seemed that COM 5th Fleet was concerned that reinforcements were being sent from Formosa to Okinawa, bypassing Ishigaki and Miyako. So a direct attack on the airfields around Formosa was proposed to counter this move).

It had already been decided that, although both pilots and aircraft were beginning to feel the strain, the possibility of carrying out a 5th operational period against Sakishima Gunto was acceptable, provided it would be on a light scale.

The Formosa operation, involving our maximum strength and flying 50 miles over enemy land would probably preclude further operations before a return to Leyte. These extended operational periods put considerable strain on the maintenance and handling crews on the carriers which, together with the operational fatigue of pilots, are of great concern.

AC 1 was informed that should we undertake the Formosa operation and COM 5th Fleet was informed that the fifth operational period would not take place. Approval for this was received in the early hours of the 10th April (Operational Summary).

Got on with re-fuelling. Sea calm. Everyone was all set to return to the friendly islands of Ishigaki and Miyako. The Americans were looking after them in our absence. But at 1930 hrs [9 April] the picture changed. A signal was received saying operations cancelled for tomorrow, so we naturally assumed that a rumour about Formosa was true. But all thoughts of this were pushed from our minds by many gins and a pantomime act by Gammy Godson. (John Hawkins)

11 April

Weather bad, strike postponed a day. No briefings, no nothing. What a peaceful existence. (John Hawkins)

The fleet arrived in flying-off position 30 miles from Yonakumi Shima at 0600. There was a fresh NNE wind, a moderate sea and a short swell. The cloud base was about 1,000 feet with intermittent rain and drizzle. Course was reversed and in daylight it was soon apparent that conditions were unlikely to improve in the flying area during the day, while weather reports showed conditions over Matsuyama precluded any hope of attack.

Task Force 58 reported being under heavy air attack all the afternoon, with the enemy showing a preference to commit suicide on the decks of radar pickets. (Operational Summary)

The Japanese, still undeterred by huge losses, pressed on with its bombing and suicide attacks. But they were tending to strike the ships doing picket duty and not the main fleet or the transports. As a result, the USN could still put hundreds of aircraft up to protect itself and strike the Japanese on

Okinawa or wherever else they thought fit. Meanwhile the transports got on with their business of supporting the troops on shore, with barely a delay due to enemy attack. The bombers did occasionally get through and find a bigger ship but the damage they inflicted tended to be light. The battleship *Maryland*, a Pearl Harbor survivor, was hit on the 7th, with 53 men killed or wounded, but stayed on station. The *Enterprise* was struck by two D4Y3s on the 11th, without sustaining any serious damage. But many destroyers and other ships in the protective shield took many hits and a number were sunk or badly damaged.

And so it went on, with stronger attacks between the 12th and 16th, when many smaller ships would again be damaged or sunk. But this time they would be joined by the battleships *Missouri* and *Tennessee* and the carrier *Intrepid*, which all sustained hits, but remained operational. The pace and violence couldn't be sustained indefinitely though. Japanese losses were huge and their efforts hadn't really disrupted Allied assaults and so a pause to regroup seemed likely. However the attacks came again on the 17th, 22nd and 27th. Yet the return on their investment was diminishing with only one ship sunk and 22 damaged, for the loss of huge numbers of aircraft and men. Inevitably the Allied fleets would also reach an unsustainable position, with their crew growing increasingly weary, but for the moment they were coping. It was truly a game of blood, with casualties mounting on both sides.

12 April
The weather was poor and for a while any operational flying seemed doubtful. But the Avengers and the escorts did get airborne and all shoved off to Formosa. The weather got worse as they neared the target and it was decided not to cross the mountains, where in the clouds we would have to fly in a much looser formation without any real co-ordination. No one knows why, but Lt Morris led his group and bombed Shinchiku and not the primary targets. There was no air opposition but the flak was very accurate.

The fleet meanwhile was having fun. This was indeed the day for CAPs. A Firefly with 'Dumbo' [flying a CAP protecting an American air sea rescue plane] shot down three Sonias and another probable, and damaged a fifth. Bill Foster and Fenwick-Smith got two each. At the same time Bill Atkinson and Sammy Langdon despatched one apiece.

Smithwick was badly shot up by a Zeke and after getting two, proceeded to return to base. Next thing we knew he had ditched 12 miles north of the fleet and as he hit the sea blew up in a mass of flames. He wasn't seen again. All in all a good day for the squadron – eight Japs for the loss of one. (John Hawkins)

The enemy really didn't stand a chance that day and we sent five or more down without a struggle. It was sad losing Johnnie Smithwick. He'd been with the squadron since the beginning and was very experienced. We believed that he shot down two Zekes after being hit by another, but he didn't return so couldn't make a claim. (Bill Atkinson)

You really couldn't miss their fighters, they just seemed to be rather slow in manoeuvring. We were able to get on their tails fairly easily and shoot them down. None took to their parachutes so may have been kamikazes. (Bill Foster)

It was over so quickly that I didn't have time to think. John's loss was felt quite deeply. We had been fairly lucky over Sakishima and vainly hoped it would last. (Bill Fenwick-Smith)

Enemy reconnaissance aircraft possibly detected the Fleet at 0555 hrs and soon afterwards air activity was detected northwards. CAPs were flown off at 0615 hrs and 0704 hrs. Seafires had an encounter with four eastbound Zekes, one of which was shot down. The main strikes, each of 24 bombers and 20 fighters, were way at 0715 hrs. One strike bombed Shinchiku airfields with delay-fuzed bombs and attacked dispersals. There was flak but no airborne opposition. Due to cloud over Matsuyama airfield the other strike attacked their alternative target, Kiirun harbour, where hits were observed on the chemical plant, dock area and shipping.

Two Fireflies shot down four out of five eastbound Sonias at 0920 hrs. Corsairs attacked aircraft which had forced landed on Yonakuni Shima and set fire to a Sally. At 1135 hrs a shadowing Dinah was chased by Corsairs and destroyed. At 1530 hrs Hellcats to the north westward of the fleet shot down a Zeke.

In the evening the enemy made a sortie from Ishigaki, which was intercepted by fighters, no enemy getting within sight of the fleet. Hellcats splashed four Oscars and two Tonies [the Kawasaki Ki-61 single-seater fighter] and damaged two. The Corsairs splashed one Val and an Oscar and damaged another.

During the day all enemy air traffic appeared to have been between Formosa and Sakishima.
Enemy losses
Destroyed – airborne 16, on ground 1.
Probably Destroyed – on ground 1.
Damaged – airborne 2.
Own Losses
In combat – 3, other causes 1.

It was evident from signals received that the enemy were engaging in very heavy air attacks on American forces in the Okinawa area, and that Formosa based aircraft were taking part. We came to the conclusion, during the evening, that we must contrive to remain for a further period. It was agreed that our remaining aircraft and aircrew could manage a fifth operating period provided that our losses tomorrow remain small. (Operational Summary)

13 April

Lt Thurston, a Canadian, was shot down by our own side. There is a lot of resentment between the pilots and the fleet gunners. Apart from firing at us quite regularly they have also got a Seafire to their credit as well as a Hellcat. (Douglas Smith)

A Val flew low over the deck and seemed to get away with it. The bloody f.... ship's gunners shot down Thurston instead! (Gammy Godson in his diary)

It's hard to blame anyone for Thurston's death. It was dark and a Jap had a few minutes earlier dropped a bomb close to the fleet. Everyone was very jittery and on edge. The gunnery officers are distraught at having killed our boys. The death of President Roosevelt was announced during the day.

Strikes again made on Matsuyama and Shinchiku by two groups of Avengers. There was no opposition although the flak was pretty hot. Two enemy aircraft were destroyed by the Corsairs as they approached the fleet. (John Hawkins)

At 0550 hrs four fighters were flown off. A bogey originally detected at 0540 hrs developed into an ineffective raid by four Vals [the Aichi D3A dive bomber] accompanied by a radar-fitted search plane probably performing a dual role of pilot plane and Gestapo. One Val dived bombed, but missed, *Indomitable*. This aircraft switched on navigation lights and fired an incorrect recognition cartridge. It was engaged but probably not hit. A second was shot down by gunfire of the fleet. Unfortunately, gunfire also shot down a Hellcat.

At 0640 hrs the CAP proper was flown off and intercepted a small group of bogeys. Two Zekes were splashed by Corsairs and the remainder retired to the northwards. Shortly after the CAP was launched Avenger strikes were flown off. The weather over Matsuyama was fair and dispersal points were successfully bomber and a petrol or ammunition dump blown up. Few aircraft were seen on the airfield. Fighters shot up about 12 aircraft on Giran airfield without apparent result.

The other Avenger force bombed Shinchiku airfield through low cloud, hitting runway intersections and installations. No aircraft were lost in either attack. Once these aircraft had been recovered the fleet disengaged to the south eastwards to refuel. (Operational Summary)

My dear Mummy,

And so it goes on! No rest for the damned. Another chance to get mail off, though we shan't be seeing the letter box ourselves. This operation is getting a bit prolonged and tedious, but it is all in support of the Americans at Okinawa, so I suppose we can't complain as they are taking the brunt of the fighting. We are now allowed to say where we've been operating, namely some islands between Formosa and Okinawa called Miyako and Isigaki. The aim has been to stop the Japs giving any air support to their troops on Okinawa from these two islands. We hope and think we have fairly successful. Just recently we've moved down to Formosa, with the same object in view.

The squadron has done well and has added another nine certainties, quite apart from probables and quite a few damaged or destroyed on the ground. We had quite a thrilling fight yesterday – chased a Tony and made some attacks on it, but unfortunately he escaped into a nearby bank of cloud. I doubt if we did much damage to him. Later on my number four spotted a Zeke and sent him down in a sheet of flames.

Today (13th) we bombed an aerodrome on Formosa – no air opposition at all!

This is all the news, but after so long at sea, there's damn all else to write about. We hope to get a short rest in about a week's time, but I'm not counting on it.

Maybe the Germans will have packed it in by the time you get this. We are all following the European news with great interest. It couldn't be much better.

Much love Mick [Godson]

14–15 April – Replenishment Period
HM Ships *Formidable*, *Kempenfelt* and *Wessex* joined Task Group 57. HMS *Illustrious* sailed for Leyte at 1755 hrs, screened by HM Ships *Urania* and *Quality*. (Operational Summary)

16 April
Late on the 15th it was announced that we were returning to Ishigaki and Miyako once more. General gloom. The film *Cover Girl*, starring Rita Hayworth (much to Gammy's obvious delight!) and Gene Kelly, was shown in the lift well. Film was awful and attracted many ribald comments from the 'stalls and the gallery', but it was certainly good to see some girls. We were beginning to forget what they looked like. (John Hawkins)

At 0600 hrs the Fleet CAP was flown off in excellent operating weather. An enemy snooper escaped before our patrol could gain height. At 0630 hrs the first strike took off to attack Ishigaki airfields. This attack and a further one flown off at 1230 hrs left all the runways unserviceable. At 0930 hrs the second strike took off to attack Miyako, with a second at 1533 hrs, these left all airfields on Miyako out of action. There was no airborne opposition over the targets and the flak was moderate.

Throughout the day bogeys were plotted on radar but there were no interceptions by our fighters. A possible explanation for these mysterious bogeys is that they were piloted flying bombs (Ocha) launched too far away and which failed to reach the fleet before exhausting their fuel.

At 1722 hrs Hellcats shot down a Myrt [the Nakajima C6N reconnaissance aircraft] which was stalking an American privateer search plane.

In spite of having received no replenishment aircraft since 9 April and the lack of fighters consequently felt a sixth operational period was thought possible from 20 to 21 April. (Operational Summary)

We returned to the carrier on a dark stormy evening. The voice of *Indomitable*'s Flight Deck Officer came up, ordering her waiting aircraft to switch on their navigating lights so that the batsman could see them approach more clearly. I heard the voice of my old friend Sammy Langdon come on the air, when one of the flight spoke to him.

'I say Sammy!'

'Yes! What is it?'

'Which is the switch for the navigation lights?'

Sammy was a gentle, quiet man, with a voice which never rose above a subdued conversational tone.

'Buggered if I know, old son. Do what I've done – put the lot on and fuck the expense.'

I looked eastwards towards *Indomitable*. Sammy's aircraft, just turning in to the round-down, looked like a Christmas tree. Wingtip lights, formation lights, landing searchlights – all blazing in magnificent illumination. He never changed. A few days later he was shot down. (Norman Hanson)

Another loss. Sammy Langdon crashed in flames over Miyara after strafing some barracks. (John Hawkins)

Sammy was seen to burst into flames while strafing a gun position. This was a very sad affair for all of us. The Japanese flak had always been of the highest possible standard of accuracy, so much so that we had been ordered not to attack low unless a sitting target was seen. It seems that Sammy may have been too brave for his own good. In a few days he and I were due to be rested from operations and return home. It was another terrible waste of life, especially so close to the end of his tour. But the strain had been so severe since January that it was beginning to tell on all of us and mistakes were being made all the time. Most got away with it, but for others their luck just simply ran out. (Noel Mitchell)

Gammy Godson and I were vectored out in the late afternoon when a bogey was spotted by radar 65 miles in the distance. By this stage we were becoming so short of fighters that CAPs were often reduced to two aircraft. Some miles out we saw a Myrt [Nakajima C6N fast reconnaissance aircraft] trailing an American Privateer, a big four-engine type based on the Liberator bomber. Before it could attack we quickly dropped down to engage the enemy aircraft. Gammy radioed 'You lead' and dropped back behind my port wing. We quickly closed in and a four-second burst of fire demolished the cockpit and sent it straight down into the sea in flames. Meanwhile the Privateer flew on, seemingly oblivious of what was happening behind it. We finished our patrol and landed back on *Indomitable* in the dark. (John Hawkins)

17 April

In view of the apparent success of yesterday's attacks the number of bombers in the main strikes were reduced. First reports showed that considerable effort had been made to fill in the runway craters at Miyako but none at Ishigaki. Consequently, we concentrated on Miyako leaving all airfields unserviceable. One Avenger was shot down and one of the crew succeeded in bailing out 1½ miles offshore from Hirara town. A Walrus was quickly flown off and rescued the airman, whilst a fighter escort kept down the fire which opened up from the town. CAPS were maintained over the two islands but no activity was reported on any airfield.

At 0609 hrs a few bogeys were detected to the north-east of the fleet. Fighters sent to investigate splashed one Zeke.

At 1627 hrs bogeys were detected 110 miles west of the fleet. Fighters intercepted at 55 miles and two out of six Zekes were shot down, the others escaping in cloud.

At 1750 hrs close-range weapons on *King George V* suddenly opened fire on what appeared to be a blazing aircraft diving vertically for the ship. It turned out to be a drop tank released by a Corsair overhead. Both missed! (Operational Summary)

Highlight of the day was Jenkins shooting down two Zekes. Six were sighted by the flight, a pity the rest failed to connect. (John Hawkins)

18–19 April – Replenishment Period

20 April

More Avengers strikes and Gammy's flight ordered to destroy four-engine bomber reported at Nobara with bombs. It made a pleasant change from low-level strafing. But the aircraft turned out to be a twin-engine bomber, but they all had a go at it anyway, though none of the bombs exploded. Bill Foster clobbered both barriers when landing. This kept the CAP up in the air for 4 hours and 40 minutes while the damage was made good and the fighter cleared away. Bill seemed OK but his aircraft was a write-off.

Nothing attacked the fleet all day although a few American Liberators were given a scare when they came too close. Everybody started knocking back rum as soon as the bar opened and so closed the present *Iceberg* series. Hooray and good riddance! (John Hawkins)

Things were getting very strained on board. The spuds were finished, the cheese was finished and there was no 'squash' in the wardroom, although, rather more importantly, we had run out of bombs. (Douglas Smith)

Four bomber strikes were sent in. By the end of the day all airfield runways on both islands were left unserviceable. This was not a very fruitful day. One Avenger reported ditching 10 miles south of Ishigaki. The survivors were rescued the following day by a US naval mariner.

At 1910 hrs the fleet set course for Leyte, having completed 12 strike days out of 26.

The operations now concluded have cost us 59 aircraft against which we can claim 30 enemy aircraft shot down by fighters, 3 kamikazes self-destroyed, and 97 destroyed or damaged on the ground. (Operational Summary)

Whether it was the rum or the thought that I had survived, but I found sleep almost impossible that night and spent many hours wandering the deck. I wasn't alone. There were many other relieved souls doing the same. That morning a signal had arrived on the ship stating that many of the old members of the 5th Wing were to be relieved at Leyte. Admiral Vian, by all accounts, thought it best to keep this information to himself until the day's flying had finished. It seemed too good to be true. (Noel Mitchell)

This document has now fallen into the hands of a highly irresponsible person who will not be held responsible for anything which may follow.

Highlights of the do were – some of them anyway.

Jenkins got two in one trip – Zekes I think. Fraser Shotten got 1½ in a trip. 1839 didn't lose any pilots – 1844 lost 3. All this went on for about a month and then we stooged off to Leyte.

And it's time I left off. I've had squadron diaries. S'long! Switching off – OFF!! (Anonymous 1839 Squadron pilot)

Sakishima (March–May 1945)

En route to Sakishima the task force picked up replacement or repaired aircraft from the fleet train, as portrayed here, all freshly painted with new BPF insignia similar to USN markings. (DM)

And some were part or all painted in dark blue to replicate American aircraft to, hopefully, reduce incidents of 'friendly fire'. (DM)

Avengers in a clear blue sky begin another attack on Japanese airfields. (DM)

On 26 March whilst attacking an airfield at low level Alex Macrae was severely wounded. With little holding his leg together and bleeding profusely he carried on with his attack and then proceeded to fly his heavily damaged Hellcat back to *Indomitable* where he landed safely despite the undercarriage collapsing. His fellow pilots believed that for such gallantry he should have been awarded the Victoria Cross and were angered when this wasn't forthcoming. (AM)

Day after day the squadrons pounded the airfields on the islands at high and low level absorbing heavy casualties. But these great efforts appear to have kept the runways out of commission and helped stop the flow of enemy aircraft from Formosa to Okinawa. (JR)

On 4 May the Japanese began to engage the BPF in a sustained kamikaze attack. Here one is caught plunging down and exploding beside *Indomitable*'s port bow. Gammy Godson and Bill Foster, from 1844, watched the drama unfold from the 'goofers' platform avoiding injury by a hair's breadth. (DM)

The stomach-churning reality of a kamikaze attack. A brave and resolute photographer, with a poor sense of self preservation, captures this enemy aircraft a split second before it hit *Victorious* on the 9th. (DM)

Indomitable seemingly unaffected by the attacks powers on, but her Hellcat wing was kept on high alert to deter any more kamikaze raids. And between times they also carried on with their airfield attacks – low level with bombs, during which Gammy Godson would be lost. (DM)

By May 1945 Godson was a tired man and should have been rested from operations, but the shortage of experienced commanding officers didn't allow this. His friends and family were convinced that combat fatigue played a considerable part in his death. In his possessions the photo on the right was found, which may be the young Wren to whom he had become attached. (PG)

The type of bomb load carried by the Wing in May, quite often without drop tanks which were occasionally in short supply. (DM)

1844 Squadron's Hellcats attack Nobara airfield on Miyako (12 May) during the raid in which Godson was killed. The height and angle of the aircraft suggests that they will pass over the airfield, fly beyond, turn sharply and run in at very low level before bombing and strafing from different directions to confuse the enemy's anti-aircraft gunners. On the 12th Godson ignored all advice and returned to attack the airfield after one pass, even though the defences were fully alert and paid a heavy price for his gallantry. His aircraft split open and exploded on impact, destroying man and machine. (PG)

The BPF sails for Australia, its work over the islands complete. After a rest the fleet would be part of the force heading for Japan. (DM)

CHAPTER EIGHT

Gammy Goes West

For those in the wing who were leaving for home, arriving at Leyte seemed something of a miracle. But until the last moment they thought that orders would change, as they so often did, and back into combat they would go. Philip Vian, ever aware of the gradual erosion of his force and the continuing demands placed on them, would undoubtedly have viewed the prospect of losing so many experienced men with some disquiet. *Illustrious*, which had sailed for Leyte a little earlier, would also depart for the UK within days, taking most of its aircrew with her. *Illustrious* was now in a sorry state of repair and could barely make 19 knots, so had become something of a liability. Many other pilots, observers and TAGs on *Victorious* were due to leave too, though far fewer on *Indefatigable*.

A great deal would rest on the experienced hands staying and in the 5th Wing they were in a minority. Of their three senior officers, Harrington, Shotton and Godson, only the last would remain. And after nearly eight months of combat Gammy was feeling the strain.

In battle, individuals can draw enormous strength from the common bond of shared experience. A person's ability to withstand the rigours of war on the front line is rooted in many things – good leadership, good health, strength of character, a ready supply of food and drink, contact with loved ones, periods of rest, hope and a predicted end to a tour of duty. But friendship is also an essential part of the survival process and the old hands that remained would see this link broken. Slowly, but surely, when this happens morale begins to break down and a sense of isolation slowly spreads. The good and the brave gloss over this loss and throw themselves into their duties seeing this as some sort of balm to their jaded nerves. But often this can be a path to reckless behaviour, becoming more apparent when that person goes into combat again.

A good leader will spot these signs and take action, but when it is the leader affected, who can provide a restraining, sympathetic hand? Certainly not the very senior officers who are often remote from day-to-day activities and wish only to have sufficient numbers available to provide a fighting force. In this situation the odds of survival become very poor indeed and history is littered with cases when this was so. In the Great War many aces died due to war weariness and the blindness to risk this caused – von Richthofen, Albert Ball and Edward Mannock amongst them. This pattern continued in the next war, even though the effects of combat stress were probably better understood. In a letter written on 27 April to his mother Gammy Godson touched on this issue:

> My dearest Mummy,
>
> The last few days have been a hectic struggle of trying to do some work mixed in with a host of reunion parties and farewell parties.
>
> There have been big changes here, all but four of my old pilots are being relieved and will be on their way home soon. I have got a practically brand new lot joining me today. It looks as though they are going to try to relieve people as soon as they are due and before they get too exhausted by this new and faster type of warfare. A good show, but I am sorry to have lost them, as we were just about getting into quite good shape.
>
> Tommy Harrington is amongst those going home and will probably look Dad up in the City. Actually I don't think Tommy will be going back by a very fast route, so I have asked another friend to let you know what goes on. This is Major Ronnie Williams (RM) who will be flying home shortly on compassionate leave, as his wife is very, very ill. He looks a bit of a typical pongo, but is extraordinarily nice and has done a lot of excellent work in helping the fighter squadrons on this ship. I suggest Dad gets him out to lunch and hears exactly where we've been and what we've been up to. Please thank Dad very much for ordering the cigarettes. They will be most useful when they put in an appearance.
>
> Haven't been ashore again, as it takes an hour by boat and there's really nothing there anyway except the usual abundance of coconut trees, flies and sticky damp heat.
>
> Another of the old desert squadron arrived yesterday and came and looked us up this evening. I expect they will all be drifting out as replacements before this lot is over.
>
> Much love – in haste – have to be off to a meeting.
>
> Micky

One thing is certain though, such a good leader would have felt some relief that those who had served longer than he had were being relieved. After losing his great friend Sammy Longdon in the last days of operations over Sakishima, he was glad that no other veteran would go the same way when so close to salvation. Yet it wasn't until the fleet had been anchored at Leyte for two days that their release was finally confirmed by Admiral Rawlings, as John Hawkins wrote:

> 25 April
>
> It was announced this morning that many pilots would be leaving the ship and heading back to the UK. Everything was rather rushed, pay to be collected, trunks to be packed,

in fact it was a complete shambles with little time to say goodbye or tour the ship one last time. Before we knew we were going there had been plenty of parties and many drank too much, with Doc Stuart and Noel Mitchell hitting new heights. Mitch ended by beating up a gunnery officer and laying him out. He felt the loss of some of our boys to our own guns very keenly, as we all did. He was later found, out cold, in the bottom of a ship's boat.

We disembarked not long before midnight. The marine band turned out to play, with all the troops there to make sure we left. And with this we plunged over the side en route to HMS *Fencer* berthed nearby, which would be taking us to Australia. It seems we have 18 people coming from HMS *Speaker* (all from 1840 Squadron) and 10 from 885 who are all aboard HMS *Ruler*. This brings the wing's strength up to 44 pilots, the highest yet. The original squadron has now all gone. I couldn't help feeling greatly relieved to survive, but have a nagging doubt that we might be back if the Allies can't finish off the enemy. In April the end still seems a long way off. Finis, for the moment anyway.

1840 Squadron, which had been operating for some time from HMS *Speaker*, had been formed at Burscough, in Lancashire, during March 1944 and contained many Royal Netherland Navy pilots. They were embarked on the carrier HMS *Furious* and then HMS *Indefatigable* during July and August to assist in Operations *Mascot* and *Goodwood* – part of a series of strikes against the *Tirpitz*, which was lurking in Norwegian fjords. During one of these attack the squadron's CO, Lt Cdr A. R. Richardson, a New Zealander, was shot down by flak, to be replaced by L/Cdr Barry Nation RN, an experienced fighter pilot and leader.

On returning to the UK in September the squadron became part of the 3rd Fighter Wing being formed at Eglinton, along with fellow Hellcat Squadrons 800, 808 and 885. This new group would support four carriers – *Khedive*, *Ruler*, *Emperor* and *Speaker* – but it was the last of these that would be 1840's home from 16 December 1944 until 27 April the following year when it was disbanded.

885 Squadron originally formed at Dekheila in March 1941, equipped with Sea Gladiators and Brewster Buffaloes. Over the next three years it had a mixed history, being disbanded then re-formed twice more. Between times it was equipped with Sea Hurricanes, two marks of Spitfire and five marks of Seafire, seeing action on convoy duty in the Mediterranean, then in support of landings in North Africa from *Victorious* and *Formidable*. Despite this the unit was broken up in November 1943, only to be re-formed three months later at Lee on Solent with Seafire Mark IIIs, as part of the 3rd Fighter Wing. With the invasion of France in the offing the navy was tasked with providing an air spotting service and between June and November the squadron fulfilled this role, combining it with offensive sweeps and anti-submarine patrols. With this role coming to an end the Seafires were replaced by Hellcats and the squadron joined HMS *Ruler* for service in the Far East as an auxiliary carrier to protect

the fleet train. By April 1945 the urgent need to provide replacement pilots for the 5th Wing meant that 885 lost much of its strength. Their numbers were built up again, but they saw no more action before VJ-Day.

And with this, 28 men arrived on *Indomitable* in the last few days of April, just in time to witness the old hands leave, and wonder what might lay ahead. To Gammy Godson and Barry Nation would fall the difficult task of working up the 'new' squadrons in the few days before the fleet returned to Ishigaki and Miyako. With the Japanese on Okinawa still resisting and more kamikaze attacks likely, Nimitz and Spruance needed TF 57 to help subdue the enemy on their old stamping ground. Godson simply wrote in his diary, '27th – the full misery......', '28th – the full misery again.... Damnably hot', '1st May – Leave Leyte for a return trip in the direction of Sakishima Gunto!!!', 'Practice Balbo with the new pilots'. Depression, it seems, was setting in, but he kept his unhappy thoughts to himself and fought on, though his wingman, Bill Foster, an astute and perceptive man, realised that something had broken in his CO:

> Towards the end of the first operations over Sakishima there had been a weariness in his behaviour. He was still in command, but when talking there were a number of pauses and sighs. He seemed to be distracted and stayed in his cabin much more. The CO from 1841 Squadron, Bigg-Wither, apparently one of his oldest friends, came on board and they spent a long time together. Afterwards this very concerned friend went to speak to Captain Eccles and a little while later the Chaplain and the doc visited Gammy. I can only presume that he managed to convince them that all was well, when clearly it wasn't. With the benefit of hindsight, it is obvious that he should have been rested.

And as the fleet prepared to sail again, so the pilots who had just left made their way to Australia, enjoying the peace, but occasionally thinking of those they'd left behind:

> Life on board the *Fencer* was pretty good. We had no duties and spent most of our time sun bathing on the Flight Deck. When the sun went in we retired to the bar and kept our spirits up with the odd noggin or two. The weather was perfect – blue skies, scorching sun and flat calm sea ... and at the end of it will be HOME! What perfect bliss.
>
> We didn't arrive in Sydney until late in the evening (of the 8th). It was Victory Day in Europe. We celebrated on board by 'Splicing the main brace'.
>
> During our stay in Sydney we saw little of our hotel. Most of us were out all day and the greater part of the night as well. Just back for a quick sleep, a clean collar, some fresh cigarettes and then out again. However, all things must come to an end and before long we found ourselves appointed to HMS *Illustrious* (which had arrived from Leyte to be patched up a little) for passage to the UK. Going home only just in time too. A few more days and Sydney would have seen us all either married or broke or in jail. (Douglas Smith)

While we were happy to be going home most of us wished that all the old members of the squadron were going together. As far as we could we followed the course of the war around Okinawa, but couldn't get many details. We hoped that the Jap opposition was dying away making the next few weeks a milk run for the boys, but soon afterwards news of more kamikaze attacks on the American Fleet reached us. There wasn't a great deal of detail but it left us in little doubt that the war was far from over. A few days later we joined *Illustrious* and were sailing home. (John Hawkins)

When TF 57 returned to the battle the next phase in the campaign was codenamed *Iceberg II*. But the pilots had numbered each period of attack over Sakishima and Formosa individually and to them the next strike would be *Iceberg VII*. As Bill Foster related, 'the bigger number summed up how we all felt about the effort we made so far. Two sounded as though we'd just started. That probably appealed to Vian, who would have had us up to 20 or more without a break and called it number 1. He wasn't noted for his compassion or sympathy. Many years later I watched the film about General Patton and was struck by the quote "old blood and guts – our blood, his guts". I think this could have applied equally to Vian'.

Task Force 57 sailed from Leyte on 1 May having spent barely a week replenishing and repairing battle damage. Two days later they linked up with the logistic support group to refuel and then prepared for operations on the 4th. But by this time, based more on desperation than rational thought, the Japanese had resolved to inflict even more damage on the enemy. A torrid few weeks lay ahead in which kamikaze attacks would be sustained and the British fleet finally come under heavy and sustained assault. On 4 May TF 57 and TF 58 would feel the full force of this onslaught with three carriers being hit – *Formidable*, *Indomitable* and the US Navy escort carrier *Sangamon*.

A CAP of Hellcats was flown off at 0540 hrs in cloudy conditions, which remained throughout the day, helping to screen some enemy air activity. This made interceptions more difficult, but not impossible, as S/Lts Batham and Thomas, from *Indomitable* found. The CAP intercepted a small shadowing force and these two newcomers to the wing shot down a Zeke. Meanwhile the first strike of the day was launched from the carriers – one at 0605 hrs to attack Miyako and the second at 0815 hrs for Ishigaki.

But it was at this point that Rawlings decided to change the day's tactics. His big-gun ships had, for the most part, been employed on air defence around the fleet. A tedious, but essential business for them, which he intended to break up by employing them on bombardment duties. The runways on Miyako were proving remarkably resilient to bombs and shell fire offered another solution. So at 1000 hrs he detached both battleships and five cruisers, with destroyer screen and fighters overhead to protect them and closed the coast at 24 knots. He couldn't have chosen a worse moment to do so. The Japanese, who still had a remarkably good capacity for reconnaissance despite their huge losses, seemed to have spotted this division of strength and pressed home their attacks on the carriers.

At 1100 hrs, four incoming groups of enemy aircraft were detected – some 26 in number, with some acting as decoys allowing single aircraft to slip through the defences. One unseen Zeke did exactly that and appeared, out of the cloud, over the fleet diving down at great speed on *Formidable*. Although hit by anti-aircraft fire its momentum was so great that it had little effect and it crashed into the flight deck, near the island, shortly after releasing its bomb. The explosions and fire which erupted killed eight men and wounded another 47 and destroyed numerous aircraft ranged on deck. However the damage to the ship was slight, the armoured deck proving itself more than capable of withstanding such a blow. An American carrier sustaining such an injury would undoubtedly have been a write-off and, perhaps, even sunk.

Vian, on the bridge of *Indomitable* watching *Formidable* erupt astern, then had his worst fears confirmed when his flagship came under attack. Another small group of kamikazes had slipped through the fleet's greatly reduced protection. Gammy Godson and Bill Foster, who were due to fly again later, rushed up to the 'Goofers Gallery' when they heard the ship's alarms sounding:

Formidable seemed to have disappeared under a huge cloud of smoke and explosions could clearly be heard, interspersed with gunfire from the ship. Within seconds a Zeke passed by on the starboard side, climbed into cloud and came down from astern at an angle of about 35 degrees heading for the island and deck. Captain Eccles was clearly aware of this and began manoeuvring the ship to starboard and the enemy aircraft having committed itself couldn't adjust quickly enough to this slight, but increasing turn. Even at that moment Gammy and I didn't duck down for protection – not that there was much there anyway – and watched it come in. I'm sure the pilot was firing his guns at that moment, but this might have been my imagination. Some said later that the kamikaze flattened its approach at the last second, but I can't say whether he did or not.

One thing was certain though – that brave pilot brought her in at too shallow angle and just seemed to hit the deck a glancing blow, demolishing the portside radar array and slide over the side. Standing within about 40 yards we could feel the blast and the explosion that followed when the plane quickly sank. All sorts of debris and filth streamed back over the deck, some of it human. A few minutes later another kamikaze came down in flames, but again Captain Eccles was on the ball and this aircraft missed the ship by a matter of yards. All the time Gammy and I didn't move an inch too drawn by the spectacle unfolding in front of us.

Some of the pilot's personal effects, including a wallet and some documents were found amongst the flotsam on deck. These were passed to Captain Eccles for examination – he was fluent in Japanese. Shortly afterwards he saw Gammy and I, showed us what he had been given and handed some of the bank notes to us as souvenirs. Gammy declined and said to me later, 'I can do without those as lucky charms. They didn't do that poor sod any good!' I kept them for the rest of the war, with a small collection of other notes from places I visited, and made it through safely. (Bill Foster)

Damage-control parties on *Formidable* moved quickly to fight fires and by 1254 hrs these were under control and wreckage clearance could begin and repairs effected. For a carrier just arriving on station it was an amazing performance and by 1700 hrs it was able to recover 13 Corsairs that had been dispersed around the other carriers during the day.

Indomitable went on as usual with its fighter wing fulfilling a full range of duties, destroying a Judy at 1220 hrs, but losing a fighter to friendly fire from *Formidable*. After such a traumatic day the gunners were nervous and taking no chances and a damaged Hellcat, attempting an emergency landing, strayed too close and was shot down. Luckily the pilot wasn't hurt and was quickly picked up by HMS *Undaunted*.

Throughout the day incoming raids were broken up and in the process 14 enemy aircraft were destroyed – 11 by the fighters. But losses had been heavy. Fifteen aircraft were destroyed, but only four in the air, the rest went up when *Formidable* was hit by the kamikaze. Meanwhile the bombardment and the strikes on the islands had achieved the fleet's primary aim of subduing activity there.

With *Formidable* still restricted in what it could do, operations on the 5th were carried out by the other three carriers, each of which had some of *Formidable*'s aircraft on board. There were signs of snoopers during the day, but no attacks developed and the usual business of striking the airfields and CAPs continued. Early in the day S/Lt Ian Stirling, a New Zealander serving with 1842 Squadron, destroyed a Zeke 80 miles from the fleet at 30,000 feet, but apart from that the day was quiet though a Corsair and two Seafires were lost in accidents. As darkness fell TF 57 withdrew and set course for its fleet train, leaving the American TF 52.1 to cover Sakishima for two days.

Away from the fighting Gammy Godson, as was becoming his habit, tended to stay in his cabin. But ever conscious of the worry his parents must be feeling, especially when reports of kamikaze attacks appeared in the press, hastened to reassure them:

At sea – Same Address – 6th May 1945
My dearest Mummy,
By the time this reaches you, it should all be over in Europe – wish I were at home to celebrate with you. We got the combined news of the fall of Berlin, the surrender of German troops in Italy and Hitler's suicide at sea the day before an operation and the miserable 'silent

service' didn't even raise a cheer! Denys Evans, myself and another slipped up to our cabins to open a small bottle of Brandy Denys' wife had given him, and we drank everybody's health we could think of – yours included.

Well, we are back in the 'old hunting grounds' again – it all seems very much healthier than it was a month ago – flak is practically negligible, possibly because some of the positions have been put out of action, but more likely because they are getting short of ammunition, which they can't get replaced. We are hoping that another few weeks will see Okinawa completely in Yank hands – it should prove to be an invaluable land base.

One of my pilots got an early intruder the other morning, but otherwise we have few thrills. I expect you have heard tales of Jap suicide planes and in case you are worrying, I thought I would allay your fears. Most of them get shot down or turn back before they ever reach us by fighters, and if any do get through, they have the guns of the fleet to face. If any were to attempt to crash onto us, they would just bounce off the armour and not penetrate. Nevertheless, when there is an alert on, I always keep well below decks, so you can be sure there is nothing to worry about.

Biggy [Lt Cdr Richard Bigg-Wither CO of 1841 Squadron] landed on here a couple of days ago for a few hours and is alright.

It is considerably cooler and more pleasant up here – not much more to say I'm afraid! Don't drink all the champagne when the armistice is signed!

Much love
Mick

Children, no matter how old they get, will always be small and defenceless to their parents. In wartime parents suffer the even more crippling burden of worry, with death or injury only a whisker away, or so it seems to those back at home. Gammy was a risk taker, as were many fighter pilots, brave to the point of recklessness when the need arose. As a child hides or dissembles from the truth of what they face, so he played down the extreme danger he confronted every day in the air or on the sea. For him the dangers now seemed to be of little significance and so a pattern of risky behaviour, that many began to spot, was becoming well established.

After a few weeks delay many letters arrived from home and Gammy wrote again to his mother:

At sea – Still Same Address – 8th May 1945.

Today we were supposed to be renewing strikes, but after the first few trips had taken off, everything had to be cancelled owing to bad weather. As flying had been cancelled we were allowed to have the bar open for ½ hour at lunchtime to drink the health of all those who have done so wonderfully in Europe in so short a time. It is very hard for us out here to realise just exactly what this means, but it is enough to know that when we return we shall be returning to an England of no blackouts, no bombs and less rationing, and possibly private cars once more on the road again, and all together things will be back to normal.

From my own point of view, I have seen English papers up to about March 7th and have been rather amazed at the lack of publicity given to the Jap war – maybe things will change now that the European business is over. The war out here could end in a month or by Xmas

1946 – much depends on the speed and energy of those at home. I only hope it wont be forgotten in what must be the present period of rejoicing and to a certain extent relaxation.

Yesterday evening, I had a letter from you and Dad after you had heard from Doreen. For heaven's sake, stop this 'heart-aching business' – it was an experiment which didn't work and for which I am none the worse and possibly the wiser and have no regrets and no ill-feeling towards anybody over the matter – except to you and Dad, to whom I caused a certain amount of trouble. As I've said before, we really are too busy out here to be worried over domestic affairs. Nevertheless, thanks for your letters, they were good to receive.

Much love to you
Mick

Doreen Pullen was a young Wren Gammy had met when *Indomitable* and the fighter wing were based in Ceylon. Pat Godson, his brother, recalled that he had fallen for her in a big way and marriage was proposed. By May 1945 the relationship had come to an end, for reasons that are now lost to time. Fearing for their son's well-being, his parents sought to reassure and comfort him, but to no avail. Until her death in 1978 Grace Godson was convinced that the damage ran very deep indeed and contributed greatly to his poor mental health in those early days of May.

As Godson struggled on, attacks by the Japanese kept striking home with appalling regularity and consequences. Many thought that the enemy would surely soon run out of aeroplanes and men prepared to sacrifice themselves, but still they came on. On the 4th two British carriers had felt their sting and elsewhere ten American warships were sunk or badly damaged, but worse was to come, with the enemy seeking out the big ships again.

Returning to the firing line on the 9th, TF 57 were soon in the thick of another battle. With *Formidable* now sufficiently restored to participate in the strikes, four bombing missions against targets on the islands went ahead during the day, plus Ramrods and strengthened CAPs. Enemy aircraft didn't make an appearance until late afternoon, apart from distant snooper that was chased off by the fighters. The official summary then takes up the story of an unfolding drama – cold, understated but still resonant in its description:

> At 1645 hrs bogeys were detected very low 22 miles to the westward, coming in fast. Four Seafires intercepted at 15 miles, but allowed themselves to be decoyed away by one aircraft which they shot down. Meanwhile four other enemy planes evaded another division of Seafires, and after climbing to 3,000 feet penetrated to the fleet. From 1650 hrs onwards the fleet was radically manoeuvred by emergency turns at 22 knots. One minute after such a turn of 60 degrees to starboard was executed, a suicide made a 10 degree angle dive onto HMS *Victorious* from her starboard quarter. The enemy was well hit by close-range weapons but crashed into the flight deck near the forward lift. The resulting fire was quickly brought under control, but the bomb explosion holed the flight deck, put the accelerator out of action, rendered one 4.5-in gun unserviceable, and damaged one lift-hoisting motor.

At 1656 hrs another kamikaze made a shallow power glide from astern of HMS *Victorious*. Though hit by gunfire it struck the flight deck aft a glancing blow and passed over the side. Damage to the ship was confined to one arrestor unit, a 40mm gun director and four Corsairs which were on deck and damaged beyond repair.

At 1657 hrs a third suicide plane made a pass at HMS *Victorious* but then shifted target to HMS *Howe* further ahead and approached from the starboard quarter in a long shallow dive. This time the attacker was hit at a more reasonable range, and continued to be so until he crashed in flames 100 yds from HMS *Howe* after passing over the quarter deck.

At 1705 hrs a fourth kamikaze approached HMS *Formidable* and then HMS *Indomitable*. It then turned and dived onto the after deck of the former. There was a large explosion and fire, which was extinguished by 1720 hrs. Six Corsairs and one Avenger were destroyed on deck. The explosion blew out a flight deck rivet and this allowed burning petrol to fall into the hangar which had to be sprayed. As a result, a further three Avengers and eight Corsairs were damaged.

Due to damage to the carriers and loss of aircraft it was agreed that the fleet withdraw to refuel, sort out and make good the damage etc, and return to strike on 12/13 May.

As the fires were dampened down for the second time on *Formidable*, a series of signals flashed between its captain and Vian, later recalled by Dick Mackie:

Ruck-Keene's signal read 'Ship badly damaged – am returning to Sydney'. Vian's response was immediate and emphatic, 'You will NOT leave the Fleet until I give an order accordingly. You will remain as you can still take on a/c, to act as an emergency landing on ship'. I believe Ruck-Keene was very angry, but the signal had the desired effect and *Formidable* fought on, though I doubt whether Vian was ever forgiven.

As TF 57 withdrew, TF 52.1 took its place again, leaving the American navy to bear the brunt of Japanese attacks. On the 11th two destroyers and an LST were put out of action but then the enemy claimed their biggest prize. TF 58's fighter screen appeared to be keeping attacking aircraft at bay when two managed to slip through and find Admiral Mitscher's flagship, the fleet carrier *Bunker Hill*. At 1009 hrs one appeared out of low cloud overhead diving towards the ship. The pilot released his 500-lb just before his plane struck the deck. The two impacts created havoc and a huge fire soon erupted. But within seconds another aircraft dived down, dropped its bomb and then crashed headlong into the ship near the island. Above and below decks were a scene of devastation and it took five hours to subdue the fires and allow damage-control parties to do their work and keep the ship afloat.

Estimates of the dead vary, but seem to be in the region of 400, with another 264 wounded. Although severely damaged the crew managed to patch *Bunker Hill* up sufficiently to enable it to reach Ulithi under its own steam. From there it eventually made Bremerton Naval Ship Yard where permanent repairs were carried out, taking until September to complete.

On 10 May, as TF 57 withdrew to replenish and tend to their wounds, Gammy wrote a short letter to his mother:

> My dearest Mummy,
> Two lines to say all is well – no news – heard Churchill's speech last night – today we splice the main brace – have been kept very busy, but have had a fairly quiet time of it on the whole. In haste,
> With Love
> Mick

Too much can be read into such a brief note, but his mother believed these few words conveyed a feeling of sadness and loneliness. This, when coupled with the contents of his letter of the 8th, convinced her that a pattern of depression, which she had seen before, was emerging again. Pat Godson, after many years of thought added, 'There was no doubt that Mick was in a bad way and my mother sensed this. A parent, having seen a child grow to maturity, will understand their character and all their different moods. Did his mental state increase his recklessness or reduce his awareness of danger? We shall never know, but she believed that it did and I have come to believe this may have been so as well'.

Lt Cdr John Ramsey, the US air intelligence officer attached to *Indomitable*, attended all the briefings during the evening of the 11th and again at 0430 hrs next morning and discussed the targets which 1844 were due to hit. On the 15th he wrote to Gammy's parents:

> He had formulated his plan of attack very carefully. I saw him before he went to bed at 9 o'clock and again early next morning before he took off. We carefully reminded him of the flak position that existed, but Gammy just smiled. He had, I feel sure, already made up his mind as to just what he was going to do. In my opinion, it was his sense of duty to do a job well which cost him his life.

As dawn broke on the 12th the sky was grey and overcast. Fleet and island CAPs, plus the first bombing strikes were flown off at 0540 hrs, twelve minutes before sunrise. Bill Foster, who hadn't slept much during the night recalled:

> Sleep had been impossible for most of us and had been since the kamikaze attacks on the 9th. Once again I would fly as Gammy's wingman and we would all carry bombs, so low-level work was inevitable. Some pilots simply jettisoned them over the islands and didn't care too much about height or accuracy. But Gammy was not one of these. He believed that every bomb, bullet or rocket should count. We spoke briefly and he gave his usual instructions, 'keep in close and get down as low as possible when we attack'. And with that we made our way up on deck and prepared to depart for Hirara and Nobara on Miyako.

As *Indomitable* launched its fighters and bombers, light was just beginning to filter through the grey, watery sky. But the sun became a little stronger as they rose up from their carriers. Seafires flew CAPs over the fleet and watched as the Hellcats and Corsairs formed up and departed, followed by Avengers and Fireflies. There was no sign of enemy air activity over the islands and radar couldn't identify any threats to the fleet, even though raids were expected.

Since the 9th, ship tactics had changed. Greater use was being made of picket ships that cruised 12 miles or more away on the periphery of the Task Force in an effort to extend the radar cover and give earlier warning of incoming raids. At the same time counter-kamikaze destroyers were stationed behind each carrier to intercept raiders. Experience had shown that they tended to approach their targets from astern, where the pilot could best judge the direction a captain might turn his ship and judge his dive accordingly. But on the 12th these ships weren't called into action, the enemy choosing to keep a lower profile or simply to build their ever-diminishing numbers up again.

Bill Foster, keeping close to his leader, remembered climbing steeply to about 6,000 feet and listening to the chatter on his radio. Gammy occasionally chipped in with 'close in' and 'all looks quiet over the island, can you see anything…':

And with that we turned into Nobara, dropped down steeply and returned to the airfield a few feet above the ground shooting up anything we came across, which wasn't much, so didn't release our bombs. The flak was bad and I was hit several times, but nothing serious. We pulled up and heard the familiar voice of Commander Luard, who was directing the traffic as usual. He and his flight had spotted enemy aircraft on Hirara and Gammy peeled off and detailed half our flight to provide a diversion – a fast low-level pass to one side of the airfield – whilst he and I came over from the east to attack.

Despite our precautions the ground fire was intense and we hadn't managed to hit anything or drop our bombs. Once again we climbed away, but he was determined to attack a known gun position once more, this time by himself. We circled for a few minutes to let things settle down and he ordered me and the others to create a diversion whilst he went in. I argued very briefly with him over the sense in committing ourselves to another attack when the enemy gunners were ready and waiting. But he wouldn't be swayed. With that he came on the radio and said, 'Okay, over we go.' This we did and could see him sweeping in a wide arc around the field, beginning his pass from the east again. By this time the three of us had completed our runs and dropped our bombs. I found myself within 500 yards of Gammy's Hellcat. Just before releasing his bomb he climbed steeply to a hundred feet or so, and staggered as shells hit him. The aircraft carried on for a hundred yards downwards in a shallow dive, with a stream of flame coming from his starboard wing. With that he hit the ground, cartwheeled and exploded. Despite the flak I circled once at high speed, barely above the ground, watching the pieces come to rest and fires burning. There was no chance of survival. I fired into a gun pit and left.

Later I wondered whether he was dead before his aircraft struck because he'd made no effort to keep the Hellcat's nose up before crashing and there was no last call over the radio. Japanese gunners had clearly caught him in a cone of fire from a number of different directions. It was such a waste. But he tended to be 'do or die' and this time he chanced his luck once too often. Another good man 'gone west'.

We completed our patrol in a very sad state of mind and returned to *Indomitable* to report what had happened. Everybody was very gloomy on board the ship.

Commander Luard, in his role as air group leader, had taken off from *Indomitable* just before the main strike force to reconnoitre the islands and report any activity. He later wrote a heavily edited letter to Gammy's father, Edgar:

I was leading and could hear exactly what was going on over the wireless.

We spotted a new Japanese aircraft on the ground (at Hirara) and decided to attack it. He detailed half his flight to create a diversion and went down himself with a bomb. It was a most gallant effort, because he well knew that he was attacking in the face of heavy flak. He released his bomb, and hit the target, blowing it up, but was almost immediately hit himself, and his aircraft burst into flames and crashed very heavily.

You will realise that the censor will not let me supply any more details at present. I know I am speaking for all of us when I tell you how genuinely distressed we all are.

With Bill Foster's testimony there was no doubt that Gammy was dead and word was soon passed to the Admiralty in London and their casualty section. A telegram soon followed as did many letters of sympathy. One of the first came from his great friend Denys Evans, followed by Commander Luard and then the ship's chaplain, Russell Hawken. Captain Eccles also felt moved to write, but waited until June so that he could give his family more news:

Dear Mr Godson

I have no means at this distance of finding out your wishes about letters, but as captain of the ship in which your son was serving I feel privileged to write to offer my sympathy.

His death was a grievous loss to me as not only was he my best squadron commander but also a personal friend. When he joined the ship, he was as wild as a hawk and though splendid in the air he did not take his hum drum ground duties as a squadron commander seriously enough. We talked this over and he did all I asked of him, he then became an outstanding officer both in the air, in the ship and ashore. We have had other casualties but none of them affected the ship as did the loss of your son. We were all very fond of him and miss him sorely.

I see in today's list that my recommendations for Honours and Awards for some of our recent operations have received approval and that your son has been given a DSC and a mention in despatches.

I'm afraid there is little I can do to help comfort you except to say what a good type he was and how we miss him

Yours very sincerely

J. A. S. Eccles Captain RN

Richard Bigg-Wither was devastated by the loss of his great friend and felt unable to write to his mother for several weeks, hoping against hope that Gammy, by some miracle, might have survived:

> Some of my squadron were flying on that day and though they didn't see anything happen, heard it all on the R/T. When they told me the call sign I thought it must be him, but signalled the ship in hope. The next day the reply came back. I remember taking the signal to my cabin and staring at it. I found myself weeping though I just couldn't believe it to be true. We have so often joked about writing to 'Old mumsies' if anything should happen to us and now I am writing to you it all seems unreal and impossible.
>
> As you know he has been my best friend for a long time and I feel a tremendous loss which can never be replaced in my life, but I am so proud, as I know you will be always, that if he had to go he went that way.

Of all the correspondence received Grace Godson found the greatest comfort from Chaplain Hawken's letter, as Pat Godson recalled:

> My parents went to stay at the Grand Hotel in Folkestone shortly after they had received word of Mick's loss. A day or two later an Air Mail letter was redirected there from our home in Godalming. Keeping faith is always difficult at such a time and Russell Hawken struck just the right note, for her that is. His letter gave her great comfort at a terribly sad time, without dwelling on the means of his death.

Chaplain Hawken had written:

> We on board this ship will miss him very much. I know that all his squadron, both officers and men, will miss him, for he was loved by all. For me it was a great privilege to know him, and I valued his friendship. Only the morning before he was shot down, he attended our Thanksgiving Service for the Victory in Europe, and dedicated ourselves afresh to the task out here. He brought along with him a number of those in his squadron.

Grace, it seems, found the description of her son getting on with his life reassuring and calmed many of her worried thoughts about his mental state. It seems likely that the chaplain, and all the others who wrote from *Indomitable*, were trying to soften the blow of loss. 'Going gladly and bravely to his death' was an often expressed, clichéd Victorian view of a soldier's life, no matter how misleading it might be. But who could deny his parents this one crumb of comfort. But as Pat Godson added, 'it was only a fleeting moment of consolation before the worries returned and these haunted my mother for the rest of her life'.

No matter how great the loss, life soon moves on, not within the family stricken by the death of a child, of course, but on a carrier in war. No matter how liked and respected the person is there isn't the time to grieve. There is a cabin to be cleared and personal possessions to be packed and despatched home; any consumables or items the family may not wish to see handed out to friends or auctioned off to provide cash for sailors' charities. This duty fell to Gammy's friend, Denys Evans. Several pilots kept Gammy's pin-ups as souvenirs or acquired bits of uniforms and flying kit to replace their worn-out items. But another day and another battle soon arrived and for two more weeks the squadrons would continue their battles over Sakishima.

Lt Cdr Peter Leckie RN arrived on board to replace Godson as 1844's commander on the 13th. He was a pre-war naval officer who transferred, as a lieutenant, to the Fleet Air Arm in 1942. Before that he had served on the destroyer HMS *Vidette*. It isn't known when he qualified as a pilot, but he seems to have served with 896 and 879 Squadrons, at various times, though didn't complete flight deck training with 786 Squadron until February 1944, flying Barracuda MKIIs. Early in 1945 he was appointed CO of 840 Squadron, which had been disbanded in August 1943, then resurrected 16 months later, only to be abandoned again. His appointment just before taking over from Godson is unclear, but he must have been with TF 57 to be able to have joined *Indomitable* on the 13th. He would serve with the wing until the end of the war.

The task force returned to the islands again on the 13th and bombed and strafed the airfields all day. There were no combats or hostile aircraft near the fleet. A Seafire was lost in an accident and one of *Formidable*'s Avengers nearly came to grief when having to land on one wheel. With only a single barrier remaining on its parent ship the pilot was directed to land on *Indomitable*, which he did with 'skill, judgement and with minor damage to his aircraft'. But apart from these two incidents, and a submarine scare, the day was something of a milk run. Despite this kamikaze attacks continued elsewhere striking TF 58 and claiming a major prize – the veteran carrier *Enterprise*. A bomb-laden D4Y3 dived onto the deck and killed 14 and injured another 34, putting *Enterprise* out of action until September. Yet one American intelligence report had already concluded that enemy attacks were reducing because of losses and withdrawal of aircraft to Japan in preparation for the expected landings there. Nevertheless, another 39 ships would be sunk or severely damaged off Okinawa by the end of July, suggesting that the enemy were far from being beaten.

A two-day replenishment period followed during which the TF 57's future programme was discussed. Rawlings and Vian were concerned that battle damage was significantly reducing their ability to remain on station. COM 5th Fleet, ever aware of the problems they were facing without any operational reserve, replied on the 15th 'Not necessary to keep up coverage of Sakishima after 25th'. And so the squadrons settled down to ten more days of operations – two days in and two days out until withdrawn, with Australia their destination, to refit, replenish and rest. But first there were three strike periods to be endured.

Bill Foster, happy to be away from the islands for a while, recalled this last period before being rested:

> We weren't told that we would soon be in Australia, Rawlings and Vian not wishing us to take our 'eyes off the ball' so to speak. But by this time exhaustion was increasing daily and some were showing far less aggression than the Admirals may have liked. We still did our duty, but the promise of leave would have raised our morale considerably. And *Indomitable* was growing tired too. The state of her boilers was well known and the engineering officers were constantly shaking their heads and tutting over the 'brick arches and the defective stern bush', whatever they may have been. But the end result was that she had problems making 18 or 19 knots, barely sufficient for flying, especially when there was no natural wind across her bows. A quite common condition in that part of the world.

Bill Atkinson added:

> With a new CO, who had very little experience of flying, let alone operations, the rest of the squadron had to rally round. Our Dutchmen were transferred to 1839 – to join their former colleagues from 1840. Whilst 1839's few remaining old members came to 1844. This certainly gave us a boost and most of the new boys were fairly experienced too. In the air Peter Leckie tended to let me lead. To do otherwise would have been foolish.
>
> We had a number of near misses and the flak remained very dangerous, on one occasional an explosive shell hit my engine and I nearly bought it. Despite smoke and flames and a dropping oil pressure I got back, but only just. The same thing had happened to me on the Ramrod that killed the CO.

Each of these experienced men were battle hardened by now and though daunted by what lay ahead drew strength from a comradeship which, for many, would last a lifetime and created unity in the air, as Dick Mackie recalled:

> Despite having such an inexperienced CO, the squadron had a strong core based on Bill Atkinson, Bill Foster and a few others. They were unshakeable and resolute. 1839 were basically 1840 transferred so had a common understanding already well established. Between us we kept up the fight, but I find it hard to remember any detail of those last strike periods over Sakishima – they passed in a blur of action. Only later when reading accounts published in the June 1948 *London Gazette* did I get a complete picture of what we did until we reached Sydney again in early June.

On the 16th a full strike programme was resumed. The runways were again cratered and seven enemy aircraft damaged on the ground. But to achieve this one Corsair was lost in combat, two more, plus an Avenger ditched, and a Seafire was also written off. Several others were damaged by flak. Next day the pattern continued with no enemy aircraft destroyed or damaged but with losses totalling four, with only one, a Corsair, due to enemy action. At 1200 hrs Peter Leckie, returned to *Indomitable* from a Ramrod mission where his Hellcat had been damaged by flak. He was ordered to bail out ahead of the fleet. It seems that Captain Eccles was concerned about any delays a crash landing might cause. During the morning *Victorious*'s barriers had been severely damaged by two bad crashes involving Corsairs. One of these also wrote off two fighters and an Avenger on its way through. As a result the rest of the fleet had to take on board 20 or more extra aircraft and so could ill afford to have another deck out of commission should Leckie have messed up his landing. He bailed out safely and was quickly picked up by HMS *Troubridge* and returned to *Indomitable*, where it seems he was rested from flying for several days.

Again the fleet withdrew to refuel, but even here disaster seemed to follow them. At 1103 hrs a serious fire broke out in *Formidable*'s hangar. Someone working on a fully armed Corsair discharged its guns setting an Avenger on fire. In such an enclosed space an explosion was inevitable, especially as the fire curtains had been put out of action by the kamikaze attacks. The hangar was flooded with water, but not before seven Avengers and 21 Corsairs had been damaged to some extent, many irretrievably.

And so it went on. Strikes continued on 20th and 21st with much the same results. Airfields were again bombed, but only one enemy aircraft was destroyed in the air or on the ground, for the loss of one Corsair to flak damage, plus a Hellcat, Avenger and two Seafires to accidents. The one success had been when Hellcats from *Indomitable*, on a CAP, had been vectored out to investigate a radar plot at about 30,000 feet, 36 miles from the fleet. They found a Myrt shadowing the task force and after a brief fight it was shot down.

Accidents –both with ships and aircraft – seemed to be becoming more numerous, perhaps due to tiredness. Before dawn on the 20th the destroyer HMS *Quilliam*, attempting to manoeuvre astern of *Indomitable*, collided with her instead. The smaller ship's bow was seriously damaged and it had to be taken in tow by HMAS *Norman* initially and then by tug to Leyte. It was followed on the 22nd by *Formidable*, Rawlings and Vian having finally agreed that permanent repairs couldn't be put off any longer. It would sail, with two escorts to Sydney, via Manus, where a dry dock awaited. Meanwhile, *Indomitable*'s armour plating had afforded some protection and *Quilliam*'s bow had taken the brunt of the impact, but it still suffered superficial damage above the waterline, though insufficient to warrant immediate repair.

The next and last strike period began on the 24th with only three carriers, but by this time enemy opposition seemed to have evaporated and no attacks on the fleet were expected. This turned out to be the case and the airfields were cratered on both days, with only one aircraft lost – a Corsair which had to ditch near its carrier. The pilot was picked up unhurt and at 1700 hrs the fleet withdrew to refuel before making its way to Manus then onwards to Sydney. *Iceberg* was finally at an end.

> After many weeks of flying and fighting we had become so tired that the moment of departure barely affected us. For most just getting in and out of the cockpit had become too exhausting, though adrenalin soon rushed into our system when over the islands and someone shouted 'Rats!'. Most of our logbooks recorded 7 or 8 hours a day on standby, of which 5 or 6 could be in the air. It was only three months since we'd left Sydney but it seemed more like 30 years. I for one didn't want to go back, though it seemed unavoidable with the Japanese still resisting so strongly. But we expected to stay in Australia for some time and hoped that the Japs might surrender before we had to return. (Bill Foster)

By the time TF 57 stood down it had been at sea for 54 days, and of these 23 were spent on operations. During this period Vian's staff calculated that the squadrons had flown 4,691 sorties, dropped 927 tons of bombs and fired 950 rockets. Seventy-five enemy aircraft were claimed as destroyed, but the cost had been a heavy one. Twenty-six aircraft were lost in combat, with another 134 destroyed during kamikaze attacks, when ditching after being hit by flak or as a result of accidents – with deck landing incidents being held responsible for 61 of these. Forty-one aircrew were killed or missing, with another 44 men killed and 83 wounded as a result of attacks on the ships. By comparison with the American fleet the numbers were comparatively small. But the BPF didn't have the reserves enjoyed by the USN and so could not make good losses in men and ships so easily. Then there was combat fatigue to consider; the gradual erosion of morale that such prolonged and intense campaigns engendered. The attacks may have subdued the enemy, and taken some pressure off forces trying to take Okinawa, but to achieve this the rate of attrition had become almost too much to bear.

When the figures for *Iceberg* and *Meridian* were added together they made gloomy reading. For the probable destruction of 150 enemy aircraft, the damage to oil production and airfields, the British Pacific Fleet lost some 201 aircraft to various causes. Statistically this was slightly more than 94 per cent of the aircraft with which the fleet began each operational period. But it was the loss of aircrew that was of greater concern – 74 in all, and this didn't take account of the badly wounded, such as Alex Macrae, or those judged unfit for further flying due to combat stress. With some 310 aircrew needed to fly the fleet's 218 aircraft on day one of *Iceberg*, they had lost a little more than 23 per cent of that number. Indeed, it was safer to fight on the Somme in 1916, where the dead and missing totalled nearly 19 per cent, than fly from carriers in early 1945; though the aircrew did have clean beds at night and regular food.

When the fleet returned to sea on 28 June *Indomitable* would be absent. She had entered a long overdue period of refit, which would last until July. Rear-Admiral Vian transferred his flag to *Formidable* in the meantime, and with him went one crucial element of *Indomitable*'s air group; its small and highly effective team of night-fighter and photo-reconnaissance pilots and their aircraft. From the deck they would see out the war and write one final chapter in the 5th Wing's history.

CHAPTER NINE

Night and Day

When the fleet arrived in Sydney they found *Formidable* already in dry dock being repaired. Having been hit by four kamikazes the gang of workers swarming all over it would have been expecting far more damage than they found and they must have been pleasantly surprised when it took only two weeks to put right, freeing up the dockyard facilities to tackle the host of other problems afflicting the returning fleet. Fraser, Rawlings and Vian must have looked on with a certain amount of anxiety to see if their ships could be made ready for the next round of operations, which were due to begin in July. With *Illustrious* out of action for an indeterminate period, *Indomitable* due for a partial refit and *Formidable* still under repair, albeit in far better condition than expected, they must have been heartened by the arrival of a new carrier, HMS *Implacable*, in the Far East. There was also the promise of a new lighter class of carrier on the way to share the burden and provide a fighting reserve. During July the first of these ships began to appear in Sydney, to be designated the 11th Carrier Squadron.

The *Colossus*-class, as they were called, had been long in planning and construction. Britain's shipyards, being overburdened with work to make good huge losses in the Atlantic and on the Artic convoys to Murmansk, had struggled to complete these new carriers. But with the invasion of Europe a success and the defeat of Hitler's U-boats virtually complete, capacity in the yards grew allowing the light carrier programme to pick up. In December 1944 the first of them, HMS *Colossus*, was commissioned and by July 1945 three more were available – *Venerable*, *Vengeance*, and *Glory*. Though not packing the same punch as the fleet carriers, in terms of aircraft and armour protection, they were still an impressive force. But the admirals had two considerable reservations about the new arrivals. All new ships suffered from teething problems and their men, particularly the flight personnel, lacked battle practice and experience.

Aircrew training programmes were still producing the numbers required, but the programme was a long and complicated one, and the number of veterans to lead them in combat were diminishing rapidly. The losses over Sumatra and Sakishima had been more wasteful than usual and made the problem still worse. This was in addition to all the other campaigns in which the Fleet Air Arm had sacrificed its men in considerable numbers in the preceding five years. With the war in Europe coming to an end there were also fewer recruits coming forward – men once eager to serve were now more eager to begin civilian life before the mass returned – and the FAA had always relied on volunteers to fill its aeroplanes, regarding conscripts as less likely to fulfil this role successfully. The war in Japan might struggle on for another year or longer, and the numbers of men available to fight it were diminishing in numbers and quality too rapidly. It was a problem of which the Admiralty were only too aware – the larder was almost bare and the enemy were still fighting.

Amongst the squadrons soon to arrive in Australia there was a hope that extended leave would be possible before the next round of operations began. In particular the New Zealanders – many of whom had missed out between *Meridian* and *Iceberg* – had been promised an extended break this time around. With *Indomitable* due for a refit, the Kiwis took advantage of this offer and flew home on the first available transport aircraft leaving Australia. For many, including Jack Ruffin, it was the first time they had seen New Zealand in two or three years, but it would prove a short visit for some. In their absence the fleet was called back to service, this time against the Japanese mainland itself. The sailing date was set for 28 June and their destination was Manus, where they would join the American 3rd Fleet, under the command of Admiral William Halsey, as Task Force 37.

Vian took a very close interest in all that his squadrons did, but he paid particular attention to their photo-reconnaissance and night-fighting pilots. Good intelligence was always essential and PR aircrew flying Hellcats had proved excellent at delivering the information he and his staff needed. The ability to intercept enemy aircraft at night had also grown in importance and only the Hellcats had proved effective in this role. But, with the loss of *Indomitable* and its fighter wing for an indefinite period, the admiral had nothing to replace them in these crucial roles. With the fleet likely to be tested as never before by the operations over Japan, Vian hunted around for solutions. Only one presented itself – recall 5th Wing pilots with these specialist skills and embed them with an air group on another carrier. Jack Ruffin soon became aware of these plans:

> After a short leave in Sydney it was decided to send the New Zealanders with the longest service home on extended leave and be virtually grounded from operational duties. I myself made application for appointment as a batsman. But my leave came to a rather quick halt when Vian began organising the new fleet for operations over the Japanese mainland. What happened next was passed on to me by word of mouth of the admiral's secretary.
>
> As he went through the list of staff going onto his new flagship he apparently said, 'I don't see Ruffin's name here'. Reply, 'No Sir, Ruffin is on leave'. Vian's retort, 'In that case recall him – I want to see him'. 'That's not possible Sir! He's on leave in New Zealand'. Vian, banging the desk with his fist,' Well then get him back and I mean now!!!'
>
> Person-to-person phones started to ring and I was eventually found in Invercargill and things began to hum. The NZ Air Force put on a plane and I was flown to Auckland where a civilian flying boat was waiting to take me to Sydney. This was just two weeks after arriving at home and deprived me of time with my family and friends and the chance of a rest. As it turned out such speed wasn't necessary because there were weeks and weeks to spare before operations began.
>
> The reason for all this was that Vian wanted me to be on the Japan job because of my experience with the aerial survey of targets. I don't like the term PR, it was a bit more professional than poking a camera over the side and pulling the trigger.

Dick Mackie was similarly affected by this sudden change of plan and flew back to Australia having barely begun his leave. When he arrived there he found four others from 1844 Squadron waiting for him, Bill Atkinson, Bill Foster, Richard Goadsby and Harry Taylor. They were joined a day later by Jack Ruffin, plus a petty officer and six ratings. More pilots were promised and four others duly arrived in late July – Campbell, Greenway, Bell and Chappel. Briefings followed, aircraft were assigned and *Formidable* was announced as their parent ship. Bearing in mind how Vian's exercise in leadership had upset Ruck-Keene in May when the latter sought to pull his damaged ship out of the firing line, Mackie foresaw problems ahead now that *Formidable* was the admiral's flagship:

> Ruck-Keene was pleased to get back to Sydney, but never believed he would soon be joined by Vian and his staff. Captain Eccles had always been aware of having a 'back seat driver', but made light of it. He was a stronger character than the Admiral and there was a professional respect too.
>
> The problems with the US CinC over the need for night fighter cover came to a head when we reached Australia in June. When I was recalled from leave I reported directly to Vian and he discussed with me how best to meet this need. Although still a sub lieutenant, but shortly to be promoted to lieutenant, he ordered me to set up such a unit and combine it with the PR role. In reply to King, Vian told me that he was sending a signal forthwith saying that, 'the BPF is fully operational, with the night cover quite capable of looking after all RN vessels'.

Vian ignored my personal record on night flying when appointing me – never in a Hellcat, never on a carrier, nor ADDLs on land, in fact no night flying for 2¼ years. Fortunately, Bill Atkinson, Bill Foster and Harry Taylor had more experience and Jack and Richard were expert PR pilots. I had to admire and respect Vian's confidence in me.

We also took from *Indomitable* Lt Cdr Colin Keay as the officer in charge of all the aircraft in the fleet as regards 'Fighter Direction', another to become CO of an Avenger squadron and a Marine Lt Colonel (Peter Nelson-Gracie), as air group leader. None of us were well received by Ruck-Keene. And this hostility remained for the time we spent on his ship, despite a list of outstanding achievements. But he seemed to reserve his greatest dislike and resentment for the Hellcat squadron. Shortly after arriving, he told me that we were 'Cluttering up his ship and could not fly to his satisfaction etc'. In fact, he ordered that our aircraft be struck down until shortly before launch and again as soon as we landed on. He couldn't allow his shiny new Corsairs to be seen beside our dog-eared old Hellcats.

He disliked all *Indomitable* personnel – Vian included – but being the great man he was he did much to assist our 'special group', and keep Ruck-Keene at bay most of the time. But there were times when he still behaved very badly. On one occasions I went to Ruck-Keene, out of courtesy, to request that he consider commendations or 'gongs' for Jack Ruffin and Richard Goadsby. I was made to feel like a spendthrift son who had asked his father for a million-pound loan – the truly prodigal son. 'People of your rank don't even make such suggestions to me – just who do you think you are?' We parted and nothing more was forthcoming. Luckily the attitude he displayed wasn't shared by others in his command.

My team arrived to find there would only be two cabins available to us – one for me and the PR boys and one for the others. They weren't ready for our occupation so we slept in the passageway for a couple of weeks – a poor, uncomfortable place as passers-by had plenty of comments to make and physical gestures to see if we were still alive. It was just as well that the other four didn't arrive immediately!

Philip Ruck-Keene had been with *Formidable* for two years by this stage of the war and had seen it through many operations. Despite the contretemps with Dick Mackie he seems to have been a well-respected captain, although as a submariner for most of his career, he had had little or no experience of carriers before joining *Formidable*. Undoubtedly he was a brave and resourceful leader and had already received a Mention in Despatches whilst in command of the 1st Submarine Flotilla in Alexandria. But like all senior naval officers at that time he hadn't been a pilot or aircrew so only had the haziest idea of what they faced each day. When it came to understanding their physical and mental tolerances this was a distinct disadvantage, and when this failed he tended to fall back on the well-trodden path of naval discipline. Eccles on *Indomitable*, Denny on *Victorious* and Lambe on *Illustrious* seem to have been better suited to coping with this aspect of their command, realising that a lighter touch with these young men could prove beneficial.

As soon as the small squadron was assembled the men quickly deposited their possessions on *Formidable*, then departed for Nowra to collect their aircraft. Dick Mackie was first there and spent the next few days, and nights, practising

night flying and landing. Then they exercised in pairs. Ruffin and Goadsby
meanwhile flew over Sydney at different heights observing and recording all they
saw. At the end of three days they reported to Admiral Vian on their progress.
The Hellcats then flew aboard the carrier in darkness on 28 June, at sea off the
coast. Next day they began a full flying serial, fitting it into a tough Corsair and
Avenger work-up programme. Practice and more practice followed until, as they
approached the war zone, the business of night and day patrols began in earnest,
made slightly more difficult with American Navy aircraft operating in the area
at the same time. But it was a good rehearsal for the dangers that lay ahead.
These early operations weren't without their excitement as Dick Mackie recalled:

> We did a very long and strenuous CAP and during this located two Allied aircraft in the
> ocean very late in the day and waited for the arrival of relieving US aircraft, including a
> seaplane. Then headed home as dusk fell, with two of the team very low on petrol. I changed
> our speed revs to ensure we had enough juice to get back to base. I called Formid on radio
> got a vector and then a lot of abuse as the fleet had already turned out of wind. Within
> minutes we arrived at the rendezvous, just as the fleet was turning back into wind. I headed
> for the deck and overshot and told Bill Foster to go in, followed by the others. We were all
> aboard in about 1 minute and the fleet turned back onto its course again. On reporting to
> Commander F I was sent to the Captain, 'Why was I so late – who was I to hold up the fleet
> etc etc' I tried to explain but left him 'disappointed' to say the least. A little later I received
> a signal from Admiral Vian offering me his congratulations. All wasn't well on the bridge!

Richard Goadsby and Jack Ruffin, whilst being part of Dick Mackie's team
for 'pay and rations', were really a small unit on their own:

> En route to Manus, Jackie and I spent many hours in the hangar, helping our maintenance
> crew polish our two Hellcats until they were silky smooth all over. The object being to
> gain a few precious, extra knots. We also received permission to have all the machine guns
> removed – again in the interests of speed. We had carefully considered the matter and
> decided that it would be a better tactic for a lone pilot to try and out run any attacking
> fighters, rather than engage them.

TF 37 was due to rendezvous with the main American fleet on 16 July and
arrived on time, having spent three days replenishing at sea, ready for their
first operation. *Implacable* had suffered mechanical problem during the voyage,
but was again fully operational. Meanwhile *Indefatigable* was on its way to
re-join the Task Force having had to return to Sydney after its high-pressure
air compressors failed – without this equipment it couldn't operate its aircraft
so would have been a liability in the front line. *Indefatigable* missed the first
strike, but was back on station on the 20th.

The 3rd Fleet's task, with the BPF as one component, was to destroy the
remainder of the Japanese air defences – at sea and on land. In addition, they

were to attack targets on their mainland to soften up their defences before an invasion was launched. The Manhattan Project was waiting in the wings, but the hope remained that the systematic destruction of cities and armed forces by conventional means might drive the enemy to the negotiating table first. With each attack though, Japanese resistance seemed to harden and the possibility of slaughter on a huge scale continued to haunt the Allied leaders planning the invasion. Atomic weapons were nearing completion, but not yet ready, so conventional attacks continued in the hope that they might encourage a collapse and surrender.

For the soldiers, sailors and airmen tasked with defeating Japan the existence of a 'super weapon' was a matter of science fiction not fact. All they knew was that the enemy was not going to surrender quickly or easily and the casualties in taking Iwo Jima and Okinawa would soon be magnified many times. As Bill Foster later said:

> We didn't expect to see our homes again. As that final period of operations began there was an air of gloom and despondency. We were all prepared to do our duty, but knew the likely cost. If we'd known about the 'bomb', and its potential to end the war in one stroke, there would have been great relief at it being dropped. Was it the right thing to do? I have often thought about this, but eventually came to realise that it was an issue that could only be judged at the time and not in hindsight. Perhaps it was the lesser of two evils when faced with the possibility of millions of deaths in the months that lay ahead.

Task Force 37 closed the Japanese coast on 17 July, with the gigantic resources of the 3rd Fleet close by. Richard Goadsby was in one of the first aircraft to be launched:

> In the pre-dawn darkness, I trotted down the deck and climbed into the cockpit of my Hellcat, JV303. I was not covering a strike – these were going elsewhere – but was carrying out a PR mission over the naval base at Akita, on the far side of Honshu, the main island of Japan. First, I would have to fly 200 miles before making landfall, and then a further 150 miles across the width of Honshu. It was going to be a long haul, with not much fuel to spare at the end of it. I hoped the task force would be in the same position when I returned.
>
> Crossing the coast at 25,000 feet I wondered how the enemy might react to a 'spy' aircraft penetrating their country from one side to the other. But the trip turned out to be uneventful, chiefly because cloud covered the island, restricting observation from the ground. Over Akita the cloud was more broken and I was able to carry out several short runs before it was time to set course back to the Fleet. Helped by a tail wind I was soon over the coast and heading out to sea and, after 3 hours and 10 minutes in the air, I dropped over '*Formy*'s' round down. Some of my photos were marred by cloud, but the clear ones showed a variety of enemy warships.

With the start of this new offensive the detachment, as they called themselves, began keeping a war diary with two pilots in turn providing a commentary of each day's activities. This slim volume was not only a record of events, but also captures their thoughts, reactions and their language. Each generation tends to develop their own colloquialisms and here the idioms of 1945 are revealed in all their understated glory. It is also a record of a war viewed through the prismatic eyes of one small unit, largely kept in ignorance of the bigger picture. They were in their own hole in the ground with all the intensity, irreverence and myopia of that world laid bare. With a few modifications to reflect different times it is an account that could have been written in any war, by any small unit of fighting men:

> 17 July
> Total war against the Japanese mainland!! In filthy weather Ruffin (now promoted lieutenant) and Goadsby flew over Japan. Mackie and Atkinson helped the Corsair squadrons out and flew CAPs with them – in 10/10th cloud from 12 to 26,000 feet. Four Corsairs ditched during the day.

> 18 July
> Weather still u/s. Ramrods flew off about midday to sweep the Tokyo area. Four Hellcats did CAP at 20,000 feet and in clear weather but the fleet had lost itself in a fog which extended from 1,000 feet to the deck. Delay while a clear patch was found when we almost ran into the US Task Force. A clear patch with ceiling at 100 feet appeared and in a very crowded circuit we all landed on safely – to be brought to immediate readiness as a bogey had appeared. By now it was dusk and visibility nil. Fortunately, the bogey was friendly or he disappeared.

> 19 July
> Utter chaos – aircraft ranged for State 11 and told to fly off – then State 12 and no State 11 – go back to bed!! All this took place at 0300 hrs. Disorganised confusion reigns on this ship – no one seems to be able to decide what he wants and then be able to stick to it. Return to oiling area. No enemy aircraft have been sighted at all yet. Two Corsair pilots were shot down in the Tokyo area. (Ashbridge and Stradwick)

Despite the poor weather the combined fleet flew a full programme on the 17th and 18th, with airfields, shipping and installations in the Tokyo area their primary targets. *King George V* even managed to get in on the act and joined TU 34.8.2, with the battleships *Iowa, Wisconsin, Missouri, North Carolina* and *Alabama*, for a night bombardment targeting industrial areas around Mito and Hitachi. The damage they did wasn't great, but they weren't attacked and retired safely to take up their normal duties. An incendiary raid 24 hours later, by B29s flying from the Marianas, in the same area had considerably more success. Upwards of 80 per cent of the built-up area around these industrial targets were sent up in flames.

After two days of strikes a third was planned on the 19th but after the first CAP had flown off at 0415 hrs the weather was deemed so poor that the day's activities were cancelled. In the event, and having been briefed on the weather for the next few days, Admiral Rawlings sought Admiral Halsey's permission to bring forward TF 37's refuelling period from the 21st/22nd. And so, on the 19th, they broke off and joined the tankers and supply ships.

20 July
It will be noted that the 'Saga' of 1844 NF & PR flights is being continued in a strange hand. It is the scrawl of the Foster, for he has been detailed by his CO to write the aforesaid 'Saga'.

The Hellcat outfit, that is us, was to have received one Hellcat II and Foster arose at 0645 hrs to go to the Woolworth's to collect same. It wasn't until he had lugged parachute and kit onto the FD that it was announced that no Hellcat was available. At 0930 hrs we were harangued (good word!) by the group leader, whose main point seems to have been that fingers are kept out with regard to deck work. Nothing else worth mentioning occurred today so I am now at liberty to get my head down, unless I am duty boy, in which case I must clean the CO's shoes.

21 July
To say that little was accomplished today is a gross exaggeration, though it is rumoured that Taylor and Mackie cleaned their 'cabs'.

The afternoon was spent 'zizzing' until 4 o'clock when Mackie, Atkinson, Taylor and Foster turned out with PO Evans and AF Scott to do battle with 1842 in a game of deck hockey. The result was either a draw or a win in our favour, no one was quite certain. When the final whistle blew, or should I say when both sides had had enough since no ref was present, we all limped off and stood under the showers. Bill Atkinson being unable to stand due to rough handling lay in a bath.

FLASH – Atkinson has haircut!!!!!!!!

22 July
Today being Sunday we rested!

At about 1000 hrs 'Flying Stations' sounded and a Corsair and three Avengers landed on and out stepped all the 'Big White Chiefs' from the other carriers. We left the oilers in the afternoon and close-range firing commenced after tea.

True to Life (starring Mary Martin and Franchot Tone) was shown in the lift well after dinner; on return Atkinson decided to start 'dhobeying'. It was then 2330 hrs and a 'harry dimmers' was taken.

23 July
The targets this time are on Shikoku and once again they are airfields. The weather forecast for tomorrow is good – this is a change. No flying for us today.

First Hellcat flight is a CAP at about 0645 hrs, this being the case I must get my head down early and so shall write no more diary today. PO Jenkins just reports 125 temporarily u/s but remainder on the top line.

24 July
Ruffin and Goadsby off at 0545 hrs for PR over Shikoku and Kyushu. Weather much better. Mackie, Atkinson, Foster and Taylor off an hour later for CAP. Arrived at 20,000 feet and saw B29s on the way. Naturally we received no vector. Atkinson tried hard to get us to dive off all our height to attack one of the DDs of TF 37. He insisted it was a picket boat!

PR boys off in the afternoon and remaining four at 1745 hrs. Dick Mackie became a repeater of vectors to what seemed like a dozen lost Corsairs: eventually all got back to the fleet except Maclisky who ditched by the 'Tomcat'. Landed on 1920 hrs.

Yank fighters destroyed a Jill (the Nakajima B6N torpedo bomber) during the night.

25 July

This morning Ruffin and Goadsby off on their usual PR trips and the remainder of the outfit took off one hour later on CAP. All landed on at 0845 hrs nothing unusual having happened. The dusk CAP took off at 1700 hrs and Taylor's R/T went for a very smart burton. At 1845 hrs Foster's engine began doing queer things and it is believed that the drop tank could not have been completely full as all went well on main.

Five minutes later Mackie and Atkinson were sent off on a vector to 20,000 feet and Foster told to stay at 5 with Taylor and both to land. At 1915 hrs the two types at 20 caught up with a number of Graces (the Aichi B7A) carrying torpedoes. Atkinson hacked down two before you could say 'Bob's your uncle' and Mackie brought the score to three and a probable fourth in no time at all. Atkinson then perceived a Jap making what might be termed 'an ugly dash' at him, so to quote our hero 'I did a tight loop and rolled out on his tail!' This statement is believed to be one of the best lines we shot, but the fact remains that he badly damaged this aircraft and it has been claimed by him as a probable. It was last seen in a 40-degree dive towards the 'oggin'. From that moment signals came in thick and fast, the all-important one from Rear-Admiral Vian, 'Hearty congratulations' and Admiral Halsey, 'May I congratulate your CIC officers and CAP pilots'.

Churchill's famous statement, 'Never was so much owed by so many to so few' was written about such gallant men as these two dashing young pilots.

Many years later Dick Mackie recalled this night interception:

We were brought to immediate readiness because the ship's radar had detected a formation of unidentified aircraft approaching the fleet. Having lost Harry Taylor and Bill Foster to mechanical faults, Atkinson and I flew on various vectors given to us by *Formidable*'s FDO, but all were blank. Finally, Colin Keay's voice came on the intercom and we clearly heard him say to the duty FDO, 'Give me that control' then called 'Dick vector 260 degrees – climb maximum speed – enemy aircraft very close. Buster – Buster'. I did as directed and success was there almost immediately.

We peered into the murk and, sure enough, we picked up the exhaust flashes of four aircraft with others further away. For a moment I hesitated because they appeared to have gull wings – could they be US Naval Corsairs? I warned Bill to hold fire while I edged in closer to positively identify them. No – they were Japs alright. I confirmed this with Bill and we both attacked. My first target blew up in front of me and I crossed over quickly to get my sights on a second one. Bill in the meantime had shot down the other two. He went after another, guns ablaze and I had lost him. He called to say he was out of ammunition and was returning to the ship. I remained in the area for a while until I was intercepted by long-awaited US night fighters from *Bon Homme Richard*. By this time I was about 100 miles from our carrier and Colin recalled me giving me a course to steer for 'home'. When we returned we received a joyous welcome.

It was only due to Colin's skill that we had any success that night (the junior FDO he had shoved aside was, I believe, given a DSC for this interception).

26 July
More congratulatory signals rolled in and Mackie and Atkinson have made a statement for all
the world's greatest broadcasting corporations. A rumour has it that newspaper correspondents
from Chile and Peru are on their way to get a statement too.

Jacky Ruffin and Dick Goadsby were congratulated by AC1 for taking such pretty pictures.
Good show! In fact everybody has been congratulated except Foster and Taylor who slunk
away into the background or like Brer Rabbit, 'laid low and said nuffin'. Two more pilots
joined us today, their names are Frank Greenaway and Colin Campbell.

27 July
Very little to report. 153 will not be serviceable tomorrow, so only one PR will be available.
Once again Hellcat personnel have put up a black. If there is anything darker than jet black
this must be it. The padre has handed in his resignation from the Mess Committee over the
question of whether Jacky's paintings shall be hung up in the ante-room or thrown overboard.
Dirty looks have been handed out by the Sky Pilot to all the Hellcat boys.

Jack Ruffin was a talented, amateur painter and like most young men going
to war liked pictures of sexy young women around to adorn their quarters or
their aircraft. It was quite common for planes to be adorned with nose art,
particularly in the American flying services, but far less so in the Fleet Air Arm.
But cabins were adorned with 'tasteful murals' and, when a rare opportunity
arose, so were wardrooms. Jack received permission to paint two large pictures
for *Formidable*'s public rooms, much to the delight of his fellow officers. But
a rather prim chaplain objected and Jack received a rather conciliatory note
from the mess secretary asking him to take them down, 'With many thanks
for your co-operation and help, and I do hope that you will realise that this
is no reflection upon your ability as an artist.'

History is made up of many small events and some that are much larger.
For those fighting and dying these different elements can quickly become
merged and have an impact out of all proportion to their importance. But the
pettiness and petulance of non-combatants, out of tune with the age or the
minds of young men being asked to make the ultimate sacrifice, was a bitter
pill to swallow. As Dick Mackie later said, 'The best thing that could have
happened to this Sky Pilot was to be strapped into an Avenger and taken over
Japan for an hour or two. He might have had his moral stays shifted a bit'.

Each day during this second period of operations the joint fleet hammered
away at the enemy. The Americans, still determined to take revenge for Pearl
Harbor, reserved an attack on ships around the Kure Naval Base for themselves,
although they relied on intelligence gathered by Ruffin and Goadsby. They
attacked this target en masse on the 24th, with B29s bombing industrial sites
around Tokyo and a huge fighter sweep of P51 Mustangs, from Iwo Jima,
hitting airfields around Nagoya. Meanwhile the RN continued their attacks

on airfields around northern Shikoku and shipping in nearby bays. During the second raid of the day they sighted and attacked a light aircraft carrier discovered off Shokoku's coast. Aircraft from each carrier claimed hits on this ship, breaking its back and leaving it in danger of sinking.

This schedule was repeated on the 25th, but the early strikes were aborted due to the weather conditions and the rest of the day's operations were washed out as well. With little prospect of an improvement the fleet withdrew to refuel and it was during these hours that Mackie and Atkinson intercepted the night attack by the Japanese.

Whilst replenishing, the war went on with the Americans continuing their bombing campaign with an increasing intensity, but seemed to meet little opposition. Some hoped this was a sign that the Japanese air forces were on their last legs. But the more pessimistic believed that they were carefully martialling their reserves ready for American marines to hit the beaches. In July 1945 such an undertaking was still some way in the future, as the losses taken during the Okinawa campaign needed to be made good and so late 1945 or early 1946 seemed the most likely time for an invasion. Meanwhile the first atomic bombs were close to completion, offering another option.

On 16 July the first nuclear detonation took place in New Mexico. On the same day components for the first two bombs – one an implosive type and the other a relatively simple fission weapon – began the journey to Tinian, where the B29s of the 509th Composite Group were making ready to attack Japan. Late in the month all was in place and just awaited authorisation to strike selected targets. This wasn't long in coming.

There is little doubt that very few people in the 3rd Fleet and TF 37 knew what was brewing, just as few people knew how devastating the devices might be. With fire bombing raids already killing tens, if not hundreds of thousands in Japanese cities, some couldn't imagine that two bombs could have a more profound effect. With this in mind conventional forces were still sent into battle and planning for an invasion was underway.

TF 37 returned to the operational area on the 28th and began the next round of attacks:

28 July
Dick Goadsby and Jack Ruffin went off early today to take more pictures (photographing aerodromes, harbours and shipping – including Kure). About 1100 hrs a Hellcat Flight was piped for, so Mackie, Atkinson, Greenway and Campbell dashed off to the AOR. First they were briefed for a CAP then for a Dumbo CAP but they were not told where the Dumbo was. Thus briefed they manned their aircraft and started up only to be struck down the forward lift and told the trip was off. Dick Mackie nearly taxied over the bows when he went through a pool of oil.

The afternoon passed and suddenly at tea time we were once again piped and flown off at 1715 hrs (a DADCAP, all flying by braille). Once again, the cloud base being between 150 to 250 feet, we had to keep a good look out for destroyers on the screen. Mackie returned after 20 minutes his aircraft being u/s.

Atkinson, Foster and Taylor were then vectored on to 'friendlies' for 1 ½ hours and narrowly escaped death on numerous occasions. All pancaked at 1905 hrs.

29 July
A very ordinary day until we were brought to Condition 11 with 10 minutes notice. This is the thing we are getting quite a lot off lately, only we normally get scrambled.

30 July
Dick Goadsby and Jack Ruffin took off on PRs as usual, one going very early and the other in the afternoon. Mackie, Atkinson, Greenway and Campbell did the 0630 hrs CAP and received not one single vector. Dusk CAP off at 1700 hrs which as usual was 30 minutes before schedule. Went to 20,000 feet and Dick found his oxygen was running away like water and returned to 10,000 feet. Remainder followed him own almost immediately. From then on we tried to pancake about half a dozen times, but whenever we approached we were sent off on another vector. Finally pancaked at 1910 hrs and were told to sleep in admiral's day cabin as we were at Condition 12 throughout the night.

Jimmy Ross killed (1842) on take-off. Wings folded and he sank like a stone. Smith floated past the QD during the afternoon and was picked up by Quality. Hit the drink taking off.

Richard Goadsby, during a long flight on the 30th, was able to observe the results of the Allied pounding of Japan:

I carried out another long-range mission this time to Maizura on the west coast of Honshu, where it met the Sea of Japan. American heavy bombers, based on Okinawa, had been pounding the naval installations and airfield at Maizura, and my task was to photograph the damage. The ground defences must have been in a state of paralysis, because I received no attention whatever and managed to take some excellent pictures. But on the way back I saw my first Japanese fighters. A flight of four Georges – similar to American Thunderbolts – climbing up to intercept, and so I gave my Hellcat full throttle and found cover at 28,000 feet, remaining there until well over the sea.

The aerial photographs I brought back were interesting. In addition to showing the immense devastation caused by the bombing, they also disclosed some quite extraordinary attempts by the Japanese at camouflaging the airfield runways. Sections were painted with intricate designs, but could never even begin to fool the camera.

Once again TF 37 withdrew to refuel and take stock. Bombing raids, Ramrods and CAPs had been left largely untouched by enemy action – fighters or flak, both of which seemed to be less venomous or being preserved to counter the expected invasion. The squadron's main attention had been focussed on attacking strategic targets, whilst TF 38 had attended to the last units of the Japanese Navy, which Halsey described, in rather an overblown way, as 'A smashing victory'. But despite the lack of really strong defences the steady drip of losses continued each day. Three Corsairs were lost to flak on the 17th, all three pilots being picked up later, and two more the following day with both men killed. Four were lost on the 24th, including a Seafire and an Avenger, another eight on the 28th and two Seafires and a Corsair to flak during the 30th. But in return the bombing was deemed a success and claims for at least 31 enemy aircraft destroyed and another 33 damaged had been made.

Once more, and after a slightly longer break than usual, the fleet planned to return to the firing line on 5 August. However a signal arrived from Halsey on the 4th postponing the next strike for three more days. No reason for the change was given due to the secrecy around the Manhattan Project, but Halsey had been ordered to withdraw his fleet for their own safety because the first atomic bomb was due to be dropped on Hiroshima on the 6th. The young men on *Formidable* enjoyed the break and dabbled in the minutiae of life completely unaware of their passage into the nuclear age:

> 31 July
> Once again we oil. Campbell fetched JW 880 from Ruler during the day and Chappel and Bell finally caught up with us at last. So we are now a squadron of 10 and although Dick Mackie gets his second stripe today it is rumoured that he is demanding the extra half due to heavy responsibilities. We've just received the very good news that Bill Atkinson has been 'Mentioned in Despatches' for the *Iceberg* operations. Hearty congrats William!!!!

> 1 August
> Sunbathing or zizzing was the order of the day, most people doing a bit of both. At 1600 hrs there was a general briefing and the main target will be shipping in the inland sea. Apparently the PR boys are going with the strike this time and not all by their lonesome.

> 2 August
> No strikes today.

> 3/4 August
> As for the 1st and 2nd. If this goes on much longer I'll be unemployed.

At this point Dick Mackie chipped in with a brief comment:

> Signal received referring to Lt Atkinson's 'Mention' to add to his DSC and we feel sure to WMCF who, as usual is hiding his light under a bushel. A DSC was awarded to a 'CPPT Foster' and there can be no doubt that it is our Willy. So congratulations to him and here's hoping that our fourth member HT – our Yorkshire stalwart – will be next on the list.

And with that Dick Mackie stuck a picture in the diary of all four men, decorating it with words cut out from an old newspaper.

> 5 August
> Although I have nothing to write about I must put something in this book or I'll get four days' duty boy for slackness. A dive-bombing exercise was carried by Avengers and Corsairs without much success.

6 August

Oiled once again. We were challenged by 1841 to another game of deck hockey. Their best team turned out, only to be beaten again. We're not called Hellcats for nothing.

(At 0815 hrs the first atomic bomb was released over Hiroshima and detonated shortly afterwards).

7 August

Tomorrow BPF strikes north Honshu and Hokkaido after a week of inactivity. Rumour has it that we will return to Sydney 'verra kweek'. General briefing 1600 hrs where we were given usual gen talks.

8 August

Spent today waiting to be scrambled. No strikes as weather was duff, but three Japs came out early and picked us up.

9 August

Strikes today. Our CAPs and PR trips as usual. Anderson ran out of fuel and hit round down then dropped back into the oggin and was killed. Gray killed on strafing run.

(Just after 1100 the second atomic bomb was dropped on Nagasaki).

10 August

As for yesterday except that a three-hour CAP was sprung on us. Off at dusk and sent to orbit a Walrus in the drink and five extra types picked up by Watchdog, also a Corsair pilot in Goodyear 400 yards away. We returned to the fleet with everything against the firewall.

11 August

The Japs seem to have decided they've had enough and agreed to accept our peace terms with one exception – they may keep their emperor. No decision has been reached by the Allies as yet. The wardroom almost went mad when the news came over.

12 August

We're oiling and waiting the decision. A very convenient typhoon seems to be on its way which will stop strikes, which we hope will be unnecessary anyway.

13 August

Final decision by Japs will be made by midnight tonight.

14 August

Still no decision re cease fire. Played DCLOs again and we won 5-3. Everyone badly mauled. Bill Atkinson is a marked man!

15 August

Today is VJ day. American radio networks don't let you forget it either. At home there is a two-day holiday. The main brace was spliced at 1800 hrs. What an orgy! Never have so many folk, with the sole purpose of getting tanked, got into so small a room. 'Seventh Cross' was shown in the lift well.

Peace, when it came, took many by surprise, as did news about the two atomic bombs dropped on Japan only days earlier. For many it would be some time before they saw film of the explosions and their aftermath. Only then would they begin to understand what had been unleashed and the way it had changed the world, as Bill Foster recalled:

> It was hard to believe after all the death and suffering that we'd experienced that two bombs should have had made such an impact. Before they were dropped we had seen a lessening of the enemy's defences and they seemed to be on the point of collapse. But no one in their leadership seemed able to say stop and it took the emperor's intervention to bring it to an end. Would this have happened without the bombs? Probably not and invasion would have been the sole means of ending the war. Was it the right thing to do? Faced with millions of more deaths, including my own, I believe it was. But what a terrible way of achieving it, though no worse than the fire-bombing of Japanese cities which probably killed many more people.

My father, who was on his way to the Pacific at the time to fly Seafires, always felt thankful that these weapons brought the war to a rapid end, probably saving his life in the process. On one occasion, shortly before he died in 1993, he jokingly called me a 'child of the bomb' – it's difficult not to conclude that I and probably many millions of others owe my life to the Manhattan Project, though, sadly, at the cost of many other lives.

Dick Mackie, who had been with the 5th Wing since its formation in late 1943, could hardly believe he had survived and remembered, until his dying day, the sense of relief he felt and his pride in all they had achieved. But he also mourned the many men who had died on the path to this wonderful day, little realising that one of them had survived in captivity, but wouldn't experience the freedom for which they had fought so hard and so gallantly to achieve.

With HMS *Formidable* (July–August 1945)

Formidable in dry dock undergoing repair following the kamikaze attacks in May. (DM)

Bill Atkinson and Jack Ruffin find a quiet corner to relax amongst *Formidable*'s guns between operations. To many on the carrier the small Hellcat team were simply interlopers, particularly Captain Ruck-Keene, who seemed to go out of his way to make their life difficult. (JR)

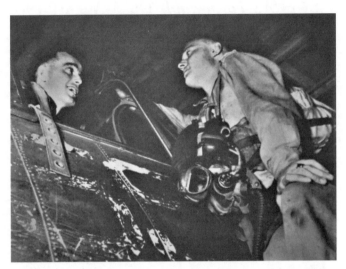

On 25 July Dick Mackie and Bill Atkinson accomplished an almost perfect night-time interception shooting down at least three Japanese aircraft that were about to attack Allied shipping off the coast of Japan. Immediately on landing their Hellcats were struck down into the hanger with the pilots still in their cockpits. This photo was taken shortly afterwards. (DM)

The Hellcat detachment's logbook records the success of four of its night fighters. (DM)

Part of the detachment's work was to undertake extensive photo-reconnaissance flights across Japan in unarmed Hellcats. Richard Goadsby and Jack Ruffin proved particularly adept at this dangerous work. The thousands of photographs they took provided invaluable data for the many strikes being made by Allied aircraft, but also much-needed information to support a possible invasion of the mainland. These two pictures represent a minute part of their essential work. (JR)

CHAPTER TEN

Murder at Changi

Death and disfigurement in war are unavoidable. Casualties are inevitable. Dictators and aggressors are very generous with other people's lives and have to be fought aggressively if freedom and peace are to be restored. Nevertheless, there are grey areas particularly where one society in protecting its own culture may seem to be inflicting their sincerely held views on others with a very different view of what freedom means. Depending on your viewpoint a defender can soon be seen as an aggressor. It is a complex issue and one with many pitfalls, even for those with honourable intentions.

Those fighting in World War II were faced with no such problem when it came to resisting Germany. A repulsive, genocidal regime inflicting its repulsive will on free people. 'Reaping the whirlwind', as Bomber Command's chief, Arthur Harris, termed it as his force laid waste to German cities and industry, had few critics at the time and many supporters, particularly amongst the tens of millions who had suffered at the Nazis' hands. The Japanese, who had committed genocide in China and treated anyone in their way abysmally, received the terminal accolade of an atomic strike that few, if any, thought undeserving at the time. In such an unremittingly savage war, fire was met with fire and some elements of morality had to be temporarily shelved, to be treasured and preserved for saner times.

But brutality, once unleashed, tends to know no bounds and even when surrender and peace have been achieved the depraved continue to inflict terrible pain. German death camp guards continued killing innocent prisoners even when Allied soldiers looked on in horror, believing, in their depravity, that American and Empire troops would approve of their actions. And in the Far East the Japanese continued murdering military prisoners in the belief that they were criminals who deserved punishment.

In August 1945, with the war over, one more case of this vicious cancer was played out on an isolated beach in Singapore. The victims were nine Fleet Air Arm fliers, including John Kerle Tipaho Haberfield, late of the 5th Fighter Wing.

With a proud Maori heritage, John Haberfield was born in 1919, and brought up in Greenhills, a small village in Southlands, New Zealand. When still a teenager his father died and 'Boy', as his family called him, left school and was apprenticed to the New Zealand Railway as a cadet engine driver. Fascinated by aviation, he invested his pay in flying lessons and in 1938 was awarded his pilot's licence.

When the Fleet Air Arm began recruiting young men from across the empire to train as aircrew in 1940, John seized this opportunity, passed all the tests and waited anxiously for joining instructions and passage to England. Finally, in the summer of 1941 his papers arrived and he began the slow and perilous voyage to the UK, stopping in obscure ports awaiting escorts and convoys to form along the way.

Even though a qualified pilot, he began the training programme at *St Vincent*, then Sealand, as though still a beginner. He formally soloed on 7 May 1942 in a Tiger Moth, after 11 hours of dual control. Though, in reality, his log book records that he was doing aerobatics well before then with the instructor as a passenger.

After this his progress was rapid and in July he transferred to 31 SFTS in Kingston, Ontario, for more advanced training, but was back in the UK, serving at RAF Errol, Scotland, by January 1943. During this period, he accumulated 200 flying hours, received his pilot's badge, being rated 'above average' and was preparing to fly Hurricanes and Spitfires to complete his training. The year passed with many hours in the air learning advanced fighter tactics and at the end of it all he received his first operational posting, to 1839 Squadron, with whom he would go to war:

> John, or Jack as he was known to one and all, was an unforgettable character. A keen rugby player and swimmer who had boundless energy and good humour. He was always friendly and unassuming, but had inner steel and great courage, which he showed in the air. He was a very fine pilot and could fling a Hellcat around in great style, but not so good at gunnery. He was always practising but it didn't seem to make any real difference. It was often the way. Some of the top fighter boys were quite ham-fisted pilots and very rough on their aircraft. But when they spotted an enemy, which they usually did before anyone else, something seemed to click and they rarely missed. A killer instinct I suppose. Where Jack excelled was in being able to hang on to anyone's tail and protect them from behind so they could focus on the enemy. He was a first-rate wingman and would have become an exceptional squadron commander. (Noel Mitchell)

The squadron had seven months to work up to full effectiveness, before joining HMS *Indomitable*. Within five months they would see action over Padang, Sigli, Cab Nicobar and Pangkalan Brandan, before sailing to join the United States Navy in the Pacific. When faced with the enemy the Hellcats had given no quarter, pressing home attacks with little regard for their own safety. Luckily, such a whole-hearted assault resulted in few casualties, but aircraft were regularly peppered with shell holes and survival often seemed a matter of a few inches either way.

John Haberfield was at the forefront of all these attacks and for one action, on 21 October, was commended for his gallantry with a Mention in Despatches. Then came two attacks on the Palembang oil refineries in Sumatra during January 1945 and with this the loss of 31 men and 16 aircraft. Amongst them Reggie Shaw and Evan Baxter from 1833 Squadron, Bill Lintern, Jim Macrae, John Barker, Donald Roebuck, Ken Burrenston and John Burns from the Avengers and Haberfield, the sole casualty from the 5th Fighter Wing. All were lost on the 24th and were believed to have taken to their parachutes, crash landed or ditched in the sea when their aircraft sustained serious damage. John's squadron commander, Fraser Shotton, later wrote a letter to his mother describing her son's fate. It arrived shortly after a 'missing in action' telegram:

> We made an attack against oil refineries at Palembang: our squadron was escorting some of the bombers and Jack was leading a section. Over the target we were attacked by enemy fighters and a fierce fight developed, during which it was not possible to see what was happening in a small part of the sky where there were aeroplanes everywhere. Jack's wingman saw him attack an enemy fighter and followed it down in a deep, fast dive, then lost sight of him. He was not seen again after that. Several pilots reported having seen aircraft crash into the ground, but none could say with any certainty whether they were our own or the enemy's.

In the melee of aircraft twisting and turning over the target it was almost impossible to see who had gone down and where. Some reported by returning aircrew as having dived into the ground managed to bring their aircraft under control close to the ground and escape. But when there was so much activity, involving so many relatively inexperienced combat pilots, confusion reigned. In a life or death struggle simply surviving was all that many could do and their inexperience, fired up with the desire to make 'a kill', often led them into danger. Sound advice – don't follow them down when damaged – was often ignored in the excitement of the chase.

Intelligence officers back on the carriers faced a difficult challenge when they tried to extract a picture of events from weary, but excited minds. All they knew with any certainty was who had made it back and who was lost, with only the haziest idea of what may have happened to the missing.

Death for some captives came quickly, local reports later confirming that two pilots, one believed to be Mike Blair from 1836 Squadron or 'Bud' Sutton from 1833, were hung from the gateposts of a local POW camp, having been savagely beaten and mutilated. Another fighter pilot, assumed to be Ian Grave also of 1836, who appears to have survived a collision with another aircraft, crash landed and was then pulled from the wreckage of his Corsair, although badly injured. Some accounts suggest that he was chained to its remains, where he remained for days without food and water, his wounds untreated, before death came. Others managed to evade capture for a few hours or days, hoping to make good their escape. But there were no friendly forces to take them in and so they fell, one by one, into Japanese hands.

Sometime later POWs held around Palembang described the impact the attacks made and their first view of the aircrew who had been captured. After years of incarceration the prisoners were in poor condition, half-starved and suffering from all manner of illnesses, and the newly captured men looked large and well fed by comparison. But few of the longer-term inmates would have changed places with these unfortunate young men. The Japanese treated all prisoners appallingly, but reserved a particular hatred for enemy fliers and subjected them to extremes of brutality. The Palembang survivors would feel the full force of this bitter, merciless treatment.

To trace the path taken by these men after capture took some years. As soon as hostilities ended war crime investigators tried to establish the fate of these lost airmen, but were thwarted by the sheer scale of the horrors perpetrated. It was left to the New Zealand Defence Department to bring the enquiry to some sort of conclusion and it took them some years. The files they kept, which still exist in Auckland, are extensive and bear witness to the depth of this investigation. What follows is a simple precis of their work.

After capture the survivors were handed over to the Kempeitai, the Japanese 'Gestapo' and every bit as bestial. At their hands the prisoners faced a regime of beatings and interrogations. They were also placed on display for public humiliation and to be photographed; their pictures appearing in local papers to remind others of the penalties they faced if they helped airmen who were shot down. In the face of such cruelty their condition soon deteriorated; compounded by lack of food and untreated wounds. From the witness statements of fellow prisoners, we learn of their plight:

> A Chinese who had been interned in Palembang recalled that he had been in a cell with some British service personnel. One was Lintern and came from London and the other bore the name Haberfield. There were five men in the cell he didn't know and five in the cell next door, all thought to be aircrew. Haberfield was badly beaten up on several occasions during

questioning. He was not seen again after 11th February. Sometime later Lintern and the other prisoners were taken away blindfolded on a truck.

If they hoped that their captors would eventually release them to a POW camp, where their chances of survival were marginally better, they were sadly mistaken. Singly, or in small groups, they were transported to Singapore. Witnesses later reported that their vacated cells were scraped clean and whitewashed – covering up the names and messages scratched on these walls, removing all traces of their recent occupants. The Kempeitai, with one eye to the future perhaps, preferred to keep these atrocities hidden for as long as possible, hoping to avoid responsibility for their actions.

For the remainder of their lives the Palembang survivors were held in Singapore's notorious Outram Road Gaol, but unlike most other prisoners of war they were kept in solitary confinement, as a fellow prisoner recalled:

> These cells had large iron doors, which had vent holes along the bottom, and spyholes at eye level. A piece of cardboard was placed over the spyholes, so that inmates could not look out or make conversation with anyone passing by. Being hit over the head with a sword was the most moderate form of punishment for such transgression, followed by reduction of rations that were already at starvation level. Dysentery, cholera and typhoid were common and went untreated.
>
> When in solitary confinement prisoners when taken out for a bath went in single file some yards apart, and were not allowed to talk by the many guards present. When taken for interrogation, which was often, all other prisoners were locked in cells, so we couldn't see their faces.
>
> I was detailed to keep solitary confinement areas clean. By lying on their sides along the bottom of the cell doors, facing the vent holes, a prisoner could make attempts at talking to a man sweeping outside. As the guards were only yards away, they could only whisper. Only once, when I was free of the guards' vigilance for a few seconds, I did see part of a man's face as he lay flat. His skin was dark. That was all I could see. I pretended to be fussy about the step's condition, to allay their suspicion, and in that time the man whispered that his name was Haberfield and he was from Auckland. He told me he had been in the cell for two months.

The airmen were kept in these conditions for six months, slowly starved and regularly beaten. If the Kempeitai expected to extract vital information they would be mistaken. After so many months of incarceration any information the prisoners could impart was long out of date. Anything of any use would have been extracted in the first days following capture. The continued violence could serve only to feed the sadistic pleasure of the guards.

During July and August 1945, the Japanese intensified the ill-treatment of prisoners. Their High Command even considered using them as bargaining tools, threatening their slaughter if Allied forces set foot on their homeland.

The sudden end of the war prevented this threat from being enacted. As it was, localised acts of 'revenge' did take place, provoked by orders from the dying regime in Tokyo that any prisoners treated 'unkindly', who lived to bear witness to this cruelty, should be eliminated. Surrender, when it came on 15 August, served only to hasten the slaughter – a final act of brutality before the curtain fell.

Executions continued for some days; the Palembang survivors being included in this purge. Yet, in the confusion following the armistice, those responsible managed to slip through Allied hands. Intelligence officers belatedly arrived to investigate rumours of atrocities in Outram Road Gaol and questioned many Japanese officers amongst them, Major Kataoki, late of the Kempeitai in Singapore. In a bid to divert attention he reported that '… nine airmen had been shipped to Japan in March 1945 for interrogation, but were presumed drowned after an enemy sank the ship.' At first Allied officers believed this to be true because:

> as a rule in a big centre, the Japanese did not execute POWs without a court martial. After a few weeks General Atsuka, who was Chief of the Judicial Department, let the cat out of the bag. He did so because he thought we knew that these men had been executed without trial and did not want to be blamed. Within 24 hours we had the whole story, or a good part of it, and sent out orders for the arrest of the culprits (including Major Kataoki). They were not prepared to face the music and apparently committed suicide on 26th December.

In a will that came to light after his supposed death, Kataoki admitted his part in the affair and provided the only record of their last hours:

> When nine British naval airmen made prisoners following the aerial attack on Palembang in January 1945, arrived in Singapore, I put them in the Army gaol here, and later obtained necessary information by interrogating them.
>
> After interrogating them I was not able to decide whether to put them in a POW camp here or send them to the Japanese Main Island. I could not help despising them for what they were. Under such circumstances I decided to personally execute the nine men.
>
> My plan was carried out with the assistance of Lt Miyashita, Intelligence Officer (HQ 3 Air Army) and Captain Ikeda of the Intelligence Office (HQ 7 Army Area).
>
> After office hours I drove a lorry myself and went to the gaol with the above mentioned. We took out the nine prisoners, brought them to the beach at the northern end of the Changi area, and executed them with swords on the beach. The bodies were then put in a boat prepared beforehand, and sunk in the sea with weights attached to them.

It is impossible to imagine the thoughts of these young men as they waited such cold-blooded executions. Starved and brutalised over many months, kept in solitary confinement without contact and support, they must have lost all hope and been in despair. Even the means of their death was chosen to terrorise and torture – decapitated one by one, the sounds and smell invading their consciousness. No escape and no compassion.

With all evidence carefully removed, the guilty attempted to hide themselves and their crimes. Although some may have committed suicide or faced judgement and punishment, it's likely that others managed to flee and return to their homeland – a fairly common outcome in post-war Japan and Germany, which were both in turmoil. However, there is much evidence to suggest that men such as this were often recruited by Allied powers to help police these defeated and lawless lands. Such were the vagaries of a world fighting for peace and order. But Lt General Fukuei, who was in overall charge of Changi didn't escape justice. He was captured before he could commit suicide and stood trial. Found guilty he was executed by firing squad, whilst a Sergeant Okayana, one of the guards, was sentenced to seven years in prison.

It is very easy to view death in war by simply recording numbers and then viewing them through the anonymity granted by statistics. How often do we hear that 'there were 60,000 casualties in one day during the battle of the Somme in 1916', or 'six million died in the Nazi gas chambers'? History and our understanding of these horrors shouldn't be left to these dramatic yet misleading statements. If we are to truly evoke the scale of the loss, we must remember and mourn each individual. Each statistic was once a son or daughter, conceived, raised, educated and nurtured to contribute something to the world, and simply not be anonymous fodder for the guns. This is no better demonstrated than in the life and death of John Haberfield, a man of great courage and honour, who deserved far better.

It wasn't until February 1946 that his family received news of his death. A telegram from the 'High Commissioner' coldly informed John's mother that he had 'been executed by the Japanese' in March 1945, later amended to August. For the rest of her life his last letter home, dated 9 January, became one of her most precious possessions. He had written, with the exuberance of a young man:

> I have just received some more letters, thanks a lot. The one mentioning my name on the wireless, we actually didn't do very much, you don't want to worry. Since I last wrote we have been over Sumatra twice. The last time another chap and I shot a Jap fighter down, and I also set fire to a tanker and silenced an AA position and strafed a number of things. Quite good fun.
>
> Had a quite hectic Xmas and NY. At Xmas a few of us went ashore and cut down a tree and brought it aboard, then lit it up and put presents around it for the ratings. I was a fairy with a wand etc, it was quite a good show. At NY we did some fishing in a boat round some of the ships and finished up having a swim at 2 am. Unfortunately, we forgot we still had our clothes on. The ones who were a little shy about swimming were thrown in.

Thanks a lot for the cakes, the boys wish to thank you too – they were very welcome over Xmas.

Lots of love to you all and don't worry,

Your loving son, uncle and brother
Boy

Although he and the other eight men murdered have no known graves, the efforts of their families and many veterans eventually resulted in memorials – one in Changi, a second in New Zealand, and a third in St Bartholomew's church, within sight and sound of the Naval Air Station at Yeovilton, from where the nine men had once flown.

Murder at Changi

Changi Prison as captured in a contemporary drawing. It was in this complex of buildings that the 'Palembang Nine' were housed and tortured. It was from here they were taken for execution a few days after the war ended. (KM)

Two of the nine. Left to right – John Haberfield (on right), Ken Burrenston. (KM/DM)

Four of the nine. Top row left to right – 849 Sqdn and Evan Baxter 1833 Sqdn, Bill Lintern 849, Bottom row – Reggie Shaw 1833 and Don Roebuck also 849 Sqdn. The three airmen who are not shown were John Burns, Ivor Barker and John Macrae, all of 849 Squadron.

Epilogue

For the Rest of Our Lives

Although the war had come to an end, the British Pacific Fleet couldn't disperse immediately and allow its men to return home en masse. But it wasn't necessary to keep all the ships on the front line. After nearly six years of war the pressure to release men and women back into the civilian world would soon grow and with it disenchantment if discharge wasn't achieved quickly. For Britain's political leaders it was a case of trying to get the balance right between policing the defeated aggressors and allowing the natural rights of individuals to be re-established. Churchill's defeat at the general election in July was a warning to all politicians that tardiness and austerity wouldn't be accepted for long. Having fought and won another world war, servicemen and women had greater expectations from peace this time. Lloyd George's hollow promise of a 'land fit for heroes' in 1918, the debacle over demobilisation, and the economic and social decline that followed, were too well remembered for it to be allowed to happen again.

With American armed forces so dominant in the Pacific there was little to keep the British fleet in the area for long. But there was a demand for help mopping up Japanese resistance in the Far East, particularly in Burma, Singapore and Honk Kong and help undo some of the damage caused by occupation.

When *Formidable*, and the rest of FT 37, reached Manus on 18 August they were soon joined by HMS *Indomitable* and the rest of the 5th Fighter Wing. Refit complete, *Indomitable* had sailed for the Pacific, arriving too late to join TF 37 but in time to be deployed as the flagship of Task Group 111.2, one of three set up to re-occupy Commonwealth territories: 111.2 would sail for Hong Kong, 111.3 to Shanghai and 111.4 to Singapore, though this one would later be re-directed to reinforce the Hong Kong operation. The creation of these strong units had been made possible by the arrival of four light fleet carriers – *Colossus*, *Glory*, *Vengeance* and *Venerable* – and the battleship *Anson*.

Before *Formidable* sailed for Sydney Dick Mackie managed to slip across to his old ship 'on business' to receive a warm welcome and congratulations from Captain Eccles. He did wonder whether he and his special detachment might be transferred back to the wing, but Eccles reassured him that they had 'done their bit' and were now going home for a well-deserved rest. As Dick left the carrier for the last time he recalled, 'feeling loath to leave and couldn't help thinking about all those boys I'd served with now dead or scattered to the four winds. It was a very sad moment'.

TF 37 arrived in Sydney on the 24th, its squadrons flying off as the fleet approached the coast. Dick Mackie and his Hellcats flew overhead as *Formidable* made its way passed the protective boom and headed for the harbour. As Bill Foster recalled:

> She wasn't our ship, though we'd grown attached her, less so to her captain and chaplain. So we dipped our wings in salute as we flew over her and departed for Nowra. Even in the few days since surrender discipline had become lax, and this increased as we began the slow process of becoming civilians again. After so many years in uniform, when every part of our lives was directed by the Navy, it was a little unsettling to be facing an uncertain future. We were little more than boys when we joined up and were forced by circumstances to grow up very quickly and accept huge responsibilities. Yet when we reached home this would count for little and we would be stripped of the status we had earnt. It was a very sobering experience to be on the bottom rung again and having to make a fresh start. Some found this adjustment difficult and seemed perpetually stuck in the world of 1945, trying to recreate squadron life.

By this time *Indomitable* was working up its squadrons for what lay ahead in Hong Kong, but since departing from Sydney, accidents continued to occur. The worst of these happened on 23 August and involved S/Lt Peter Cornabe of 1844 Squadron. When landing his hook caught the number three wire which failed to check his forward momentum; instead the flailing cable dragged him over the ship's port side and he drowned as his Hellcat quickly submerged in the ship's wake.

As the task group sailed on the pilots took on additional duties. With the Japanese around Hong Kong likely to resist despite the surrender, the wing were given small-arms training by the marines. For most this proved to be a pleasant distraction, until they realised that they might be part of a landing party and have to fight hand to hand. As things turned out the Japanese complied with instructions flashed by signal to Hong Kong and the smaller ships of the task group entered harbour on the 30th, preceded by a group of Australian minesweepers. *Indomitable* and *Anson* stayed at sea until the mines had been swept, aided by charts supplied by the Japanese. Whilst they waited some suicide craft were observed leaving their moorings on Lamma Island, presumably with the intention of striking the Allied ships. Hellcats soon attacked and destroyed them before seeking out those still in harbour and despatching them as well. This proved to be the last action involving the wing before it was disbanded.

Captain Eccles, a Japanese interpreter, was tasked with setting up a military administration to assist in the transfer from war to peace, under the overall command of Admiral Harcourt, who had flown his flag on the carrier. Harcourt and Eccles fulfilled this task until 11 September when Major-General Festing arrived to take over as head of Military Administration. Les Rouse, a Hellcat pilot with 1839 Squadron, remembered these last few weeks with mixed feelings:

> We were a month in Hong Kong doing all sorts of things – but not flying – and towards the end I went down with a fever. I returned to Sydney in the ship's hospital and was unable to fly from the ship with the others. As our Hellcats had been supplied by the Americans under Lend Lease we left them in Australia and returned home without planes. We docked in Portsmouth on 30 November when my parents came aboard and the following day I went home on leave.
>
> London was a cold and cheerless place. My friends there were either still in the forces or dead. Although, with overseas leave I remained in the RN until May 1946, I decided that it was time to get back to work and early in January I started in the CID at Savile Row Police Station.
>
> At least then I had a future – something that I had thought impossible a mere five months before when I was on the other side of the world.

By early 1946, all the 5th Wing pilots were in their home countries enjoying leave and looking to the future. Some, like Les Rouse, took up their careers where they had left off, but for most it was a case of starting their lives over again in a country struggling to come to terms with peace. They had fought for strong moral reasons and helped win the war, but achieving victory had bankrupted Britain. It was to a bomb-damaged and depleted country that many of these young men now returned, scrambling to find work and come to terms with all they had seen and experienced.

Tommy Harrington, Dennis Jeram and Peter Leckie stayed in the navy with mixed fortunes. Harrington rose to become a captain and died in 1989. But Jeram and Leckie remained lieutenant commanders, one dying in 1977 and the other in 1952, whilst flying near the RAF station at Strubby in Lincolnshire, leaving a young widow. John Hawkins, John Northeast, Dick Neal and Bill Foster took advantage of military sponsorship schemes for further education and went to college. The two Johns went to Cambridge and

Oxford, respectively, where they rowed against each other, without realising they had both served with the wing. Dick and Bill, after graduating, became teachers and seem to have found great satisfaction in their careers. Gradually the others too found a route into civilian life.

In New Zealand and Canada their former comrades made the same transition. Dick Mackie returned to his law practice, whilst Alex Macrae, disabled for life, became closely involved in environmental work. Dick Mackie described his old friend as 'living by himself in the wilderness of Northland, New Zealand, engrossed in his research'. In his last letter to me Alex wrote, 'my kicks now come from propagating and tending hardwood timber trees and consequently pruning to 20 feet'. But he never forgot the stress of flying in combat and, at times, relived these experiences, on one occasion when hearing news from another war: 'At the time of *Desert Storm* I suffered a period of high temperature and blood pressure when reports noted Tornado losses whilst interdicting Iraqi airfields. Needless losses were confirmed by a senior RAF officer.'

When I spoke or corresponded with the survivors I was struck by their stoicism and their reticence in describing the dark side of all they had experienced. In an age where mediocrity is celebrated and the most mundane actions are described as 'brave' or 'awesome', it is important to contemplate the real meaning of these words. This is personified best by the lives and actions of these gallant men, who faced death, fought for their country, and sacrificed so much for our liberty.

As their lives came to an end they displayed the same fortitude and strength. In 1971 Dick Mackie suffered terrible spinal injuries when crashing his motorcycle. Paralysed and confined to a wheelchair he still lived life to the full and kept in contact with many of his old comrades; gently contributing to their lives as he had done in the war. He recorded with great sadness the deaths of Jack Ruffin and Bill Atkinson as they both succumbed to cancer. He also recalled the death of Keith McLennan who in 1950 disappeared without trace while sailing off the coast of New Zealand.

From the recollections of all these men and their families emerged a story of great endeavour and true bravery. I was privileged to be the medium through which they conveyed their memories and I feel privileged to have been trusted with their thoughts and reminiscences. I hope that something of their spirit has been captured in this book.

As these final paragraphs were written and the story came to an end I was left remembering a difficult day in 1993 when John Hawkins, in a moment of great understanding, gently engaged my imagination. 'Did I recognise anybody?' he'd asked and I eventually realised what he meant. The question, as he intended, went far beyond recognising the faces of young pilots soon to face death. It was the subtlest way of saying have courage and fortitude when all around you is crumbling to nothing and the future looks grim.

Epilogue

Even though combat had ended for the squadrons on *Indomitable*, accidents still occurred with great frequency. Above: S/Lt Speak landed too fast and failed to stop and entangled himself in the cables. A number of pilots felt that the arrestor wires and mechanism were in so poor a condition as to be rendered useless by this time. (BN)

And sometimes it may just have bad luck. On 23 August S/Lt Peter Cornabe of 1844 Sqdn caught the No 3 wire when landing which failed to check his momentum. The aircraft went over the side and he drowned. (BN)

Even in the middle of a battle there could be calm times in which to relax. The coming of night as the fleet left the operational area was just one of those moments. Copies of this photo were kept as reminders of their time afloat and these brief periods of peace. (DM)

ST. JOHN'S CHURCH
DEVIZES

A CELEBRATION
of the life of
JOHN HAWKINS
23rd April 1923 ~ 24th November 2001

John Hawkins as a young man (DM) and the celebration of a life well lived.

Glossary

A25	accident report form
ADDLs	Airfield Dummy Deck Landings
Batsman	Deck landing signals officer
Big F or Wings	Commander (Flying)
BPF	British Pacific Fleet
CAP	Combat Air Patrol
CinC	Commander in Chief
CPO	Chief Petty Officer
Dhobeying	washing your clothes
DSC	Distinguished Service Cross
EA	Eastern Fleet
FDO	either Flight Deck Officer or Fighter Direction Officer
Gestapo	in naval terms an enemy aircraft shadowing the fleet looking for an opportunity to order up bombers to mount an attack and then observe events from a distance
Goofer	casual observer of life on the flight deck, sometimes noted as having a morbid interest
Gremlin	a mythical being that causes accidents
Harry dimmers	taking a dim view of proceedings
Heads	ship's toilets
HMS	His Majesty's Ship
IJN	Imperial Japanese Navy
Jimmy (or Jimmy the One)	1st Lieutenant
Kempeitai	secret police with reputation on a par with the German Gestapo
Little F or Little Wings	Lt Cdr (Flying)
NF	Night Fighter

Pipe	outpourings of the ship's loudspeaker
PO	Petty Officer
Popsylating	flirting
Prang	a crash
PR	Photo Reconnaissance
RAA	Rear Admiral Aircraft Carriers
RFA	Royal Fleet Auxiliary
R/T	Radio/Telephone
Rigger	rating responsible for the airframe of an aircraft
RNAS	Royal Naval Air Service
RCNVR	Royal Canadian Naval Volunteer Reserve
RNVR	Royal Naval Volunteer Reserve
RNZNVR	Royal New Zealand Naval Volunteer Reserve
Senior Pilot	second in command of a Naval Squadron
Sky Pilot	naval padre
Strafe	to repeatedly attack a ground level target at low level with bombs and gunfire
STD	sexually transmitted disease
TAG	Telegraphist Air Gunner
TBR	Torpedo, Bombing, Reconnaissance Aircraft
TF	Task Force
TG	Task Group
USN	United States Navy
USS	United States Ship

Index